Theorising Teaching in Secondary Classrooms

Theorising Teaching in Secondary Classrooms is for all teachers who wish to fully understand and improve upon their own practice. It encourages you to reflect on and conceptualise your teaching, and helps you understand how your practice is connected to the social, cultural, political and institutional contexts in which you teach.

Considering the latest international research literature and extensively illustrated with quotes from real beginning and experienced secondary school teachers talking about their teaching, it explores nine fundamental aspects of teaching that make up the sociocultural 'jigsaw'. Key issues considered include:

- the relationship between teacher and student
- classroom management
- teaching and communication for learning
- formative assessment
- teaching in diverse classrooms
- ethics in the school.

Theorising Teaching in Secondary Classrooms both challenges and supports you as you explore and endeavour to makes sense of the many facets of professional practice. It is highly valuable reading for all those engaged in initial teacher education, professional development and Masters degrees.

Beverley Bell is Associate Professor in the Department of Professional Studies in Education at the University of Waikato, New Zealand.

Theorising Teaching in Secondary Classrooms

Understanding our practice from
a sociocultural perspective

Beverley Bell

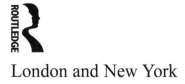

London and New York

First published 2011
by Routledge
2 Park Square, Milton Park, Abingdon, Oxon OX14 4RN

Simultaneously published in the USA and Canada
by Routledge
711 Third Avenue, New York, NY 10017

Routledge is an imprint of the Taylor & Francis Group, an informa business

British Library Cataloguing in Publication Data
A catalogue record for this book is available from the British Library

Library of Congress Cataloging-in-Publication Data
Bell, Beverley.
Theorising teaching in secondary classrooms : understanding our practice from a sociocultural perspective / Beverley Bell.
p. cm.
Includes bibliographical references and index.
1. High school teaching. 2. High school teaching--Social aspects. I. Title.
LB1737.A3.B45 2012
373.1102--dc23
2011022531

ISBN: 978-0-415-58419-7 (hbk)
ISBN: 978-0-415-58418-0 (pbk)
ISBN: 978-0-203-15475-5 (ebk)

Typeset in Times New Roman
by Fakenham Prepress Solutions, Fakenham, Norfolk NR21 8NN

Printed and bound in Great Britain by
TJ International Ltd, Padstow, Cornwall

For Susan

Contents

List of illustrations

Acknowledgements

I wish to thank the following people:

- the teachers who spoke with me about their teaching;
- the Teaching and Learning Research Initiative, New Zealand Council for Educational Research, and the Ministry of Education which funded the 'Making a Difference' Project;
- my colleagues in the 'Making a Difference' research project 2005–2007 on initial teacher education and induction of secondary teachers: Glenda Anthony co-director, Ruth Kane co-director, Ronnie Davy, Sylvie Fontaine, Mavis Haigh, Susan Lovett, Ruth Mansell, Kate Ord, Brian Prestidge, Susan Sandretto and Cheryl Stephens;
- students in the masters class on teaching as a sociocultural practice, for their feedback over the last eight years;
- colleagues, both former and present, in the Professional Studies in Education Department, Faculty of Education, University of Waikato, and in particular the late Nola Campbell, Helen Findlay, Dianne Forbes, David Giles, Mary Hill, Pare Kana, Heather McRae, Michele Morrison, Pam Schon, Jill Skerman, Jane Strachan, Bill Ussher, Jayne White, Noeline Wright and Russell Yates;
- doctoral students Dianne Forbes, Desmond Lee Hang, Ai-Hsin Ho, Suxia Gao, Elly Govers, John Lockley, Lesley Murrihy, Emily Nelson, Patricia Rodie, Bill Ussher and Xue Qing Yao, for the many conversations we have had on teaching and teacher education;
- Dr Carol Scarff Seatter of the University of British Columbia, Canada, an academic visitor in 2010;
- Elisabeth Joseph, a Summer Research Scholarship holder in the summer of 2009/2010, who did much preparatory work for the book and helped write the chapter on teaching as a cultural practice;
- Donn Ratana for the cover design;
- Michael Collins for the jigsaw diagrams;
- Yvonne Milbank for her librarian help.

I wish to thank the editorial staff at Routledge for their support and help: Anna Clarkson, Helen Pritt and Claire Westwood.

Preface

This book has its origins in my wish to theorise teaching, after many years of research into learning and its implications for teaching, teacher development and assessment. I first theorised learning from a personal constructivist perspective in the 1980s, in work on students' alternative conceptions of science (see Bell, 2005a). The personal constructivist position was also used in associated research on teaching which took into account students' prior and existing thinking in science classrooms, and the contexts in which the science was learnt and used (Bell, 2005a, 2005b). In the 1990s, I developed my theorising further to theorise teacher development from a social constructivist perspective (Bell and Gilbert, 1996) and assessment for formative purposes from a sociocultural perspective (Bell and Cowie, 2001). Now I wish to theorise teaching.

In my masters study in the late 1970s, teaching was theorised as a process and product within cognitive science (Dunkin and Biddle, 1974), which appealed to me as a science graduate and teacher, but which seemed dull, uninteresting and uninformative as to how to improve my teaching, compared to my masters research on finding out as a teacher what students were thinking of and what sense they were making of the science lesson. Whilst appreciating that Education draws on the disciplines of psychology, sociology and philosophy, I wondered what theorising would arise out of teachers making sense of their practice of teaching. The theorising in this book represents a snapshot of my thinking to date.

In the 2000s, I sought to theorise teaching in ways that are congruent both with what teachers think and do in the context of their classrooms and schools, and with current sociocultural theorising in the research literature. I first edited a special issue of the *Waikato Journal of Education* on theorising pedagogy to start a conversation with colleagues about theorising teaching (Bell, 2003).

From there, I developed a masters paper for teachers on sociocultural ways of theorising teaching. The one-semester education paper has been taught in both online and face-to-face formats. The paper is divided into 12 sessions, each based on the chapters of this book, with the final session being on teaching as a learning practice, in which the masters students discuss what they have learnt from being a teacher and from the masters paper. The sessions were developed over eight years of reading the education research literature in which teaching had been theorised as a sociocultural practice. Each session has a study sheet outlining the topic and including questions for self-study and questions for class discussion. An important part of the paper is the students re-storying, sharing and theorising (explaining) their own teaching thinking and practices using the theorising in the readings. The assignments are based on the masters students theorising teacher accounts of teaching. Likewise in this book, each chapter contains the readings, beginning and experienced teachers' accounts of their teaching, and study and discussion questions for other masters students reading the book.

The strength of this book is its breadth in considering nine sociocultural aspects of teaching, not just one or two as is typical in the research literature. Therefore, I have had to limit the depth of writing on each of the nine practices. However, there are many references given for readers to study the detail. The list of references given is not exhaustive, but they are ones my students and I have found helpful and of interest.

The nine aspects of teaching are important for several reasons. First, the nine aspects are present in the accounts of teachers talking and explaining their own teaching. Collectively, they represent how teachers (and not classroom observers, or people outside of the classroom, or theorists from other disciplines) theorise their teaching. Second, the nine aspects each have a research literature base upon which we can draw in masters teaching and learning. Third, the nine aspects are those that have been theorised using a sociocultural perspective. The sociocultural perspective is important as it asserts that, to understand teaching, we need to consider the teacher's mind (cognition, affect and conation), the teacher's action and the context in which the teaching occurs. To neglect one of these (mind, action and context) is to only partially understand teaching. For example, to view classroom management as behaviour modification is at times a useful perspective for teacher thinking and action, but it is only a partial perspective of teaching – one in which the teacher is viewed as a technician, competently implementing techniques. To consider classroom management within the context of the teacher–student relationship in classrooms is to see a bigger explanatory picture. It shows how respecting students builds up the teacher–student relationship as a part of teaching, and how this relationship impacts on the management of classroom activities and student learning. It views teachers as professionals, able to make judgement calls and professional decisions.

This book is primarily written for secondary teachers who have some experience of teaching and some of the language of the discipline of education, and who wish to learn the bigger explanatory picture of teaching, to understand their teaching so as to make informed improvements to their teaching. Each chapter forms the basis for one teaching session or module. Each chapter provides references for further reading, study and class discussion questions, and quotations of teachers talking teaching to reflect on.

The book is also suitable for students in secondary initial teacher education who are learning the language of education after having learnt the language of another discipline in their undergraduate degree. The book provides an insight into the professional knowledge, thinking and practices of secondary teachers – the community into which they are being inducted. The first three chapters will be of particular interest for initial teacher education students as they address their immediate learning needs.

The first chapter gives an overview of sociocultural theorising with respect to teaching, and introduces the nine aspects of teaching as a sociocultural practice, using a jigsaw model of teaching. The overview and introduction is done through reflection on one beginning secondary teacher talking about her teaching.

The second chapter explores the notion of teaching as a relational practice, including relationships with students, colleagues, and parents and care-givers. The notions of classroom management and teaching as a spiritual practice are also discussed within teaching as a relational practice.

The third chapter explores teaching as a social practice, which highlights teachers' use of language and communication as a part of teaching, including mindful planning, the use of different knowledges to inform teaching, the co-construction of shared meanings and understandings, mediated action and scaffolding, and assessment for formative purposes.

The fourth chapter on teaching as a cultural practice discusses the ways in which the culture of the teacher and student influences teaching. The notion of culturally responsive teaching is discussed.

Teaching as an emotion practice is discussed in the fifth chapter, linking emotion and teaching, and introducing the notions of emotional work and emotional labour as a part of teaching.

The sixth chapter explores teaching as a caring practice, discusses the caring done as a part of teaching – caring for students, colleagues and self.

Teaching as an ethical practice is discussed in Chapter 7, with a consideration of the ways in which teaching is an inherently ethical and moral practice, including ethics of justice and ethics of care, and ethical relationships in teaching.

The eighth chapter considers teaching as an embodied practice, meaning that we use our bodies as well as our minds in teaching, and how using our bodies influences our teaching. Topics include teaching with a sick, tired, disabled or differently coloured body.

Chapter 9 addresses teaching as a spatial practice. The spaces in which we teach can be seen as relational spaces existing in time and space, physical spaces, or the virtual spaces of online teaching.

Teaching as a political practice is discussed in Chapter 10, addressing how we as teachers address the discourses of power in schools and education. The topics discussed explore the power dimensions in teaching with respect to social justice, curricula, government policy on education, teachers' unions and school politics.

The last chapter summarises the chapters of the book and rebuilds the bigger picture of theorising teaching as a sociocultural practice, using a revised jigsaw model of teaching.

Beverley Bell
May 2011

1 Theorising teaching as a sociocultural practice

As teachers, we use our professional knowledge of teaching to theorise our practice as teachers. When theorising, we are explaining and giving an overview of a phenomenon, with theory being seen as 'an architecture of ideas – a coherent structure of interrelated concepts ... [that distinguishes] good scholarship from even the best journalism' (Anyon, 2009: 3, 4). Theorising takes our thinking beyond description to explain and account, linking what we notice to a broader perspective (Anyon, 2009; Bruce, 2010). In theorising, we are using theory to add depth, interpretation, meaning, explanation and significance when making sense of what we do and notice when teaching (and when doing educational research).

Theorising is important as we currently work within the neo-liberal discourses of teachers as technicians for efficiency and effectiveness, rather than professionals (Ball, 1995). As Ball states: 'there is a kind of theorising that rests upon complexity, uncertainty and doubt and upon a reflexivity about its own production, and its claim to knowledge about the social' (Ball, 1995: 269), rather than solely seeking claims to truth. 'Theorising is a vehicle for "thinking otherwise"' (Ball, 1995: 266) and a foil against reductionist and technocratic thinking. And, as such, theorising is not just something that researchers do, it is also done by teachers reflecting on our practice, with theorising being reconstructed or rejected accordingly.

Sociocultural theorising has been useful to educators (of science, for example) to make sense of the teaching and learning in the classroom (Bell, 2005a). Teaching has been theorised in the research literature as a sociocultural practice, with the main goal being to create an account of human thinking and action that recognises the essential relationships between mind and action, and their social, cultural and institutional settings (Nuthall, 1997; Wertsch, 1991, Wertsch *et al.*, 1995). In other words, to understand the thinking and practices of teachers and students teaching and learning in the classroom, we need to take into account the sociocultural contexts in which the teaching and learning are occurring, and the relationships between mind and action.

In addition, the notion of 'practice' communicates something wider than a technique and skill, something incorporating, as well, knowledge, making judgements, intuition, and the purposes for the action (Beckett and Hager, 2002).

The term 'teaching' is used here in the sense of the broader term 'pedagogy' (Bell, 2003) to indicate that teaching is considered not just as a skill set, but as a professional practice, with reference to values, aims and the philosophy of education (Winch and Gingell, 1999); the linking of power and knowledge (Bernstein, 1971; Gore, 1993), and acknowledgment of the situated nature of teaching (Leach and Moon, 1999b). Hence, teaching as pedagogy is viewed as being more than 'best practice', more than the techniques or strategies of arranging the seating in the classroom, choosing the materials and equipment to be used, preparing a lesson plan, or 'managing' learning activities for the students during the lesson. Seen as a sociocultural practice, teaching as pedagogy is the encompassing of dispositions, knowledges, minds, ways of knowing, languages and discourses, epistemologies of the learner and the teacher; educational goals, purposes, values, expectations, curriculum; the interactions and relationships between participants; the prior knowledge, motivation, the affect, the diversity of students as well as the more widely known facets of teachers, teaching, learners, learning, assessment (Leach and Moon, 1999a).

The aim of this book is to explore the sociocultural theorising of teaching, and in particular nine aspects of teaching as a sociocultural practice, namely teaching as a relational practice (including teaching as a spiritual practice), social practice (including teaching as a knowledge practice), a cultural practice (including teaching as a gendered practice), an emotion practice, a caring practice, an ethical practice, an embodied practice, a spatial practice, and a political practice. In each of these practices, we are invited to explore the relationships between person and context, and between mind and action.

The format of the book is around three strands. First, for each of these nine practices, a review of relevant but not exhaustive educational research is given. The reviewed research literature is from early years, primary, secondary and tertiary educational research. These nine practices have been identified previously in the research literature, but only one or two of them tend to be discussed in any one research article, with few if any articles making reference to all nine (Bell, 2010).

Second, each of the nine practices is illustrated with quotations from beginning and experienced secondary teachers talking teaching. Details of source of the quotations are given in Appendix A.

The third strand in the book is the sociocultural framework or jigsaw (see Figure 1), which is a distinctive feature of this book. Each jigsaw piece of the sociocultural jigsaw is not new knowledge, with each piece or chapter containing a review of existing literature. What is new is that all aspects are reported together here in one publication, and that the jigsaw is used to analyse and theorise the talk of beginning and experienced secondary teachers talking teaching (Bell, 2010; Bell and Scarff Seatter, 2010). The purpose and

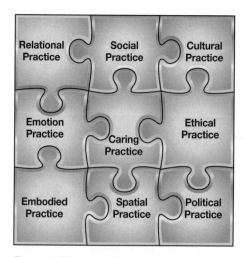

Figure 1 The sociocultural jigsaw

usefulness of the jigsaw is to retain as far as possible the complexity of teachers talking teaching, while at the same time providing a structure or patterning to enable us to make sense of the complexity. The jigsaw is further discussed at the end of this chapter and in the final chapter, Chapter 11.

A case study

As an introduction to the nine aspects of teaching as a sociocultural practice, each practice is briefly discussed with respect to the relevant literature and illustrated by quotations from Sally, a beginning secondary teacher of English, talking teaching (Bell, 2010).[1] Sally had come to teaching as a second career.

1. Teaching as a social practice

One aspect of theorising teaching as a sociocultural practice in the research literature is theorising teaching as a social practice (Bell, 2005a, 2005b; Bell and Cowie, 2001). Teaching involves social interaction with others; it is not something a teacher does without students. The dialogue between teacher and student is a social practice and we call this teaching. It requires the teacher to use her or his knowledge, and hence teaching as a knowledge practice is included as part of teaching as a social practice.

One aspect of teaching as a social practice is that of teaching as a knowledge practice. Teachers know and use many different kinds of knowledge to teach (Shulman, 1987; Shulman and Shulman, 2004), including pedagogical content knowledge, which is seen as important as it is unique to a teacher's professional knowledge (Loughran *et al.*, 2006; Hume and Berry, 2010). Sally indicated that she used different kinds of knowledge in her teaching practices, including her knowledge of content:

> ... and academically I feel very confident and very strong in especially English, it's been my passion for years ... it's not say I know everything the kids ask obviously. There's content questions I don't know or I haven't read the book or whatever. ... in terms of grammar or structural stuff like that, I don't have any problems at all. [Sally]

She had a knowledge of her students; for example, what interested them and engaged them:

> [The department] suggested to me two extended texts and two films and I just looked at the kids ... and I thought 'it ain't going to work, there's just no way this is going to work'. ... [I spoke with the] Year 12 coordinator in English and told her of my concerns. ... I said 'I just can't see these kids interacting with either of these things' and she said 'well it's your call, you know, you do it'. So I went with my gut instinct and it was exactly right. I mean it ended up with things that the kids loved. ... I got huge satisfaction out of realising that I was right in terms of my gut instinct ... I was spot on with them ... just the match between the film and the girls was perfect and they are not good writers but at least they had something that they did engage with and they were happy to talk about. [Sally]

---

1 This section is a revised version of Bell 2010.

She had knowledge of their home situation, as indicated when she talked about what it means to be a 'good' teacher:

> ... I think a good teacher is more than the classroom. I think a good teacher looks at the pastoral role, but also the greater community ... and I ring parents a lot, I involve parents a lot ... [Sally]

Sally indicated she had a knowledge of the students' prior knowledge and skills, educational theory, how to teach the content (pedagogical content knowledge) and planning. She also spoke about teaching as a social practice: that is, explicit teaching of the content or subject matter through talking, discussion and dialogue between teacher and student or student and student, either face-to-face or online.

Sally spoke of how she set up interactive activities in the class so that the students could co-construct shared understandings:

> ... the way I work in the classroom is that I use that peer appreciation all the time ... at age 18 their peers are their model and I notice it in the classroom. I can see it happening in front of my eyes and I use that in the class and a lot of that group work is because they work well together. You know, they do listen to each other. They're more inclined to listen to each other than they're ever going to listen to me. So group work works in those situations provided you can keep the classroom management. You know, the structure has got to be there. [Sally]

She indicated the ways in which she engaged the students with the thinking and learning. For example:

> I am very controversial and I like to, for instance we did [the book] *Whale Rider* recently and I said to them ... 'Aren't whales just cows in the water?' ... and everybody was up in arms, and I love doing stuff like that because then that promotes a discussion and they're able to prove to me that what I'm saying is incorrect. So playing the devil's advocate sometimes encourages that sort of thing as well and I don't mind them challenging me and I don't mind when I get it wrong. ... and I say to them that's wonderful because that shows me that you're being responsible for your own learning, you're not dependent on me, you're thinking for yourself. [Sally]

Sally spoke of how she mediated her students' learning, for example via another teacher, by having a specific dialogue with the student on language use:

> I have, for instance, a child in my Year 11 extension class, very, very bright young woman, but her first writing ... and I picked a consistent grammar problem. So in the first week of her writing ... I took that [the student's writing] down to the ESOL teacher and she's been on a programme ever since, one period a week, and her writing just improved incredibly. It was just a grammatical hitch that's all ...she's obviously going to do something wonderful at university. Incredibly bright, very talented young woman. [Sally]

She spoke of how she had scaffolded the units of learning so that the students could succeed in each step of the task:

... I spent most of last summer, and that was a big advantage, getting myself organised, so I had all the units prepared and I made extra scaffolding steps for them [the low ability class] so that they weren't ever put in a position to fail because that's what they've done for six years ... and that really changed the attitude. ... [But] even at the end, I had one girl who would start every unit [with] 'Miss, I can't read' and 'I can't write'. Every unit, and she did, I think, six of the units and achieved and wrote particularly well. What was astounding [was] the quality of the work that came out of these kids. [Sally]

While Sally did mention assessment for summative purposes in responses to questions on her preparedness to do assessment for the (New Zealand) National Certificate of Educational Achievement, when she discussed her teaching her talk was mainly about assessment for formative purposes, that is, assessment for learning:

[In what ways have your assessment practices developed over the past 18 months?]
I'm not so structured on the test as I was; I use different forms of assessment now in terms of formative assessment than I did before. ... I do it with my senior Year 11 extension class. ... I gave them a task, they had to do an essay, 200 words ... And then, I gave them a structured template to have a look at ... they felt they could judge for themselves where they might have gone right or wrong. If they were happy with that, they didn't have to rework it. ... and they got another person of their own choosing to go through and check grammar and spelling and punctuation and things like that, and then they got it back again, then they had to rework it. And then I gave them an assessment sheet, the one I used for the marking criteria, and they had to mark it themselves. ... I went over to see what they had done and in fact they marked themselves incredibly harshly, but they also had moved. There were individual differences in the way they were writing, and they had moved away from that [initial] format ... I wanted to see some thinking and some different levels of thinking ... so that was very successful. [Sally]

2. Teaching as a relational practice

Teaching may be viewed as a relational practice, with relationships being seen as very important by teachers (Bauml, 2009). It is within a relationship that the work of a teacher is done. After six months of teaching, Sally identified her relationships with the students as a key priority for her:

[When you graduated last year, what did you think teaching would be like?]
... it is exactly what I thought it would be and I really, really enjoy it ... it's a comfortable sort of, very satisfying feeling that I get from it and I love the challenges and I love the kids and I never realised the relationship you would form so easily with them and I've never laughed so much, I love every class, they're just gorgeous ...'

[... What have been the most rewarding experiences as a beginning teacher?]
The relationship with the kids without a doubt, I just, I really enjoyed that from Day 1.

[... And what's the most important thing to you about being a teacher at this time?]
I think the most important thing is my relationship with the kids I teach and I think I've

realised that unless I have a good relationship with them then I'm not going to teach them anything basically. [Sally]

After one year of teaching, Sally spoke of classroom management as a relational practice and the two-way nature of relationships:

> *[... Tell me what it's been like since we talked in June?]*
> ... and I also think relationships manage classrooms. ... I think I want to have a relationship with my students that's professional and friendly, but I don't necessarily feel that I have to please them. [Sally]

Sally also spoke of teaching as being a relational practice with colleagues:

> *[So what about informal support, did you have a buddy or ...]*
> Oh yes I meet [with] my buddy, we're meeting once every six days, in the six-day period, we still meet one period every six days, she's lovely. She runs a Te Reo Pākehā [unit], lovely young woman and I'm trying to think how long she's been working, but very efficient, very organised and was somebody I was able to be quite frank with at times and we established a rapport very quickly and she was a good sounding board at times about different things. [Sally]

In summary, Sally talked about the relationships she had with students and staff, relationships in which she practiced teaching.

3. Teaching as an emotion practice

Another aspect of teaching as a sociocultural practice addressed in the literature is that of teaching as an emotion practice (Hargreaves, 2001a, 1998; Zembylas, 2004b). (The term 'emotional practice' is not used here to avoid 'emotional' being linked with 'irrational'). Sally discussed what she had learnt in her first year of teaching, about working with other staff:

> Gosh, learnt how to write reports. ... The software system the school uses is pretty pathetic and so that causes problems and it causes frustration amongst other staff and that's an area I don't particularly like because it causes a lot of tension because it's just the wrong system and it falls apart every time people do reports, so the tension rises, so I don't like that. I've learnt to be very diplomatic around report time and give [other] teachers their space. [Sally]

This quotation illustrates Sally talking about her own and her colleagues' emotions as a part of what teachers do. Sally expressed her own feelings when talking about her teaching – for example, the negative feelings she had had in her first 18 months of teaching – by using words such as 'nervous', 'not feeling confident', 'awful', 'horrified', 'battling', 'so annoyed', 'discouraged, 'irate', 'feel the tension', 'grumpy', 'exasperated', 'tired', 'pathetic', 'frustration', 'cried', 'huge pressures', 'did not enjoy', 'not done a lot', 'upset', 'demoralising', 'unfair'.

Sally also expressed her positive feelings about her teaching, using such words as 'amazed', 'successes', 'inspiring', 'enjoyable', 'very relaxed', 'laughter', 'smiled', 'very sweet', 'pleasure', 'passionate', 'supportive', 'helpful', 'impressed', 'pleased with', 'interested', 'celebrate', 'wonderful', 'fabulous', 'formidable', 'fascinated'.

4. Teaching as a caring practice

Teachers practice caring as a part of teaching (Noddings, 1992). Sally talked about how she cared about her students' achieving learning outcomes at school:

> ... these girls are either stood down on daily report, detention, usually out of uniform. It took a whole term for them not to swear, not to swear at me, to stay in their seats, either engage with the class or at the very least not interfere with the class ... at the end of the first term I felt quite discouraged until I talked to some of the teachers and especially the deputy head. I said I didn't feel like I had got anywhere academically ... and she said 'I think you've done wonders because of the nature of them' and this term, this last term, we've actually made some progress academically and looking back I think I was a bit impatient ... they needed that whole term just for them to have some trust in me. [Sally]

Sally showed her teaching as a caring practice in the interest she took in her students and in getting to know them:

> It took me probably a term for them [the students] to trust me and I spent a lot of time getting to know them and what sports they played, where they worked, I gave them each a little questionnaire thing when I first started about their likes and dislikes. [Sally]

Sally cared about how other students spoke about her Year 12 class, using her own values as a basis for her caring:

> ... I was horrified. The next class coming in one day said 'what's this, the cabbage class?' Well I haven't lost my temper, but I was so annoyed with that child and I said to them 'Don't you dare come into my classroom, and say anything like that to my students'. And in the next class, I told my Year 12, I said 'Don't you dare stand for anyone telling you that. Everybody has strengths and weaknesses'. [Sally]

Sally discussed her caring practice of keeping students safe, for example, emotionally safe, when the topic of child abuse was included in a book which the class had to read. She also commented on her practice of caring about the students' emotional lives, noting their emotional situation when they entered the classroom. She also mentioned the way the students cared for her when she hurt her ankle by opening doors and carrying her books.

5. Teaching as an embodied practice

Teaching is not just a practice of the mind, it is also a practice of the body (Shapiro, 1997). Sally discussed the time when she hurt her ankle and had trouble walking:

> *[The next question is about your best day or experience, so ...]*
> That was easy, that was an unplanned lesson. ... I'm usually very organised, it's only ever happened once. It was only several weeks ago. It was a Year 9 class and for some

reason, I have a locked cabinet, I left my key at home, and I'd left my planning book in the staff room, and my ankle was sore. I walked into the classroom, and I thought, 'Oh' ... and I thought about my sore ankle and I thought about the locked cupboard and away I went. And we had a fabulous lesson and the kids were really [engaged]. ... it was a great confidence booster because I knew then, that if all I had was a white board marker and I knew my class, I would be okay. ... [But it was also my worst experience] managing the three lots of stairs with a sprained ankle and trying not to get grumpy by Period 6 in the afternoon. ... I was just tired, and the ankle [was] sore and so I didn't have the concentration or the energy or enthusiasm level. [Sally]

When her ankle was sore, Sally was aware of how her body had influenced the way she taught and how she felt.

6. Teaching as a cultural practice

Teaching as a cultural practice is seen to be evident when we, as teachers, take into account, value and build on the lived cultural experiences and knowledge of students and hence their cultural identity (Bishop et al., 2009). For example, Sally noted:

[X, a Māori[2] teacher educator] said in his lecture that he thought the best teacher of Maori students was a Pākehā teacher that he observed. And so, I took that to mean that his methods probably were across the board, and certainly at the school that I'm at, [there is a] huge diversity in ethnicities. I've used them [pedagogies for Maori students] and had huge success with all sorts of different nationalities, so I find that extremely interesting. [Sally]

She stated that she was aware of and took into account the culture of students – in this case, the ethnicity of students. Sally did not directly address teaching as a gendered practice.

7. Teaching as a spatial practice

Teaching as a spatial practice refers to the way the spaces in which we teach influence and determine what we do as teachers (Jenlink and Jenlink, 2008). Spaces may be physical spaces, e-spaces, social spaces in relationships, and linked to time. Sally discussed at length her thoughts about not having her own teaching classroom. She had commented that it was unfair that the senior, more experienced teachers had their own rooms, but not the beginning teachers. A hierarchical distribution of power via the allocation of teaching spaces was implied:

... a lot of the senior teachers [are] teaching senior classes of 16 to a class, and they might have three classes because they have other responsibilities [and they are teaching] in their own room. And junior teachers, meaning junior in experience, not in age, have five or six classes of 30 junior students each and they are moving around. To

---

2 Māori is the word for the indigenous people of New Zealand. Pākehā is the Maori word for people descendent from the largely British colonists of the nineteenth century. Both words are in the everyday language of English speaking New Zealanders.

me that seems totally unfair because 1) they [the senior teachers] are better managers, 2) they have half the students, and 3) they have all that experience. ... I don't agree with it. I don't think it's right. [Sally]

In her second year, she was expected to move between 11 classrooms, which meant she had to carry her teaching resources for student-centred teaching with her:

> ... if I'm moving all the time as a new teacher and I haven't got my resources with me, because I can't carry boxes of dictionaries and boxes of reading material and stuff like that, it must affect my students. ... And in fact it would have made it impossible to teach my Unit Standards girls the way I do, because I have all my Units running concurrently and they can pick whatever they want. ... So it would have changed my teaching practice, it would have been terribly detrimental to it ... [Sally]

Sally was very much aware of how the spaces in which she taught influenced her choice of teaching activities.

8. Teaching as a political practice.

The literature indicates that teachers undertake teaching as a political practice, that is, they address the discourses of power in schooling, especially with respect to inequities and social justice (Gore, 1993). Sally expressed concern with the allocation of teaching classrooms:

> ... because I did go to her [Head of Department] with my classroom allocation and she thought that that classroom allocation was okay ... so she didn't support me in that. [So] I went to the PPTA [Post-Primary Teachers Association, the secondary teachers' union] and it says under the national agreement that PRT 1 and PRT 2 teachers [year 1 and year 2 provisionally registered teachers] should not be put under undue stress in their first two years of teaching because they are new teachers and that fitted the criteria. So I went to the Principal on my own bat and negotiated and it would have been nice to have some support. I mean I'm a quite strong individual and I'm in a position that if I had felt they weren't going to compromise I would have walked. ... Financially I could do that but for a lot of young teachers with huge [student loan] debt, they are not in that position and that's not good for students, it all comes back to me and I had this discussion, my Principal probably didn't appreciate it. [Sally]

This is an example of one of the ways a teacher might use political practices as a part of teaching.

9. Teaching as an ethical practice

In the literature, teaching is viewed as an ethical practice, as teachers need to be ethical, respectful and responsible to protect the welfare of the students, given the students' dependency, vulnerability, and powerlessness; to ensure fairness and equity of opportunity and outcomes of students; and to not abuse their power and status (Hall, 2001). Teachers also need to be ethical to teach and model ethical behaviour for the moral development of children, reflecting society's and culture's expectations, norms, values and mores – for example, social justice, democratic rights and human rights. Being ethical also requires teachers to be competent and appropriately qualified as teachers, to practise ethical collegiality and to manage ethical conflicts (Hall, 2001).

Whilst Sally did not use the word 'ethics', she did discuss professional caring for her students, and in particular that her students succeeded academically. She was also mindful of her teaching practices as relational, and she indicated a keen sense of social justice and fairness – for example, in her differentiated teaching practices and treating the girls with respect and expecting them to do likewise to each other as well.

A sociocultural jigsaw

When it is theorised as a sociocultural practice, the literature suggests that teaching may be viewed as a number of related and interacting classroom practices, which teachers indicate they do in the classroom. Nine such practices are discussed in this book. These nine classroom practices can be seen as forming a framework or jigsaw. This can be represented as shown in Figure 1.

The metaphor of the jigsaw is used here to emphasise five key points. First, whilst each jigsaw piece has a picture on it, the picture on each piece is partial. The whole picture on the jigsaw is only visible when all the pieces are in place. In a similar way, if we theorise teaching as a sociocultural practice, we can only understand teaching in its fullness and complexity when we understand the multiple aspects of 'sociocultural', here the nine practices. Hence, the purpose of the jigsaw of the nine sociocultural practices is to make more visible the sociocultural theorising of teaching as a 'coherent structure of interrelated concepts' (Anyon, 2009: 3) to explain and provide an overview of teachers talking teaching.

Second, in a jigsaw, the pieces are related to each other through the shape of the interlocking pieces and the partial picture on each piece. Where each piece is placed is related to the other surrounding pieces. Likewise, the nine teaching practices discussed here as aspects of teaching as a sociocultural practice are related to and interact with each other. Often, the teachers interviewed discussed two or more practices in a segment of their teaching talk. The teachers tended to not to discuss one practice without referring to others of the nine practices.

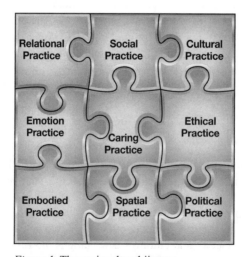

Figure 1 The sociocultural jigsaw

Third, the sociocultural framework or jigsaw of the nine practices tentatively appears to be a fruitful way to analyse and theorise the talking of both beginning and experienced teachers about their teaching, indicating that the framework is not a narrow partial perspective of teaching, but is holistic. Theorising using the nine related practices appears to preserve the complexity and richness in the talking and theorising of both the beginning and the experienced teachers.

Fourth, the framework indicates that the teachers were both describing and theorising when they talked about their teaching.

Last, the value of teachers reflecting on, talking about, re-storying and making sense of their lived experiences has been documented in the literature over many years as promoting teacher professional and personal learning and development in the teaching profession, whether it be in initial teacher education or in ongoing in-service learning (Brown, 1996; Loughran et al., 2008, Loughran *et al.*, 2004; Palmer, 2007). It is hoped that the framework developed in this book will be useful for teachers learning to teach in initial teacher education and for teachers starting more in-depth theorising of teaching at the master's-level programmes.

Each of the nine practices is discussed more fully in Chapters 2 to 10, with a review of the relevant literature and illustrations of beginning and experienced secondary teachers talking teaching.

Study and discussion

- What do you understand by the term 'sociocultural theorising'?
- Why are the nine aspects of theorising teaching as a sociocultural practice depicted as a jigsaw?

2 Teaching as a relational practice

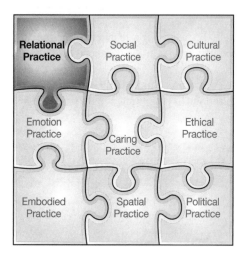

When we view teaching as a relational practice, we are acknowledging the teacher–student relationship – the essence or crux of teaching. Effective teachers and award-winning teachers are noted for the quality of their relationships with students.

> Teaching is at heart a relationship, [the teachers] said, and everything else depends upon and flows from that relationship (Tate, 2007: 7)

It is within the teacher–student relationship that students feel included or excluded from a discipline of human knowledge; academically successful or failing; belonging to or disconnected from schooling; valued or not valued for who they are – the beliefs, ideas, experiences, values they bring to school learning; trusted or not trusted; and worthy or unworthy members of their school communities. How we as teachers relate to students impacts on their lives (Noddings, 2003).

The relationship between teacher and student provides the context for the teaching and learning of a range of cognitive, social, personal, moral and behavioural learning goals, and not just the learning of interpersonal or relational skills by the students, when modelled or taught explicitly by the teacher. And more importantly the teacher–student relationship influences the outcomes of learning, including academic learning (for reviews of the research evidence see Davis, 2003; Murray and Pianta, 2007; Newberry, 2010).

Within the teacher–student relationship, teachers communicate with students to: teach the concepts and skills being taught and learnt; set expectations for student learning (Murray and Pianta, 2007); ensure ethics in teaching of honesty, truth, caring, fairness, justice; nurture the holistic wellbeing and growth of students (Tate, 2007); provide a culturally and emotionally safe environment for students; model interpersonal skills and values – for teachers teach who they *are* (Tate, 2007); get to know their students; and build up a rapport to support behaviour management in early-years, primary and secondary education (Davis, 2003), in special education (Murray and Pianata, 2007), in tertiary education (Cranton, 2006), and in teacher education (Bauml, 2009; Giles, 2008b, 2010).

The teacher–student relationship can be theorised in several ways (Giles, 2008a, 2008b) and, here, three ways are noted. First, it can be theorised as a physical, social, or emotional space between teacher and student, a space for the meeting of two minds and hearts. For example, the teacher–student relationship may be described as close or distant, warm or cold. Cranton (2006), for example, writes of tertiary teacher–student relationships based on a respectful distance, collegiality, or closeness, according to what the teacher finds professionally and ethically comfortable:

> When respectful distance is the basis of knowing students, the relationship occurs primarily through the subject area and focuses on the learning. In collegial relationships, the educator views the learner as a future or current colleague, works collaboratively, and engages in mutual sharing of experience and expertise. In a close relationship, teachers and students come to know each other as people (Campbell, 2008) both inside and outside the classroom (Cranton, 2006: 10).

Students also construct meanings for the perceived distance in the teacher–student relationship, and students may see a teacher as being 'present' or 'not present'; being in the relationship or not and with or without reciprocity and mutuality (Giles, 2008). The teacher–student relationship is seen as the space in which trust, respect, empathy and a sense of belonging for students are co-constructed (Davis, 2003). It is also the place in which teachers practise ethical behaviour to protect students in their dependency and vulnerability (Tate, 2007) which 'cuts to the core of human relationships' (Campbell, 2008: 377). The relationship is a space in which teachers get to know their students, and therefore rely less on stereotypes to inform their thinking and actions (Davis, 2003; Cranton, 2006). It is a space in which teachers learn of students' cultural practices and worldviews (Bishop and Berryman, 2006). It is a space in which students develop resilience in relationships (Davis, 2003). School culture and social norms may be supportive of or constraining of the creation of a space for the interaction needed for teacher–students relationships (Davis, 2003; Murray and Pianta, 2007). When interpreted from a sociocultural perspective, the relationship and the relational space are seen as 'dynamic, changing and culturally bound' (Davis, 2003: 225).

Second, the teacher–student relationship may be theorised as discursive, drawing on post-structural theorising (Bell, 2005a; Middleton, 1993, 1998). If we use discursive theorising to make sense of the teacher–student relationship, we are mindful of the power constructed within the relationship, particularly with respect to ethical responsibilities (Tate, 2007), advocacy for students and social justice. This theorising of the teacher–student relationship also enables us to reflect on discursive positioning: how others in the relationships use language to position us, and how we position ourselves, and on the discursive co-construction of what it means to be a teacher (Devine, 2003). A teacher's identity or understanding of themselves is always in relation to their students, for the student is not absent in teacher identity (Vogt, 2002). Relationships may be constructed in relation to time and space, which may be configured differently in different cultures – an aspect that is foregrounded when considering relationships with indigenous and Pasifika students[1] (Kalavite, 2010). For example, during a total immersion professional development, living as Māori, Baskerville noted: 'I learnt the importance of the time and space given to establish relationships, roles and responsibilities for Māori' (Baskerville, 2009: 463).

Third, the teacher–student relationship may be seen as teachers in relational connectedness with students (Gibbs, 2006). Relational connectedness 'describes a basic bond of the relationship such that, as human beings we live to relate; connectivity being basic to our humanity' (Giles, 2008a: 2). To use the term 'relational connectedness' is to highlight the inherent and integral nature of the connectedness in the relationship, rather than seeing it merely as the 'meeting space' between teacher and student. To acknowledge the deep-seated relational connectedness is to acknowledge the spiritual:

> Spirituality is the eternal human yearning to be connected with something larger than our own egos (Palmer: 2003:377).
> Rather than a religious orientation, the spirituality of relational connectedness is a "awareness of something greater than ourselves, a sense that we are connected to all human beings and to all creation" (Giles, 2008: 2, quoting Nugent, 2003).

In this sense, we are viewing teaching not only as a relational practice, but also as a spiritual practice. The notion of relational connectedness is central to teaching as a spiritual practice. It is within this related connectedness that we consider that 'good teachers love their students' (Tate, 2007: 10), not in the sense of romantic or sexual love but in the sense of care, commitment, knowledge, responsibility, respect, trust (hooks, 2003), and patience, devotion, dedication and commitment (Tate, 2007). As one of the experienced teachers said:

> ... I think a good teacher has to like kids, it's as simple as that; and I've always loved kids, so I think that's stayed through me the whole time. I don't know why anyone is teaching if they don't like kids. [Harry]

In Chapter 1 we read how a beginning teacher also mentioned her love for the students:

> I love the kids and I never realised the relationship you would form so easily with them and I've never laughed so much, I love every class. [Sally]

One's relationship with oneself is also of interest when we consider teaching as a relational and spiritual practice. 'Knowing myself is as crucial to good teaching as knowing my students and my subject' (Palmer, 2007: 3). 'Who is the self that teaches?' is a key question for us to reflect on, as is 'How does the quality of my selfhood form – or deform – the way I relate to my students, my subject, my colleagues, my world?' (Palmer, 2007: 4. Palmer

1 Pasifika is a term used to refer to Pacific peoples in the context of Aotearoa New Zealand.

continues that knowing oneself is to know the intellectual (one's thinking about teaching and learning), emotional (the way one feels when teaching) and spiritual (one's connectedness with people and with the larger world). Hence, teaching as a spiritual practice highlights the whole teacher and holistic teaching (Schon, 2005). It also views students in their wholeness: their intellectual, emotional, embodiment, and spiritual selves. It is when teachers know the self-who-teaches that they are able to be present in the connectedness with students, and therefore also vulnerable to the fear of having 'a live encounter with another', the fear of the 'conflict that will ensue when divergent truths meet'; and the fear of 'losing identity' (Palmer, 2007: 38). Knowing the self-who-teaches is seen as a part of a teacher's identity and integrity in teaching, with identity being seen as the mix of all the forces on our lives, and integrity as recognising the whole of who we are, both good and bad. Being and doing what flows from one's identity, and integral to one's nature, is seen to lead to good teaching (Palmer, 2007). To know the self-who-teaches is to know our inner landscape (Connolly and Clandinin, 1999). For example, beginning teacher Ellie, after 18 months of teaching, commented:

> *[Are there any areas of your teaching that you still want to develop?]*
> And you start to identify who you are as a teacher, what you are as a person. And although you used to look at what other teachers are doing, and kind of think 'I want to do that' or whatever, you know that you can't now. You've got to do your own adaptation of things. You have to be comfortable with what you are doing, and you can also be yourself and also be a good teacher. So it's just coming to terms with it ... I think when you leave [Teacher's] College, you see someone and you think 'I will adapt that completely' but of course you can't because, as I said before, you've got to become yourself within the profession as well. [Ellie]

To teach from the spirit is to inspire and give hope. Such a pedagogy of hope (hooks, 2003) is seen as transforming lives, advancing social injustice and healing. In a similar way, Shahjahan (2009) talks of pedagogies of love and hope. A pedagogy of love is seen as offering protection so that students feel safe to express themselves in the classroom, and to give voice to the silenced as well as the oppressor. 'This support and healing was necessary in order to move towards social change rather than maintaining the status quo' (Shahjahan, 2009: 125). Likewise, Palmer (2003) uses the term 'pedagogy of the soul' to describe a pedagogy which creates a safe place for the soul/spirit of both student and teacher; and which meets the needs of the soul/spirit.

The above ways of theorising the teacher–student relationship – a relational space, a discursive relationship and a spiritual connectedness – provide three ways of making sense of teachers talking teaching as a relational practice. When the interview data from the beginning and experienced teachers were analysed, it was noted that they talked teaching as relationships, not just with students but with different groups of people. Hence the following sections are based on these groupings of people, rather than the above three types of theorising identified in the literature. Within the category of teaching as a relational practice, there were comments made by the beginning and experienced teachers on teaching as a relational practice with respect to the relationships between teacher and student for promoting student learning and development, with students with respect to behaviour management, between colleagues, between a teacher and parents and care-givers, with friends and family at home, and with the subject matter. Each of these is now discussed in turn.

Relationships with students

Developing relationships with students was seen by the teachers interviewed as an essential part of being a teacher. For example, an experienced teacher commented on how he built up and valued the teacher–student relationship to improve learning:

> 'Improving student learning?' One of the things that I think I've learnt … is actually finding out a lot more about the students' home lives and interests, where they see their interests in Science … It's kind of like, I guess, it's a 'prior learning' but in much more general sense. And I also when I start a year, I put up a Powerpoint showing them all my kids and grandkids and me at the beach, and all sorts of stuff, so they actually see that I'm a person, just like them. So … right from the start, to improve the learning, for me, is actually getting that relationship going with kids. … that's hugely important for that to happen within the first few weeks. [Harry]

The teacher–student relationship was seen as going beyond the classroom, for example to the sports club:

> *[Have there been any things that you might call rewarding experiences in your first six months?]*
> Rewarding, probably the students themselves. I really haven't met any students that I teach that I dislike, and I know that sounds unusual, but being involved with 150 or 160, which is a lot of kids, the thing that's really surprised me is how enjoyable it is actually to be in class. … I'm the … teacher in charge – cycling [at a boys' school] which has been quite good … mountain biking and the road cycling. … I've had experience in the past with event management with cycling, and the fact that I come from a cycling family and my husband and children are involved in it, and I'm involved with the club, so it's something that's been easy to get contacts. And that's been great because you get to know the students in a quite different, casual sort of way. It's been really good and they're keen at what they do, so they join in with the cycling, because they want to and so you get a group of very enthusiastic boys, and it is a chain reaction because they … they tell their friends … if you have one of your students that you teach … and they work in your class, it makes teaching that bit easier and enjoyable. Sort of leads on, but no, it's been good. [Stephanie]

The teacher–student relationship was also seen as extending beyond the year in which it is first formed: extending the initial time and space constructions. A beginning teacher said:

> Kids often say 'thanks for that lesson', or 'that was fun' … I suppose the best feedback for me in a way is the kids that came back from last year – that come in and want to tell you about how well they are doing. [They] come in uninvited to tell you that they've just got Excellence for a speech or something like that. Not necessarily feedback on your teaching but they do want to come and share with you their successes and tell you what is happening in their day. [Sandy]

Relationships for behaviour management

The beginning teachers discussed behaviour management as an aspect of teaching as a relational practice, which they were still learning to do. Most found it challenging and mentioned that they would have liked to have spent more time on it in their initial teacher education, even though they realised developing their practices of behaviour management was better suited to learning 'on the job', with help from mentors and senior management in the school. It was an aspect that most said they would still be working on in their third year of teaching. For example, beginning teacher Sandy talked about behaviour management in all three interviews. In the first interview, she discussed a challenge she had faced with a student who was abusing his power in his classroom relationships:

> I had an issue with a boy who tried to intimidate me as well as some of the kids. And I just said 'No you don't, I will not be intimidated' and … they're not used to not being able to bully people. But, yeah, I sort of think well 'Hey, you are three times the size of the little girl up the front.' [Sandy]

In the second interview, at the end of her first year of teaching, she discussed how she had asked for help when the teacher–student relationships in a class were stressed:

> … I very nearly lost a class on Thursday. … class management issues and that's actually my form class. So that's the one I had to have extra teachers in today, to help manage them, they're basically starting to hang off the ceiling. So yeah, that was my worst day.
>
> *[So what sort of things were the students doing?]*
> Oh, just a range, like not settling and then just taking a long time to get them to settle, and backchat starts, and try to settle again, and that just built up and built up and built up. And … I kept a lid on it until another teacher unfortunately chose that moment to come and ask me a question. I took the opportunity … she took my class for ten minutes, while I just went out and took a deep breath. …
>
> *[In what areas have you still got to, or want to, develop over the next year?]*
> For me probably still, I'd really like to do more work on class management in terms of wait time, tone of voice and control and also developing some more strategies for engaging students. [Sandy]

In the third interview, halfway through her second year, Sandy was viewing classroom management and good relationships as aspects of good teaching:

> *[Has your view of a 'good' teacher changed since you began teaching? In what way?]*
> I don't know whether it's changed completely or maybe refined a bit that I see an effective teacher as still being someone who can, I think to a certain extent you have to have effective relationships with the students. To be a good teacher obviously I think the classroom management is an extremely important part that can't be overlooked and being able to really communicate that desire to learn rather than just a knowledge imparting type activity. [Sandy]

The experienced teachers were also asked about their classroom management. When experienced teacher Harry discussed his classroom management views, he spoke of his knowledge of students and of building relationships with them within a bounded space:

Classroom management. ... I like setting up boundaries, kids want to know that – they pretend like they're grownups. When you first come in as a year one, two teacher, the hardest thing is you think you've actually got through to them and converted them into adults but, you know, they're just big kids. ... Right through to year thirteen, you have to keep a boundary with kids – you can still have a bit of fun and respect but you must keep that boundary. The kids like to know their limits, you've got to establish those very clearly, try and establish them with your junior classes, with the students participating [in a discussion] to say 'what's good and not good' rather than 'dos' or 'don'ts'. It's better to give reasons for why you're setting things up with the kids. And fairness, consistency with how you deal with students ... there's a whole heap of exemplars of that but one of the big problems that starting-out teachers have is backing kids into corners ... and not giving kids options. Like, instead of 'you will go and sit there' [it's] 'right, you can either sit here, or sit there, which one is it going to be?' So they feel they have a choice and you get the same effect without [backing them into a corner]. [Harry]

Later in the interview, Harry referred to the power of teacher authority in the teacher–student relationship:

... I think a lot of teachers my age struggle because they're still thinking of those days in the past when the kids 'respected the system' and the system meant that you could go in your classroom and teach, because the system looked after the kids who weren't respecting it. And I think there's been a bit of change in there. So I guess in terms of behaviour management and classroom management there have been some changes. [Harry]

He also discussed the responsibility of the teacher to establish the teacher–student relationship for learning, rather than for misbehaviour:

And I guess, the other thing [that] happens when you're at a school for a couple of years, is that the word goes round ... 'oh, that's Mr (...)' ... the kids have a view of you, if you teach their older brothers and sisters. Of course, as you get older ... you just have to raise your eyebrows. But if your kids want to be there because you're providing a bit of fun for them, and a bit of interest in Science, a bit of thinking skills, then your classroom management doesn't become so much of an issue. Kids will bring things into the classroom, their baggage from outside, but by and large they can leave it outside if you're providing a programme [of learning] for them. So to me, classroom management, if you're having difficulty, you actually do have to look at yourself and what you're providing – is it relevant and right for that group of students, for their ability levels, that kind of stuff. And I guess we all find that out, I talk about it a lot with my year one and two staff. [Harry]

Another experienced teacher explicitly mentioned relationships:

[So what is your key to success for classroom management?]
Good relationships with your students. I think that's a key part ... I think in lower decile schools [schools in low socioeconomic communities] ... a lot of your success is based on the relationships and how well the children know you. [Megan]

Megan also discussed how she positioned herself in the teacher–student relationship to manage classroom behaviour:

> I try to communicate to the students what I'm about in the classroom, and I'm not about somebody who we're going to have a personality clash with, I'm not about somebody who you can have an argument with, I'm not your mother, I'm your teacher and my job, my function, is to get you to learn. So when students will come in late or those sorts of things I sort of say, well … try not to pick arguments I think is one of the key fundamentals of success and always try to look at the positives … so for instance if somebody comes in late and they're chewing gum and all those kinds of things, what would I do? I'd make sure I've greeted them really warmly and said, 'good morning, it's really lovely to see you. … I'm glad you're here. But before you sit down I just want you to remember that we've got some classroom rules in here so could [you] just make sure that you get yourselves sorted out before you start, thank you?' … We're not here to create an argument. [Megan]

Relationships with colleagues

The beginning teachers commented on how their relationships with colleagues were a part of being a teacher. First, the beginning teachers commented on their induction and enculturation into the communities of practice in schools, and the support and assistance they experienced from colleagues. For example:

> *[What's it like being a beginning teacher in your school?]*
> There's a lot of support. It's an incredibly supportive school and that was one of the reasons I came here, because I knew that when I was interviewed … that I wanted to work with those people. So there's a lot of assistance and support. Because it is a smallish school of 700 … teachers tend to know each other and it's a good experience, positive experience being a beginning teacher here. [Ellie]

After 18 months of teaching, Ellie had become aware of the complex web of relationships between staff, and how she was positioned by herself and others in terms of what it means to be a teacher:

> *[Reflecting back on your induction programme since you first started teaching, what aspects would you recommend as essential for beginning teachers?]*

> Obviously things about getting yourself into the school systems as quickly as you can. Working out who are the negative people and they are the ones to avoid. Systems … And working out where you are going to have your lunch, when you do have lunch, where you are going to sit, working out what is best for you rather than being told what to do or thinking everybody does that, I will go and do the same. You realise you don't always sometimes want to be in the staffroom. I noticed that the most effective teachers don't spend much time in the staffroom at all. Things like that, they are system things. … moving paper [on] that is another thing that you work out. You are not really told that, but you have so much paper to work through … and if you've got to fill out something or pass something on, do it really quickly, because you notice there is quite a big collegial disapproval of teachers [who don't]. [With] certain teachers you think

'Oh, that person never does that' and you get this label on you right at the start. I don't really know what the label is on me, but you do get this label right from very early on. So when you are a beginning teacher you've got to be really careful about that, because you are going to be labeled, and if you are seen as being a person who holds things up or stuffs up systems or something you just get that label really early so that is a really important thing to watch out for. [Ellie]

Being able to form and maintain working relationships with colleagues in a school team was seen as a crucial skill for teachers by beginning teacher Sandy:

[And lastly, working with colleagues in a teaching team? Did you feel prepared [by your initial teacher education programme] to do that?]
Well, I think I've worked in teams for a long time [in a previous career] ... there was a lot of team work that we did do here [in the teacher education programme]. The difficulty is, I think, it's a bit false because people can walk away from the university [student] team. Whereas, when you're in the [school] teaching team, and if you don't get on, well you have to get on. I think they are life skills that you take with you, not sure if people can teach you that or not, but some people learn better than others. [Sandy]

Colleague–colleague relationships for professional development were also seen as important, for the discursive construction of what it means to be a teacher, and for the support and connectedness. Experienced teacher Mary commented:

I don't know if you've seen in the *Education Gazette* at the moment but they're running a series about 'collaborative colleagues' and the recent one is about two people who have worked together for several years and planned together and they're asking for other people to write in and share their stories and things. And for me that person particularly is (X) ... Because we don't necessarily always agree on things, but we can have a professional-level conversation, and agree to disagree, and we can have those conversations at a level where we come out thinking we reached agreement, and an end point. But there never is an end point. So one or other of you will come back and say, 'when we did such and such, we ...' ... I like being in the classroom and I like working with the students and I get satisfaction from that, but I also get a huge amount of satisfaction from that professional reflection and checking where I'm at, I suppose; but having a colleague I can sound off with on that level. ... I think having a – I don't know if you'd call it a 'critical friend' or a 'collaborative colleague' or whatever you'd call it, but I think it's useful to have someone that you can do that with or – and someone that will say to you, 'no, that can't be right,' or 'have you really thought about that? I don't think that actually works,' or 'are you sure about that? Have you read this?' or 'here's a paper you really need to read; if you don't know why that didn't work, here's something you should read.' Because I think too often the conversations are at a superficial level that don't necessarily challenge you to think professionally about what you're doing. And it's very easy to say 'I'm a reflective practitioner' or 'we need to reflect on what's happened' but, you know, reflection isn't just saying 'well, that was a good lesson'. ... So I think for me having a colleague that I can actually have a deeper-level conversation with and somebody ... who also likes to read academically and challenge themselves with doing some sort of postgrad work, and those sorts of things. [Mary]

Relationship with the community

Some beginning and experienced teachers mentioned their relationships with students' parents, care-givers, families and the community. For example, experienced teacher Mary described how a Somali community member became an advisor to the teachers of Somali students in her school; and beginning teacher Ellie discussed how she had established contact with families of Pasifika students, with the support of the Pasifika teachers on the staff. These two examples of relationships with the community are discussed more fully in Chapter 4.

Relationships at home

Supportive relationships with people at home was mentioned by the beginning teachers as being important to them. For example:

> *[What has sustained you in your first 18 months?]*
> Sometimes my husband has been very supportive, my family. Because [it's] physically and emotionally quite shattering sometimes and that's very important to me – my home life and supporters. And the excellent support of my colleagues [who] have been incredibly supportive. ... if you have had a bad day or a problem, they have been there, done that, and laugh about it, those things have kept me going. [Ellie]

> *[What has sustained you in your first 18 months?]*
> My sense of humour, and keeping fit is an important one, although it has lapsed at times. My family and again, I would say the support of younger colleagues at school. [Sandy]

Relationships with the subject matter

Another relationship teachers have is with the subject matter they are teaching, and for which they have a passion. For example, experienced teacher Megan commented:

> I think the thrill of the job for me is if we can sow the seed of enthusiasm for science, by the end of two years I've ... it's not really coming from me but if by the end of the two years if I can see a student say, 'I want to [work] in Science because this is what I like learning about it, this is how I want to use it', I think I've done a good job. [Megan]

Summary

If we theorise teaching as a sociocultural practice, teaching may be viewed as a relational practice. Being a teacher means to be in relationships with students, colleagues, parents and care-givers, and with the subject being taught. Teaching involves building up and maintaining these relationships. Teaching as a relational practice sets the scene for the remaining chapters, in which aspects of teaching seen as a sociocultural practice are further explored and discussed. Teaching as social, cultural, emotion, caring, ethical, spatial, embodied, and political practices are all viewed here as being done within relationships.

Study and discussion

- Describe a positive relationship you as a teacher have had with a student.
- Why are teacher–student relationships considered important in teaching?

3 Teaching as a social practice

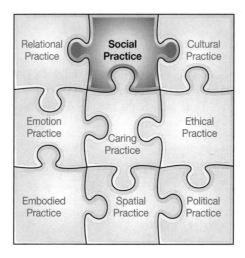

When we view teaching as a social practice, we are acknowledging that it is not a solo activity. Teaching involves social interaction, that is, communication with others, and is not something a teacher does alone, it is done with students in mind. The dialogue between teacher and student is a social practice and we call this teaching. Teaching is just not set in a social context of the classroom, it is itself a social action.

This view of teaching is informed by social views of learning (Bell, 2005a), including: social constructivism (Bell and Gilbert, 1996; Driver *et al.*, 1994); situated learning (Hennessy, 1993; Lave and Wenger, 1991); apprenticeship, guided participation, participatory appropriation (Rogoff, 1993, 1995); distributed cognition (Salomon, 1993); learning in the zone of proximal development, with mediated action (Vygotsky, 1978); (Wertsch, 1991; Wertsch *et al.*, 1995). A fuller review of these is given in Bell 2005a: ch. 3. In these overlapping views of learning, learning is viewed as a purposeful, intentional activity involving meaning making; a situated and contextualised activity; a partnership between teacher and students; and involving the use of language to communicate meaning. Such views of learning do not prescribe a way of teaching; rather, they suggest ways to think about teaching.

Social views of learning highlight the use of language and communication in teaching (Bakhtin, 1986; Vygotsky, 1978). Using the theorising of Bakhtin (1986) in an educational context (Roth, 2005; Wertsch, 1991), a teacher is viewed as mindful of the student, whether that student be in the classroom, reading the teacher's/author's textbook, or learning online. Teaching is purposeful, as it is done with the intention of promoting learning. As teachers, when we talk or write we are considering the student as listener or reader, in order to maximise the student's comprehension of what we are saying. This awareness by the speaker (the teacher) of the addressee (the student) is termed 'addressivity' by Bakhtin (1986) and Wertsch (1991). The notion of addressivity means that 'utterances are not indifferent to one another, and are not self-sufficient; they are aware of and mutually reflect one another's' (Bakhtin, 1986, quoted in Wertsch, 1991: 52). Addressivity is not inherent in the unit of language (for example, in the word or sentence) but in the utterance. For example, in talking to the whole class to explain something, a teacher is not just talking into 'thin air'. The teacher is considering the students, the addressees, taking into account their age, their prior experiences, their cultures, their prior learning, and any information that has been elicited from students during formative assessment. The teacher is communicating with the students, not talking at them.

Bakhtin (1986) uses also the notion of 'voice', meaning the speaking personality, the speaking consciousness. Voice is concerned with the wider issues of a speaking subject's perspective, conceptual horizons, intentions and worldview. It always exists in a social milieu, that is, not in isolation from other voices. Voices produce utterances – a term used by Bakhtin to focus on the situated action of language-in-use, rather than on objects that can be derived from linguistic analytic abstractions. Considering how voices engage with one another is important to a discursive view of mind (Wertsch, 1991), for it is only when two or more voices come into contact (for example, when the voice of a listener responds to the voice of a speaker) that meaning comes into existence (Bakhtin, 1986). In other words, meaning is seen as discursively constructed by two people in dialogue, meaning more than one voice. Hence, when a speaker produces an utterance, at least two voices (those of both the speaker and the listener) are heard simultaneously, as the speaker has addressivity. A dialogic philosophy is said to emphasise 'ontological notions of becoming and draws attention to forms of validity that are constructed within the community in which the dialogue takes place' (Whyte, 2010: 6). Hence, the idea of 'constructed' meanings brings with it a constructionist or relativist ontology. No distinction is made between language and any assumed underlying, internal, static mental states and processes such as cognition. In this non-mentalist ontology, the social actions *are* the cognitive processes. Thoughts reside in the uses we make of public and private systems of signs (including languages and symbols). To be able to think is to be a skilled user of these sign systems. Whilst not denying the existence of a 'reality' of the brain and its functioning, there is a denial of the value of separating language and thinking. In this view, knowledge claims are seen as socio-historical and political, and words are seen as having no objective meaning outside the social and relational contexts in which they are used:

> Language is viewed as reflexive and contextual, constructing the very nature of the objects and events as they are talked about. This emphasises the constructive nature and role of language ... As people are engaged in conversation with others, they construct and negotiate meanings, or the very 'reality' which they are talking about. (Augoustinos and Walker, 1995: 266)

For example, a teacher wishing to understand the learning by two science students doing practical work in the school laboratory needs to make sense of the social talk between the two students as they discuss, for example, why bubbles are coming off only one of the electrodes in the copper chloride solution, not both. That is, the students' discursive practices of purposefully using language, signs and symbols to explain a phenomenon.

Another useful notion for theorising teaching is Bahktin's notion of speech genre, as a type of utterance, whichs relate to typical situations of speech communication (Werstch, 1991). The typical speech in a classroom situation is a genre. As Nuthall (1997b: 729) stated: 'classrooms are language communities that develop their own forms of language'. For example, often a teacher may ask a question to which she already knows the answer, for a specific purpose – to find out what the students is thinking, and to give feedback:

> Teacher: What is the bone in the thigh called?
> Student: Femur.
> Teacher: Yes, that is correct.

This kind of questioning and response rarely occurs in non-teaching situations in everyday life. Speech genre are seen to provide a link between thinking/talking and its social, cultural and historical settings. In classroom talking, the voices appropriated by the students can be only fully interpreted if one goes beyond the individual speakers involved. In order to understand what it is that they have said and to identify 'who' it is that is doing the talking, one must look to the speech genre appropriated in the speakers' utterances. For example, to make sense of the action of a science student who reads the shop sign 'No animals allowed inside', and who then enters the shop, we need to consider who is doing the talking in the sign and who is the intended reader of the sign. The talking is from the public health authority, which has the responsibility for ensuring hygiene standards in food shops. In this case, the everyday meaning of the word 'animal' is being used, not the scientific meaning (Bell, 1981) – meaning dogs, cats, rabbits and other pets that people may not bring into the shop with them. The sign is addressed to pet owners, and not to people in general who are considered animals (as consumers) in the scientific sense, and who may carry on them millions of animals – for example, skin mites. To understand the actions of the science student going shopping, we need to go beyond the individual.

This chapter will explore aspects of teaching as a social practice, focusing on communication, through a discussion of: mindful planning; teaching as a knowledge practice; shared-meaning making and engagement; mediated actions and scaffolding; and formative assessment. In all these sections, the agency of the teacher is central if we are to view teaching as a purposeful, intentional action as distinct from viewing teaching as a socially determined performance to standards (Edwards, 2001).

Mindful planning

Initially, planning by the beginning teachers was seen by them as being based on the subject to be taught, the curriculum, and what they as teachers had to do. The planning was often packaged in the form of resources, which are a source of pedagogical content knowledge, and often exchanged between teachers. For example, beginning teachers Stephanie and Katie noted:

> … I was able to come into school with folders full of resources all ready.

> *[What sort of resources did you bring with you?]*
> Lesson plan or unit plans, a whole lot of unit plans for different subjects across the board. Printouts and different making-things resources, just a whole lot of resources

and a lot of things on disc that I've put to good use. … also I've got a big ring binder full of teaching strategies as well. Yeah, so it's been great, I've come away [from initial teacher education] with lots of resources. [Stephanie]

I also went to the SCICON 2006 [biennial conference for science educators] in the first week of these holidays just gone. … it's really inspired me a lot … as well as getting so many resources, I love it, free stuff, it was so funny, teachers are like magpies with free stuff. [Katie]

However, the beginning teachers also mentioned the need to adapt the resources for the students in their class – they were using their knowledge of the students to inform their planning. For example, beginning teacher Ellie commented:

But you know, in the end … no matter how much help you get from other people and even ideas for lessons, they don't necessarily suit your class and you always have to tailor things to your own. So I find that's my big challenge. [Ellie]

Experienced teacher Harry explained the ways he used to engage the students in his planning and teaching:

[So in what way would you involve the students in your planning?]
Ok, often I will say to the students, 'Right, guys, the topic is Energy, ok. So here's what I'm thinking we might do.' I've already done my thinking, and I'll say, 'Right, we're going to look at a big key question, and the key question is how does this mystery thing called "energy" influence our everyday lives? And that's our key question, this is the whole topic, what we're going to try and answer by the end of it. Ok, now, what I'm thinking we might do is that … I'll give you some starter questions and you guys can look up on the net and find out what is … energy. … so, for example, you guys might like to look at … energy in a house … maybe you might like to look at energy in cars and engines.' … So the idea is that you involve them and check out their ability to express [their] ideas back. So that's what I mean about involving them in the lesson … I have the bigger picture which they don't see … The second is to involve them and get them to write the assessment questions for me. Like, 'you guys have covered this. Now, right, your group … write one question, you guys write one question about what we've been doing for the others all to answer. And you don't have to answer your own question but you've got to answer the other eight. Ok, that'll be our test.' You know? It works really, really well. [Harry]

Using knowledges to inform their teaching

Teaching as communication requires that teachers use multiple knowledges in their communication with students: content knowledge, general pedagogical knowledge, curriculum knowledge, pedagogical content knowledge, knowledge of learners and their characteristics, knowledge of educational contexts, and knowledge of educational ends (Shulman, 1987: 8). A form of knowledge seen as specific to teachers is that of pedagogical content knowledge (PCK), which is described by Shulman in arguing for the need for initial teacher education as that 'special amalgam of content and pedagogy that is uniquely the province of teachers, their own special form of professional understanding' (Shulman, 1987: 8) and 'the capacity of a teacher to transform the content knowledge he or she possesses into forms that are pedagogically powerful, and yet adaptive to the variations in ability and background presented by students' (Shulman, 1987: 15). Both the first meaning (an integrative view; for example Segall, 2004) and the second meaning (a transformative view, for example Loughran *et al.*, 2008) have been developed by researchers since Shulman's seminal paper (Kind, 2009). A micro-example of PCK is a teacher using a vacuum cleaner tube to demonstrate the way that rings of cartilage keep the human respiratory tract open when the neck is bent. A macro-example would be a teacher organising the teaching of atoms to year 9 students, based on 13-year-old students' prior learning experiences and constructed understandings, rather than using the more advanced modelling of the atom of a scientist.

PCK is typically tacit, with experienced teachers often unable to communicate what they do (both the practice and its associated thinking) when they teach others – for example, pre-service teachers on practicum or beginning teachers – to teach. But, once elicited, teacher educators are particularly keen to use the examples of PCK in their teaching of teaching, both as a concept and a heuristic device (Loughran *et al.*, 2008), so that beginning teachers may use it to plan and teach in a way that reflects the complexity of teaching and learning (Abell, 2008; Loughran *et al.*, 2006; Hume and Berry, 2010).

The beginning teachers indicated that they used a range of knowledges to inform their teaching; that is, teaching as a knowledge practice. They talked about using their knowledge of students to inform their teaching. For example, beginning teacher Samantha said:

> *[What other factors influenced your learning this year?]*
> … the kids themselves certainly taught me a lot, as to how they think, and how they react, and what drives them, and definitely what doesn't drive them. [Samantha]

Samantha continued in the next interview:

> *[Have you learnt to support the diversity of student needs?]*
> I'm still learning … I am still at a stage where I am concentrating on me, and how I am delivering the text, [rather than] on how they are receiving it. And I think the second step of that will come more with time and more experience. … but I want to make sure I am getting across the information in an effective way first and foremost. [Samantha]

Beginning teacher Ellie, in her third interview after 18 months of teaching, noted:

> … I spent about 6 months of last year imposing my lessons on students, planning. And then I realised, actually I've got to sit down and look at what they are doing, where they are up to and taking it from them more. My teaching has to be student-centred or driven to some extent, a lot more than I probably thought when I started out. And you realise you've got to teach appropriately and you have to change your teaching for different classes ... And that's hugely turned [my teaching] around. Just how to do that … I'm still learning that. [Ellie]

Ellie mentioned the use of diagnostic tests to obtain information on students:

> *[What aspects would you recommend as essential for beginning teachers?]*
> Familiarising yourself with the student base, getting an understanding and a grip on that. If you are teaching a class, it's a bit more difficult with the [year 9, 13-year-old, students] because you don't always get the records. But if you are teaching anything from year 10

upwards you can get some statistics and information about the students you are going to be teaching. For example, in English there is the AsTTle [Assessment Tools for Teaching and Learning] information … If you have a list of that information before you start teaching, you can look across, and you can see who is likely to be going ahead in the class and there might be people who are a bit behind. … The stats … usually correspond very clearly to reality … I find, so that's very useful. So information on the children. Although when you start out teaching, that all is just data really, it's a bit of a blur. I suppose, maybe, as a second-year teacher you get used to reading those things. I think some way becoming familiar with your student base is really important because that is going to lead to better understanding and be able to operate more effectively. [Ellie]

Experienced teacher Megan also discussed the need to have data to enable her know her students:

The sort of teacher I could aspire to be: I really want to aspire to … have some baseline data of what I've got when I come in, and really be able to have the time to look through everybody's [data] so I get to know them, but not just personally. I really understand where they're at … and at the end of the year I'm able to show [that] it's not about what I've done, [but] to be able to … say to the students, 'look how you have progressed,' and tangibly be able to show them where they've progressed [to]. [Megan]

Knowledge of students was used to inform differentiated teaching, with respect to ability. For example, beginning teacher Sylvia said:

Probably the biggest thing I've learnt is [that the] maturity levels of the junior school are much less than I had initially thought. … I don't know whether it's the school that I'm at or just generally, I found their maturity levels quite low. And I found myself having to almost go to primary school-type teaching, or what I think primary school teaching is. … the importance of routine, especially in the junior school … I think I learnt quite a lot about teaching strategies that work and don't work in terms of what they are learning. … But after trying a few different things, I guess [it's a] different strokes for different folks-type situation. Also, the real importance of differentiating their learning [activities], and how, even in a streamed class, the abilities are quite broad. [Sylvia]

Experienced teacher Harry also talked about the need to know students:

I try and teach my staff the same thing, get to know your kids, get to know where their levels are and teach less but teach it better, rather than teaching more just because it's in the [curriculum] … try and keep the kids on board with you. [Harry]

Obviously, teachers use their knowledge of the subject in their teaching, and the beginning and experienced teachers mentioned this in the context of when they did not know the content. Some of the beginning teachers spoke of teaching a subject that they were not 'trained' to teach in their initial teacher education. For example:

I'm teaching all subjects I've been trained for, apart from accounting. They [the initial teacher education provider] wouldn't let me into accounting at university [in the teacher education programme] because I hadn't done a 300-level paper. Yet this year I'm teaching [it]. Even though I did it at university, it was a long time ago and I'm kind of suffering ... I don't know the curriculum because I haven't done it ... But then I've got the teacher that's in charge of that subject ... just next door to me and she's really good. But I mean it's just quite hard [retrieving] what's in your memory when you haven't done it for 13 years. ... And some of my friends are the same, they were let into accounting but not into economics ... we're all doing both, but we know one but not the other one. [Sylvia]

For one experienced teacher, a bad day teaching was one when she did not know the subject:

Worst days again: initially they gave me a top set Maths class; I'm not a Maths specialist, I'm very fortunate my husband's a Maths teacher so I'd go home and kind of ask him how to do stuff. But worst days ... I'd rote-learn how to do a particular equation or whatever it was that I was supposed to teach, and when the kids ... were a little bit stuck, I couldn't really unpick what the problems were and I can remember standing up by the side of that whiteboard, working through something and thinking, I really don't know what I'm talking about here. ... My professional integrity, I felt, was taking a little bit of a knock because who wants to be known as the teacher who doesn't know what they're doing? ... That's really important to me, that if I think that the students are going to learn from me, I know that they need to have confidence in what I'm talking about. ... 'she knows what she's talking about'. [Megan]

The teachers also talked about using other knowledges. Some beginning teachers spoke of using their knowledge from previous careers to inform their teaching; for example, beginning teacher Ellie noted:

I worked in the Beehive [parliament buildings] for about 10 years, I worked in the Defence Ministry and overseas in Australia and then I worked in advertising and PR in the UK. Quite different, but they all ... relate to my subject area, which is English ...all communication and language based things. [Ellie]

And beginning teacher Samantha added:

... if you come into being a teacher, you need to know about time management, you need to know about organisation, all of which are skills I already had anyway, having been a secretary. That was my life for 8 years. So that hasn't really been difficult for me, making lists, crossing things off, dealing with paperwork as soon as it comes in. I'm used to all of that, I've worked in that world and it's a white collar corporate world. [I am] totally used to deadlines, all that sort of thing. Whereas other people I know have not had that experience at all. [Samantha]

Some beginning teachers spoke of using their knowledge of the national curriculum to inform their teaching. For example:

[My teacher education has] been quite useful of recent, because we've been looking at the new draft [national] curriculum, and I definitely have a lot more background information about that. I mean we were given part of the draft document last year anyway, and we have gone over it a bit. So in that respect … the actual workings of the curriculum and all the rest, have … made me aware of how much professional development we had last year in regards to that, that perhaps people have been teaching for a long time didn't get. [Stephanie]

If teaching is viewed as a social practice, it can be seen as involving the construction of shared meanings and understandings, mediation and scaffolding, and formative interaction. Each of these will be discussed in turn.

Construction of shared meanings and understandings

Teaching and learning involves teachers and students constructing shared meanings and understandings of the content to be learnt, within purposeful communication (Bell, 2005a; Driver *et al.*, 1994; Nuthall, 1997). The construction of shared understandings is called the constructivist aspect of a sociocultural view of learning, in which knowledge and understanding are viewed as human constructs and not something in the environment to be discovered and transmitted intact or unchanged between teacher and student (Driver *et al.*, 1994; Bell, 2005a). During learning, the new understandings are constructed by the student, not received like a passive vessel waiting to be filled up; and during teaching, the teaching is the helping of students to construct new understandings, not the transmission of knowledge per se. Whilst a teacher may give an erudite explanation of a scientific concept, say, in a lecture-type teaching activity, the students still need to construct the new knowledge for themselves, linking it to their existing knowledge. The role of the teacher is to provide for learning activities for the students to construct those understandings for themselves, but not *by* themselves. The input of the teacher is discussed in the following sections. Vygotsky (1978) used the term 'the dialectic' for the dialogue in which the co-construction of understanding is done.

The construction of a shared understanding between teacher and student uses a co-generative dialogue (Roth and Tobin, 2004), in which both teacher and student contribute to the construction of the shared understanding. In this sense, teaching and learning are inextricably entwined, something that is inherent in the Māori word 'ako' which means both teaching and learning. This shared construction is also termed 'appropriation' (Rogoff, 1993), as teacher and student each 'appropriate the product of their mutually evolving partnership in the activity' (Nuthall, 1997a: 705).

One of the teaching and learning activities that is seen to aid the construction of shared meanings and understandings is co-construction, also known as 'negotiating the curriculum' (Mansell, 2009; Boomer *et al.*, 1992). In this interactive and collaborative communication between teacher and students, the students are given the opportunity to negotiate with the teacher the enacted curriculum in the classroom. By this is meant that both teacher and students have a say in what is taught and learnt in the classroom, to maximise the students' interests, goals and prior experiences being considered in the curriculum decision-making in the classroom. Therefore, co-construction can provide for student input, choice and control of their learning, while increasing relevance, motivation and responsibility (Mansell, 2009).

Experienced teacher Harry referred to the construction of shared understandings, in a broad sense:

… what I'm always developing is trying to keep in touch as much as I can with my view of the world, with what kids are seeing of the world, and to remind myself that my view isn't the same as theirs. But also to help them to understand that I have a view as well and that if they're learning then there's something that I can offer them from my view. [Harry]

Whilst teachers may not use the term 'construction of shared understandings', they do talk of the engagement of the students in the teaching and learning activities in the classroom.

Engagement can be viewed as a multifaceted construct, with cognitive, behavioural and emotional aspects (Chapman, 2003; Fredricks *et al.*, 2004). Cognitive engagement refers to the cognition of students when they are using the thinking skills needed for conceptual change, that is, recalling prior knowledge, making links between new information and existing knowledge, constructing new understandings, and testing or trialling the new understanding, for example, in communication with the teacher or other students. It also includes the cognitive skills of problem-solving, inquiry, self-assessment and meta-cognitive reflection. Effort, persistence, attention, motivation and concentration are also linked to cognitive engagement. These aspects of cognitive engagement are used in the making of shared meanings. Behavioural engagement refers to the active student response to the teaching and learning activities: for example, attending class, participating in class discussions, completing tasks, following classroom rules. Emotional engagement refers to students' emotional responses in class: for example, interest, boredom, happiness, anxiety and identification with school. The importance of engagement is due to its high correlation with higher achievement (Fredricks *et al.*, 2004).

For example, beginning teacher Ellie talked about her teaching:

["When I am teaching at my best, I am like..."]
I have the engagement of all the students and ... they are motivated and ... they are wanting to learn more. For example today we were working on a novel, this is the [year 9s], and I read the last part and they didn't want to stop, they wanted the rest of it, they wanted the rest of the story. And that is not something you do every day ... just read. But that was kind of holding them there, [with] them wanting more. They were asking when the next English lesson was. [That is] what I think is the ideal – that they are wanting to do that themselves. [Ellie]

Engagement was also discussed by beginning teacher Sandy:

[How do you know when you're supporting student learning?]
... you know that you're supporting students learning when the students are engaged, and they are also showing that they want to work on an activity. [Sandy]

Engagement was explained further by the experienced teachers. For example, experienced teacher Mary talked of a good day in her teaching with a mixed-ability class:

[Can you tell me about a good day's experience of teaching that has recently occurred for you and why was it good for you?]
The good days are the days when the lessons hum.

[by hum you mean?]
...when they are there in the ... learning mode, they are asking enquiring, [asking] questions, they are working with each other and assisting each other, and answering questions, and they are happy to give assistance to somebody else who is more

challenged by the actual work. They are wondering what comes next, or making links to what we've done previously, or talking about how what we're learning links to the real world. ... they are captured, they are interested and they are making the links, you're not artificially making the links for them, they are actually seeing that what they are learning has some relevance for them and it's important for them to know it. ... So those sorts of lessons are discussion that's on-topic and even though it might go laterally out from the actual ... my planned objective, it's still very linked to, and relevant to, where they're at. So that's a lesson that hums ... [Mary]

Mary also talked about engagement with respect to learning and constructing new knowledge in an able class:

[On a good day], with the year 10s, because it's a higher learning group, they tend to be students who have good habits in terms of learning. ... The challenge with them is to actually move them from 'give me the information, put it in front of me, tell me the answer and I'll write it down' to actually making them think. And they get quite frustrated and can be quite vocal [with them] saying 'what is the answer?' So a good lesson with them ... [is] ... moving their thinking and getting them to do more analysing and synthesising and [thinking].

[What are the sorts of things that they might be doing when you get them thinking? Can you give me an example?]
For want of a better description, it's probably around those research-type tasks, but not necessarily 'go away and find out about Ernest Rutherford' or something as specific. But if we take Papatuanuku,[1] the topic we're currently doing, our Earth Science topic: if we're looking at fossils and then we take a New Zealand example, so we look at Joan Wiffen,[2] so 'What was it about what Joan did, that made her a good science practitioner? How did she find her evidence? What did she do that indicated she was participating in science? Bringing in that nature of science strand ... is there evidence that she communicated with other scientists? Why did she go where she went? So some leading questions without totally directing them in terms of where they go. ...

[Would you be doing this in a whole-class discussion or small groups or ... ?]
Predominantly small groups ... we try to limit those group sizes to three ... [Mary]

And summing up her teaching, she said:

[How would you describe your teaching?]
For me I think there's a couple of things that make teaching work for me personally, make me keep coming back. One is, it is challenging but it's also very rewarding. It is

1 In the Māori world view, land gives birth to all things, including humankind, and provides the physical and spiritual basis for life. Papatūānuku, the land, is a powerful mother earth figure who gives many blessings to her children (Te Ahukaramū Charles Royal, 2009).
2 Joan Whiffen (1922–2009), an 'amateur' or non-employed scientist, discovered the dinosaur bones which provided evidence that dinosaurs had inhabited New Zealand.

having those lessons that hum, where students are making those connections and they are asking relevant questions; and that's the real sort of buzz. [Mary]

Experienced teacher Harry used the term 'in the learning zone' to discuss engagement:

So good days, I think, are just when the kids are ... you get a lot of teachable moments – it's the times, the lessons when you have lots of teachable moments, [those] are the good days for me.

[And a 'teachable moment'? How would you describe that?]
I think where the students are in the zone to learn, they are taking part in the learning. ... I like to think that's because they're actually finding it interesting, what I'm teaching, ... and the time just flies, I mean you just [go] ... woah, has that [lesson] gone already? And you have students approach you in the playground and say, 'hey that was cool, can we do that next time?'; that kind of stuff. [Harry]

Later in the interview, Harry talked about his changing views of teaching over his career to-date, and the importance of thinking skills involved in the construction and use of new knowledge:

... when I first started teaching I was very much more filling up empty vessels, as they say, and the students kind of accepted that premise as well, that they were here to be filled up and regurgitate it in an exam. And if [they got] thinking and learning along the way, that was all well and good, sort of thing. And I think that I've evolved over the years as education has evolved, to start looking at [how] you're actually teaching kids how-to-learn and you're using science as a vehicle for it, and you're teaching a whole lot of, a wide range of thinking skills, as well as the content knowledge and applying of the knowledge. So a good teacher now to me is the one who can turn the kids on to the science, who can actually get them thinking for themselves and applying their knowledge, and that's at the higher-level end for me. [Harry]

Mediated actions and scaffolding

Teaching may be viewed as a social practice in which teachers undertake mediated actions, including scaffolding, as a part of their teaching. Mediated actions depend on communication between teacher and student. A mediated action is an action that employs mediational means, such as technical tools (for example, a computer) and psychological tools (for example, language) to change thinking (Vygotsky, 1978; Wertsch, 1991). Vygotsky's view on learning and development brings epistemological theorising to our views of teaching (White, 2010) as it suggests possible teaching actions, and is an instructional heuristic (Moll, 2001). Examples of mediated actions are a teacher using words (for example, lemon juice, citric acid) and a formula (for example, the H+ ion) to explain what an acid is for students; and a teacher using a computer simulation to indicate where the earthquakes and volcanoes occur in the world – on the edges of the tectonic plates. The use of mediational means does not simply facilitate an action that could have occurred without it (Wertsch, 1991): instead, as Vygotsky (1978) noted, by being included in the process of behaviour, the psychological tool alters the entire flow and structure of mental functions. Hence, the agent and the means become inseparable. 'The action and the mediational means are mutually determining' (Wertsch, 1991: 119). The teacher and the teaching are inseparable, just as the knower and the knowledge are inseparable. The pedagogical practices used by a teacher are inseparably linked, for example, to the teacher's identity, goals of education, expectation of students, knowledges, and views of learning and students.

One kind of mediated action performed during teaching is scaffolding, which refers to the mediated actions of the teacher to support a student to function inside their zone of proximal development (Vygotsky, 1978; Wertsch, 1991). The zone of proximal development is the space in which a student can achieve or perform a learnt task only with the help of the teacher. For example, a parent teaching a child to ride a bicycle might use trainer wheels to help the youngster learn. Not only does it enable the child to ride the bike but the child's sense of balance and motor skills are developed. Eventually the trainer wheels can be taken off when the child can ride independently and without the support or scaffolding. The use of the trainer wheels is a mediated action: scaffolding.

The beginning teachers tended to speak of their teaching as facilitation to distinguish it from transmission teaching and, hence, were referring to mediated actions:

> When I am teaching at my best, I am like … [a] facilitator. [Sylvia]

> *[Has your view of a 'good' teacher changed since you began teaching?]*
> Still really see the teacher as a coach and a facilitator and as a mentor and someone to really help the students along the way. [Sandy]

Experienced teacher Megan also discussed facilitation with respect to what it means to be a good teacher:

> My view of a good teacher now is somebody who has got a great inclusive environment and it's a good learning environment and we've got good two-way communication and good roles, and somebody who can really support students to think – a good teacher now for me is a facilitator of learning. [Megan]

However, facilitation is not a neutral activity, with the teacher just organising activities and resources. Within their notion of facilitation, the teachers indicated that they mediated the students' learning: for example, to help students link ideas together:

> *[How has your teaching [in a boys' school] changed this year?]*
> … Probably put a lot more revision into this end of the year with my teaching, so that we go through the lessons and then we revise over the main ideas again. Whereas before, it was like just one lesson, one lesson, one lesson and there was no tying in. So I try and tie in one idea after another and make sure the boys have the main summary of ideas that we've gone through, rather than expecting them to get it. [Stephanie]

The teachers spoke of mediating a student's language when English was the student's second language. For example:

> I've got one ESOL student in particular, who is really, seems to be suffering. And that's been a big eye-opener for me recently, with the report evening we had. Because although she sits with some bright kids, who are not international students, whenever I got an assessment back from her, there would be pages not filled in, nothing even

attempted. ... I thought this girl was not making any sort of effort. I didn't know that she was a true international student, for all I knew she could have been born here, so I just thought 'well she's just not making much of an effort', so I put that on her report. And then her father, at the report evening ... came and said 'well I don't understand this, she is making the effort.' ... So that was an education for me and I backtracked and said 'I'm terribly sorry', you know, 'from the work I was getting it didn't seem that way at all, if I set tests she doesn't do the test, if I set an essay to write she doesn't write anything' ... I've been in contact with the ESL teacher here and he's got a programme whereby you can feed [in] various documents, either by a scanner or via email, through a programme that he's got and it will take the words out and put them in a word list ... [I can] help them understand it a bit better. ... that was the only time I got caught out, [with] the ESL student, who I just misread completely. So I actually apologised to her and, she said 'oh, it's okay' ... she didn't seem offended. [Samantha]

Mediating students' thinking by helping them make connections was discussed. For example:

... I can link it [the science being learnt] to the real world. ... I think it is something that sparks an interest in me and I thoroughly enjoy doing it. [Katie]

Helping students to make connections with and use the content of knowledge being taught and learnt was discussed. For example, experienced teacher Harry said:

I am unashamedly a story teller and I like to relate the stories ... from my experiences but also trying to put it into the students' everyday experiences when I'm teaching a particular area. I have had times when my staff have been out the back listening as well, apparently, so they tell me. ... For example, I have a number of ... famous moments in science history ... I'm always watching television, internet, the news, whatever's happening in science. And just bring it up in the middle of something with the students, so it doesn't necessarily have to be what I'm actually working on that lesson on sometimes. It's just a nice break, a nice little interaction, something that I think will interest them. Then I have a Friday event where I take the trivial pursuit questions from Science and we have competitions with the kids, right through to [year] 9 to 13, they come running in every day, they'd play it all week if we let them. [Harry]

Facilitation with small groups, so that students can mediate each other's learning, was mentioned by Harry:

We do a lot of group stuff at our school ... it's based on research that shows that, in the real world, science people work in teams, not as individuals, so [it's] not just the practical experiments but actually a lot of the everyday work with students in year 9 and 10 in the school, in Science, the students work in teams and they have three roles that they do within the group work: there's a technical advisor, there's a recorder and there's a person who actually does it, a technician, and they swap their roles around; and we keep the formative assessment material on the board, like a competition, like a results chart for the students and they have prizes at the end of the month for their group ... It's ... a matter of ... the kids getting confident [with] working together in teams. My view is that if you can provide success for students then they want to come to class and they will be [more] successful. Using the [team] approach, the students, when they sit their summative assessments for Science, they actually sit it in a group of three as well, they're allowed to talk amongst themselves, they produce one written answer for the three and they'll all get the mark. When they finish that, I mark the ones that are right, I don't give any corrections because I give it back to them the next period and they can have a [second] go at the ones they didn't get right ... and I give them an average of the two marks. The result of this is quite inflated marks ... but at the end of the year, when these kids [who] have done [the group assessment] and they come to sit their own tests, they do much better than if they were on their own the whole year. And so we've had some really good year 9 and 10 assessment results from using this approach. [Harry]

Using ICT to mediate the students' knowledge and learning was also mentioned by Harry:

... using ICT ... using computers ... kids working in groups to solve a key Science problem by answering [with] content knowledge – gathering problems around it, building up their content knowledge and then producing some kind of presentation of what they've been learning. And again, the students seem to do really well in the testing. What happens when they sit the same core tests as the rest, they do better, even though they probably don't cover all the content like the others. They enjoy Science, so for me it's about enjoyment, I guess, of Science. So improving learning and assessment, formative and summative assessment, that kind of stuff for me is relationships, getting kids to enjoy the science, using group work like ... and using the ICT components. ... You can't go wrong with it [ICT], we're now getting into the ... iPhone and the touch pad sorts of things. [Harry]

Some of the beginning teachers spoke of scaffolding the learning activities for the students. At the end of her first year of teaching, beginning teacher Sandy said that she breaks down:

... the elements of the class requirements so that students can [be] scaffold[ed] to the next sort of steps. Sometimes in a mixed, like in a mixed year 10 class, it does mean actually having a range of activities that students can then step through depending on their ability as well. But I find that very challenging. It requires three times as much preparation sometimes. And then the ones you have prepared the things for, don't turn up. ... those are things [that] maybe [get easier] as you get more experienced and more resources are possible. But in a mixed-ability class, I also find it very challenging to be able to meet the needs of all the students. [Sandy]

And after 18 months of teaching, Sandy said:

[What do you do to support the diversity of student learning needs?]
I do try to ... to have some different learning activities. That means that students with, say, less developed abilities in writing or reading can still access and participate. Like writing an essay. I might get some of my class ... who [have the] instructions on how to write an essay ... to work by themselves. ... The second group has more scaffolding, and the third group has almost got like a closed paragraph, and then trying to write a second paragraph by themselves. So it's just really trying to give everybody the same, to get to the same result, but give some people some more assistance, as much as you can with one person and 28 students. [Sandy]

Assessment for formative purposes

Another aspect of teaching as a social practice is assessment for formative purposes (Cowie and Bell, 1999; Bell and Cowie, 2001), which involves meaningful communication between teacher and student (or student and student). A definition of assessment for formative purposes always includes an aspect of using the assessment information gathered to improve learning (Gipps, 1994):

> [...]he process used by teachers and students to recognise and respond to student learning in order to enhance that learning, during the learning (Bell and Cowie, 2001: 8).

Research evidence shows that assessment for formative purposes does improve learning (Black and Wiliam, 1998), making it a valuable aspect of effective teaching and learning. The relationship between formative and summative assessment is much debated in the literature. Some advocate that one assessment task can be used for both formative and summative purposes, with two different lots of assessment information being collected (Bell and Cowie, 2001), while others advocate that the same data from a single assessment can be used for both: summative and then formative purposes (Black and Wiliam, 1998; Rawlins, 2010).

The key aspect of assessment for formative purposes is the giving and receiving of feedback and feedforward (Clarke, 2003; Hattie and Timperley, 2007). Feedback is information given to students about their learning with respect to the learning goals. Feedforward is the subsequent teaching which helps the student close the gap between their existing understanding and the learning goals. To learn from the feedback and feedforward, students must self-assess – they need to understand the learning goals, the criteria used to judge if they have attained the learning outcomes, and how to develop what they already know and can do. Hence, formative assessment always involves student self-assessment – it cannot be done without it.

In doing formative assessment, the teacher is taking into account the sociocultural situatedness of the teacher and the student (Bell, 2000; Gipps, 1999; Filer, 2000), that is, the curriculum to be learnt, the age of the student, the prior experiences and knowledge of the student which will also include cultural knowledge, and the language of the discipline, to co-construct a shared understanding. For example, in developing culturally appropriate forms of formative assessment, Lee Hang (2011) researched the use of written feedback and feedforward work sheets for use in Samoan science classrooms, given the Samoan cultural practices of silence; and (Phuong-Mai *et al.*, 2009) researched the use of cooperative learning activities as a context in which formative assessment might be done in Hong Kong and Vietnamese cultures.

Assessment for formative purposes can be theorised as a sociocultural practice, as it can be viewed as:

> ... a purposeful, intentional, responsive activity involving meaning making; an integral part of teaching and learning; a situated and contextualised activity; a partnership between teacher and students; and involving the use of language to communicate meaning (Bell and Cowie, 2001: 113).

The relational aspect of teaching is also highlighted when we consider formative assessment as a part of teaching. For students to disclose what they know and don't know to the teacher, there needs to be a trusting and respectful teacher–student relationship (Bell and Cowie, 2001).

Some of the beginning teachers spoke of doing assessment for formative purposes. For example, beginning teacher Sylvia talked about 'noticing' in the classroom:

> *[What tells you that you are supporting their learning?]*
> Just the way they are approaching their work. If they [are] producing and you can see them working hard. You have a look over their shoulder and you can see what they are doing and you can see that they are actually making some good progress. If they are asking good questions. Answering well or at least attempting. Just their general enthusiasm to what they are doing. And obviously … their assessment results [are] one way of finding out. So just their general enthusiasm, the work that they are producing in class, their contribution to discussions and assessments would be the way I gauge it, and also their behaviour. Like if they are not engaged in their learning, that is when they generally play up, so that is a surefire sign that they are not either not getting it or it's not interesting for them. [Sylvia]

Feedback and feedforward as parts of doing formative assessment were mentioned by beginning teacher Sandy:

> … and in terms of working with students in groups, feedback [and] feedforward. They were very useful for improving the success of Māori [students] but they're also very important tools for all students. And really they're not things that … work just because of cultural or racial differences. [Sandy]

Examples of the kinds of activities she used in formative assessment were discussed by beginning teacher Katie:

> We have little quizzes every lesson that happens as a bit of revision and I get a bit of an idea by looking back through their books to see how they went on those. And just getting the kids to answer their questions rather than me saying 'these are the answers'. I go around the students and get them to answer them so you can pick up any areas of weakness hopefully. [Katie]

Using the information from formative assessment so as to be flexible in the classroom was discussed by beginning teacher Stephanie:

> And just being able to judge the mood of the classroom and be flexible … to change lessons around … what's going to suit what classroom you happen to be in. … Thinking on the hop and thinking about how to improve ideas. You start something and then straightaway you can think of ideas on how to make it better and you sort of just change, I'm not afraid to change things if I see what I want can be better … [Stephanie]

Using formative assessment to find out what the students had learnt in a lesson was raised by experienced teacher Mary:

> At the end of most lessons – and I say 'most' because with the best of intentions it doesn't always happen – we revisit the learning intention and look at success criteria. Now, sometimes that might be a little bit more formal than others, so sometimes I might ask them to jot down three things they've learnt today, to recall three things they've

learnt for the day, [or] give me two new pieces of vocab for the day and one question that they might still have. ... So that would be more formal reflection into the back of their books. Or we might have an exit-type question; so 'before you leave today, tell me one thing you've learnt' and so that might literally be at the door as they exit or it might be while they're packing up and I move around the room and say to them, 'tell me one thing that you've learnt for today.' ... [or] 'turn to your neighbour and tell your neighbour three things you've learnt today' and then reverse it and I just circulate so I'm not actually speaking to each one of them individually but I'm getting a general gist of whether there is any learning happening. Just, questions that they might pose at the end often give an indicator as to how much understanding they had or their interest level; and ... yeah, those are probably the main ones I use in terms of what learning have we had today and how do I know that. [Mary]

Likewise, experienced teacher Megan talked of her use of formative assessment – assessment for learning:

[In] planning, I split [the topic] into little subsections that basically would be building up the knowledge for what you need to know for the end of assessment. And what I felt was really important was that for each little subsection, we had ... a little bit of a formative assessment with which those students then demonstrated to me what they knew, what they had learned, and I could sort of feedback, feedforward ... on where they were at. [Megan]

Summary

If we view it as a sociocultural practice, teaching may be theorised as a social practice. Teaching as a social practice refers to teaching as a purposeful communication activity (the talking and listening) between teacher and student (and at times between student and student). The talking and listening in teaching includes mindful planning, the use of teacher knowledges, co-construction of shared understandings, mediation, engagement and scaffolding, and assessment for formative purposes.

Study and discussion

- Can you give an example of pedagogical content knowledge in your own teaching area?
- Can you give an example of scaffolding from your own teaching, and explain why you consider it to be scaffolding?
- When thinking about the term 'co-construction', what do you understand by the prefix 'co'? and the word 'construction'?
- Why is assessment for formative purposes considered to be a part of teaching as a social practice?

4 Teaching as a cultural practice[1]

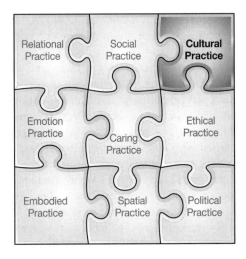

Teaching may be viewed as a cultural practice as our teaching is embedded in and determined by culture. First, our own culture informs our teaching because our taken-for-granted ways of doing things, that is, our cultural norms, inform our choice of teaching and learning activities, the relationships formed and the ways of forming them, what knowledge is valued, the expectations we have of students and the learning outcomes valued. Second, our teaching is informed by the culture of the students in our classrooms, as competent teaching may be seen as that which takes into account the culture of the students, both in research publications containing, for example, Effective Teaching Profiles (Bishop *et al.*, 2009) and in policy statements such as national curricula (New Zealand Ministry of Education, 2007; New Zealand Teachers Council, 2007). The term 'culturally responsive pedagogy' is used to refer to such teaching (Gay, 2000; May and Sleeter, 2010a; Sleeter, 2010). Both aspects of teaching as a cultural practice are discussed in this chapter.

In writing this chapter, I acknowledge my own cultural positioning – one cannot write about teaching as a cultural practice without doing so. I am a sixth-generation New Zealander; both my mother's and my father's families migrated to New Zealand in the

1 I wish to acknowledge Elisabeth Joseph, a Summer Research Scholarship student 2009/2010, who did the preparatory work for this chapter.

first wave of migration, settlement and colonisation from England, Scotland and Ireland, in the early 1840s. My ancestors were mainly literate farm labourers, who sailed to New Zealand on the hope of owning land to farm. I am Pākehā,[2] English-speaking, middle-class, educated, with an Anglican Christian upbringing.

I live in a bicultural nation, as current government philosophy, policy and practices recognise and are informed by the founding document of New Zealand, the Treaty of Waitangi, which was signed in 1840, as a treaty for power-sharing and partnership between Māori (the indigenous people) and the British Crown. The Treaty is now interpreted as a partnership between Māori and non-Māori. I live in a multicultural society, as New Zealand has changed with the rest of the world in terms of globalisation, migration and refugee resettlement. Māori and the early British settlers/colonists have been joined by immigrants from around the world: for example, from Pacific nations, China, Taiwan, Korea, Philippines, India, South Africa, the Netherlands, Somalia and Chile. At the beginning of the 21st century, Pākehā are the dominant ethnic group in terms of population size and political power.

Through the span of my teaching career in secondary and tertiary contexts, from the 1970s to the present, the ethnic diversity of students in my classrooms and office has increased dramatically. In writing this chapter, I am mindful of my own journey to become bicultural (Māori and non-Māori) in terms of being a New Zealand citizen, and multicultural in terms of the society in which I live, and to use a culturally responsive pedagogy in my teaching. This journey started with a desire to connect with and engage Māori students in learning science in the 1970s, and it is still ongoing. It has had many joys, but it was not without its trials and tribulations. I give thanks to Māori, Tongan, Samoan, Solomon Island, Taiwanese and Chinese colleagues and research students – I have learnt much from listening to you.

In this chapter, I highlight the key signposts in my own journey of becoming a culturally responsive teacher. These signposts are ones I have found myself as I reflect on my teaching, and others that I have recognised in the international research literature.

The notion of culture is here described as 'the ever changing values, traditions, social and political relationships, and worldview created, shared, and transformed by a group of people bound together by a combination of factors that can include a common history, geographic location, language, social class, and religion' (Nieto, 2000: 139).

Teaching and the culture of teachers

A teacher's teaching is informed by her or his culture(s). To articulate one's own tacit culture and worldview may be difficult for many in a dominant culture, but one's culture(s) does inform teaching practices whether a teacher is aware of it or not. Teaching is embedded in the cultural contexts of a society, and can only be understood if those contexts are taken into account (Gao, in preparation). For example, the notion of what constitutes competent, effective or accomplished teaching practice is culturally bound (Clarke, 2010b). In Western education research, learning understandings within a discipline – for example, mathematics and science – are seen to be promoted if students in small group discussions are given

---

2 Pākehā is a Māori word referring to New Zealanders descended from the nineteenth- and early twentieth-century British settlers, who are the dominant ethnic group in New Zealand in the twentieth and early twenty-first centuries.

opportunities to talk, engage in dialogue and discuss with both the teacher and other students in the classroom, using the language of the discipline (Walshaw and Anthony, 2008; Lemke, 1990; Roth, 2005). However, this valuing and promotion of students talking mathematics and science, for example, as a part of being a competent teacher is not necessarily seen in other cultures (Clarke, 2010a). David Clarke and his associates researched three Seoul classroom, finding that student–student talk using key mathematical terms comprised a very small portion of the total classroom talk (Clarke, 2010b), and yet Korea is rated highly in international studies of mathematics achievement – for example, the 2007 Trends in International Mathematics and Science Study (TIMSS) (Mullis *et al.*, 2008). Clarke notes:

> ... the Korean students were given disproportionately fewer opportunities to make oral use of key mathematical terms in whole class or teacher–student dialogue. In contrast to the teachers in Shanghai, Tokyo and Singapore, the teachers in the Hong Kong and Seoul classrooms did not appear to attach significant value to student spoken rehearsal of mathematical terms and phrases, whether individual or choral mode. (Clarke, 2010b: 10)

What was valued in the three Korean mathematics classroom researched was the 'choral utterance' by students, usually a class response in unison in reply to a teacher proposition such as 'When we draw the two equations, they meet at just one point, right? Yes or no?' (Clarke, 2010b; 9). In this case, it was the teacher who was talking mathematics. This kind of talking, choral utterances, was not universally valued, as 'the classrooms in Tokyo, Berlin and Melbourne do not appear to attach significant value to this type of utterance' (Clarke, 2010b; 8). Similarly, what teaching activities are considered to be examples of competent teaching was found to vary from society to society:

> Any international conceptualisation of accomplished practice would be arguably deficient if it did not include such activities as: mise en commun (French), pudian (Chinese) or matome (Japanese).
> Mise en commun – a whole-class activity in which the teacher elicits student solutions for the purpose of drawing on the contrasting approaches in order to synthesise and highlight targeted key concepts.
> Pudian – an introductory whole-class activity in which the teacher elicits student prior knowledge and experience for the purpose of constructing connections to the content to be covered in the lesson.
> Matome – a teacher-orchestrated discussion, drawing together the major conceptual threads of a lesson or extended activity – most commonly a summative activity at the end of the lesson. (Clarke, 2010b; 18)

Clarke was able to conclude from his several researches on this topic 'that culture shapes local conceptions of accomplished practice for both teachers and students' (Clarke, 2010b; 11).

Teaching and the culture of students

Teaching which takes into account the culture of students is termed culturally responsive pedagogy (Sleeter, 2010), and has been shown to raise the achievement of students whose culture is not the dominant Eurocentric culture in mainstream schooling (Gay, 2000) – for example, students who identify as Māori in mainstream New Zealand schools (Bishop *et al.*, 2009).

Culturally responsive pedagogy, in terms of what a teacher does, has the following features (Richards *et al.*, 2006; Bishop *et al.*, 2009; Gay, 2000; Swartz, 2009; Macfarlane, 2004; Aitken and Kana, 2010; Sleeter, 2010; Ladson-Billings, 1995):

1   Culturally responsive teaching is not ethnic-blind and takes into account, rather than ignores, the culture and ethnicity of the students.
2   Culturally responsive teaching does not use deficit theorising to explain differences in the achievement of students of different ethnicities.
3   Culturally responsive teaching includes having high expectations of students, not expectations based on stereotypes.
4   Culturally responsive teaching involves forming relationships with students for professional caring, and a commitment that students will achieve academically.
5   Culturally responsive teaching includes teachers knowing and relating to their students as culturally located human beings.
6   Culturally responsive teaching includes building relationships and communication with the families and communities of students.
7   Culturally responsive teaching involves using the cultural and ethnic knowledge, language, values and practices of the students as resources to inform teacher decision-making about curriculum and pedagogy.
8   Culturally responsive teaching is emancipatory and transformative, and hence it is political for social justice.

There is no sequence or progression intended in this list. The order of the list was determined by the author for ease of reading. Each of these features is now discussed in the following sections.

1 Culturally responsive teaching is not ethnic-blind and takes into account, rather than ignores, the culture and ethnicity of the students

Ethnic blindness is when a teacher ignores the ethnicity of the students in the classroom (Gay, 2000) and relates to them as members of the same culture as themselves, or of the dominant culture. In contrast, culturally responsive teaching takes into account the culture of the student, rather than ignoring it, with teaching drawing upon students' prior experiences, the communities in which they live, their cultural knowledge, values and practices, as well as those of the teacher. An illustration of ethnic blindness is the comment by one beginning teacher in this study in response to a question about how she teaches for the diversity of students in her classroom. One interpretation is that she is just starting to become a culturally responsive teacher:

> I don't see colour, I don't see race. ... coming from [a northern hemisphere metropolitan city], I'm just used to every colour, creed, nature, whatever, so I just see the people. [Samantha]

While this teacher meant well by implying that she does not discriminate between students, and treats them all equally, such teacher thinking is problematic in that she tacitly assumes the students have the same worldview as herself. Samantha is necessarily basing her teaching on her own cultural worldview, values and practices, albeit tacitly, and therefore she is taking for granted the assumption that her culture, Anglo-Western, is universal for the people in the classroom. Some teachers make a conscious effort not to focus on the cultural differences, in the belief that this being fair to all students and that no student is treated differently to others. This is referred to as being colour-blind (Milner, 2005) and as naive egalitarianism (Causey *et al.*, 2000). This universalist notion of equality, a central tenet of Western liberal thinking, needs to be changed from one of equity of opportunities to one of equity of outcomes for all, so that being 'equal' is not the same as 'being the same'. A level playing-field does not exist for all students. To position oneself in the discourse of ethnic blindness often means that 'teachers fail to engage the reality of learners' lived experiences and the need to do something about inequities that their students experience because of their cultural and classed identities' (Santoro and Allard, 2005: 869). Being ethnic-blind means the teacher is drawing only on his or her own cultural norms and worldviews to make pedagogical decisions, rather than viewing the students' cultural experiences and knowledge as a valuable resource in the classroom (Greenleaf *et al.*, 1994).

In this research, Samantha also expressed a view focusing on the need for multicultural, and not just bicultural, teaching, perhaps overlooking the indigenous (and not migrant) position of Māori students under the Treaty of Waitangi as the *tangata whenua*, (first people of the land) in which they are seen as members of a partnership, even though population figures suggest they are a minority group. The underachievement of Maori compared to Asian students' high achievement was also not noted:

> *[Did the ITE course prepare you for] teaching Maori students?[*
> ... one comment I had to make about the course at uni[versity] was that there was a lot of emphasis of teaching Māori, as there should be, but there wasn't really any emphasis on teaching Asian students. It was all ... How can we get the best out of Māori [students], but why aren't we looking at Asian students? ... I think because I come from [city], so you've got every ethnicity background, culture, whatever. I'm so used to [it]. [Samantha]

Samantha appeared to be unaware of the role and importance of the Treaty of Waitangi and its obligations for teachers. She again indicated her lack of knowledge and awareness of culture in the classroom:

> *[What about Pasifika students?]*
> ... I don't believe I have any Pasifika[3] students, I could be wrong but I'm pretty sure I don't. And the [students] that I have here are basically very, they're born and bred round here, it's quite a middle class sort of town and they seem to be pretty outgoing for the most part. I mean, as a class, my Level 6 class will go very quiet if they're asked a question, they just don't want to make a fool of themselves and that's not a cultural thing. It's just purely 'oh I'm too thick or something'. But if you go round them individually, it's absolutely fine. [Samantha]

However, Samantha's comments do create a space to raise the notion of the need to address all students' cultures in the classroom as a part of good teaching practice, and not assuming that all have a similar culture to us as teachers. Her views were shared by beginning teacher Katie:

---

3 Pasifika is a term used to refer to Pacific peoples in the context of Aotearoa New Zealand.

[How well prepared were you by the teacher education course for teaching Māori students?]
Yeah, not particularly well. I don't differentiate in my teaching. I don't know whether that's just a personal thing that I don't feel that they should be treated any differently. And also that the kids don't feel that they should be treated any different[ly] … There's also not a high population of Māori in the school, or in my class.

[And teaching Pacifika students?]
There are very few here so, but in terms of my teacher training for it, limited, very, very limited. [Katie]

When the teacher and student are of the same culture, there is likely to be a match of worldviews, cultural expectations and practices in the classroom and between school and home. But in situations of colonisation, migration and globalisation, this may not be so – there may be a mismatch between the teacher's and the student's cultures. For example, in New Zealand, Māori students overwhelming have been taught by New Zealanders of European descent in mainstream primary and secondary schools, despite the setting-up of total immersion Māori language and philosophy schools (*kura kaupapa Māori*) and with increasing numbers of Māori teachers being qualified. And, with increasing global migration, the teacher and student may be from different cultures, even though they both hold the same citizenship – for example, a Taiwanese-born but New Zealand-qualified teacher teaching Mandarin to non-Asian students, as well as to those from the People's Republic of China, in a New Zealand secondary school.

A key part of becoming a culturally responsive teacher is the acceptance that different cultures have different worldviews to make sense of their world and to inform their interactions with others (Clark and Flores, 2007). It is then said that the worldview of the teacher affects their interactions with students (Swartz, 2009; Milner, 2005). Worldview is here taken to mean:

> … the lens through which people see and experience the world. Worldviews are shaped by deep-rooted cultural tenets, ontology (ways of being), and epistemology (ways of knowing, views of knowledge). Cultural tenets – and the ontology and epistemology they generate – have been identified over time in the science, philosophy or spirituality, and metaphysical understandings of various cultures or cultural and regional groups. These are the basic elements of worldview that, in turn, shape the beliefs, values, and practices of cultures or cultural and regional groups. Identifying the relationship between the basic elements of worldview and the beliefs, values, and practices they produce has strong explanatory power. (Swartz, 2009: 1049)

Illustrations of the notion of 'worldview' often include those of indigenous people, whose worldviews are seen to be characterised as valuing oneness and unity (the interrelatedness of all realms of existence); the sacredness of life; the shared good of the family and community; and balance through reciprocity (Swartz, 2009). Another notion often discussed is the Cartesian worldview, from Europe's Enlightenment period, which is seen as characterised by duality or split between mind and spirit; alienation from nature and from people, which are seen as hostile and with competition for limited resources; hierarchies of 'people, ideas and methods' (Swartz, 2009: 1050); and the reduction of life into separate and discrete worlds. It is important to acknowledge that any worldview is but one, and a partial view at that, and that 'it is only a view of the world; it is not the world itself' (Swartz, 2009: 1051). In addition, worldview is communicated and learnt in schools by students through 'the structure of schooling, policies, and curricular and pedagogical practices. ... In this way ... the culture of power remains largely unarticulated yet universalized' (Swartz, 2009: 1051). In summary, ethnicity, culture, language and thinking, and hence learning, are interconnected and interactive.

As mentioned earlier, the notion of culture is here described as 'the ever changing values, traditions, social and political relationships, and worldview created, shared, and transformed by a group of people bound together by a combination of factors that can include a common history, geographic location, language, social class, and religion' (Nieto, 2000: 139). It is not a 'characteristic of individuals, and as such a set of stable practices that can be described and taught'(May and Sleeter, 2010a: 4), but 'culture and identity are understood here as multilayered, fluid, complex, and encompassing multiple social categories, and at the same time as being continually reconstructed through participation in social situations' (May and Sleeter, 2010a: 10), and politically enforced (Brown *et al.*, 2007). Hence, culture is seen as fluid and dynamic (Nieto, 2010; Brown *et al.*, 2007), not static and set in stone, even though it may also be relatively stable over time. This is especially so if we also take context into account. For example, there may be similarities and differences between being Tongan in New Zealand and being Tongan in Tonga; being Tongan born and living in New Zealand; and being a New Zealand Tongan, born and living in New Zealand (Kalavite, 2010). The identity montage is further described:

> New Zealand-born and New Zealand-raised Pasifika young people have developed unique forms of expression and identification ... They strive to be bicultural or multi-ethnic on their own terms. ... It exists, it is vibrant, and is becoming more and more distinct. It appears to blend aspects of traditional culture with the urban and the contemporary. It does not exist in any of the Pacific nations, rather, emerging within the migrant communities of Pasifika in New Zealand, Hawaii, the west coast of the USA and Australia. The conscious and deliberate construction of such a personalised Pasifika identity means it is okay not to be fluent in the mother (or father) tongue. It is okay not to be an expert in traditional art form; and, it is okay not to be knowledgeable of culturally based protocols. (Samu, 2006: 40)

Culture is also multifaceted (Nieto, 2010) and cannot be linked just to ethnicity, but also, for example, to lesbian culture, rugby culture, and the farming culture. Teaching as a gendered practice may be considered here as well (Gore, 1993; Middleton, 1993).

Culture is socially constructed and therefore influenced by social, economic and political discourses (Nieto, 2010). Culture is not something innate or inherent in the natural world, it is a human construct. Hence, the dominant discourses at any time determine what will be valued or not. The culture of power and privilege (Delpit, 1998) in schools and classrooms may enable a Eurocentric dominant culture to maintain oppression and hegemony over cultures' knowledge, language, and ways of knowing. However, other knowledges, languages and ways of knowing, which may be invisible in school classrooms, have contributed to humanity's knowledge building. For example, science as a body of knowledge and way of knowing, has been built up with knowledge from different cultures, including European, Chinese and Persian cultures. Likewise, what is valued literature to include in a school curriculum, may be more than just Eurocentric literature. Eurocentric knowledge is but a partial view of knowledge. Viewing Eurocentric knowledge as 'mainstream' in multicultural educational situations, continues its positioning at the top of a hierarchy, and minimises the contribution and value of a wider spectrum of knowledges, so that 'students and teachers gaze at "others" …'(Swartz, 2009) p. 1056, rather than participating in ways of thinking from a broad spectrum of cultures. Culture is learned, like worldviews, from interactions between members of families, communities and schools (Nieto, 2010). Lastly, culture is dialectical (Nieto, 2010), meaning that there are tensions within the complexity of culture, and identifying with a culture does not require accepting all aspects, good and bad, of that culture. Dialectical thinking is characterised by a tolerance of contradictory beliefs. For example, in order to succeed at their study, Tongan tertiary students in New Zealand may choose to not practice aspects of their culture, for example, attending church meetings on weeknights (Kalavite, 2010). 'That culture is dialectical does not mean that we need to embrace all of its contradictory manifestations in order to be "authentic" members of the culture' (Nieto, 2010: 87).

Hence, the reality for many students and teachers is that their identity is not singular but multiple, constructed, discursive and contradictory. Teachers and students may be multi-voiced and take up multiple positionings: for example, 'a man, an academic, a Catholic, an Asian, a Malaysian, a Chinese, a son who is expected to show filial piety to his parents, an American-educated person' (Lim and Renshaw, 2001: 12). And the hybridisation or (re) combination of forms and practices of cultures into new forms and practices also contribute to the multiplicity of voices and realities (Lim and Renshaw, 2001; Samu, 2010; Siteine, 2010). As Siteine (2010) comments with respect to Pacific identity:

> The idea of singular identities does not allow for the idea that individuals have multiple, fluid identities. One person can be, without contradiction, a New Zealand citizen, of Samoan heritage, with German ancestry, a Christian, a woman, a heterosexual, a feminist and an All Blacks supporter, and none of these identities can be taken to be the person's only identity. (Siteine, 2010: 9)

Therefore there are concerns about basing one's teaching on a singular identity for students. For example, in the context of Pasifika students in New Zealand classrooms:

> The way in which teachers understand identity, and therefore select the content of their educational programmes, has significant implications for their students. The selection of [a] national or ethnic identity leads to an unconscious allocation of identity and privileges one form of identity over another. (Siteine, 2010: 9)

Pasifika people in New Zealand belong to one or more of the cultural groups of Samoan, Cook Island Maori, Tongan, Niue, Fijian, Tokelauan, Tuvalu, the Solomon Islands, Vanuatu, Kiribati and French Polynesian. Each has its own unique social structures, languages, histories, values, perspectives and attitudes (Samu, 2006). Therefore, there are calls against using a pan-Pasifika identity in the classroom but to teach in such a way to ensure that 'Pasifika cultural identities and values are not compromised, or smothered by other influences' (Samu, 2010).

Identity is also linked to place and space. For example, Somali refugee students in Christchurch, New Zealand, may find schools a contested space, 'where identities of "race" or ethnicity, gender and class intersect. In challenging dominant understandings of "past–present", "secular–religious" and "private–public" space differences for men and women, Somali students found school was often a "culturally unsafe" place' (Humpage, 2009: 80).

For example, there was an expectation that school should be a space in the present, which meant that their past experiences as refugees, often with disrupted education, were often not taken into account, for example, in placing the students in classes. Sometimes the students struggled to be academically successful in the classes to which they were assigned. For example, the students found themselves in schools that were secular but in which Christian festivals, such as Easter, structured the school year. In Somalia, half of their schooling was religious study, and students were able to practise their culture safely within the Islamic school structures.

In this chapter, culture will be used in the sense of ethnicity, as this is a major field of interest in my country at the present time. However, one aspect of focusing on the ethnicities of students is that ethnicity becomes a synomyn for 'non-European' and 'other' (Santoro and Allard, 2005).

2 Culturally responsive teaching does not use deficit theorising to explain differences in the achievement of students of different ethnicities

Research findings indicate that indigenous students and students from minority groups may underachieve, and have higher rates of absenteeism and behavioural problems in Eurocentric classrooms where their culture is ignored and not taken into account (Bishop *et al.*, 2009; Sleeter, 2010). These low educational outcomes in turn are seen to result – for example, for Māori – in higher levels of unemployment, higher levels of imprisonment, illness and poverty (Bishop *et al.*, 2009).

Deficit theorising is one way educators may explain the disparity in achievement between students of different ethnicities and cultures by viewing the low-achieving students as the site or agency of the low educational outcomes. The student is said to be deficit in some way: for example, in having low ability, low motivation, and low expectations of their own schooling (Shields *et al.*, 2005). Deficit theorising is evident in this instruction given to me as a Year 6 student in a co-ed class: 'You girls may find this lesson on science difficult, so you can sit up the back and do some reading.' Here the girls in the class were problematised, not the teacher's deficit thinking about girls and science. Despite this, I went on to be awarded a BSc.

Deficit theorising is based on stereotypes, which may lead to blaming the student, and to teachers lowering their expectations; and the curriculum may be watered down (Milner, 2005). 'In short, deficit thinking occurs when teachers focus on what students do not have or know rather than what students have or know' (Milner, 2005: 771). With lowered expectations, teacher tend to change their pedagogy accordingly, offering reduced educational opportunities (Greenleaf *et al.*, 1994). Culturally different and classed students may be positioned 'as "problems" to be "managed"' (Santoro and Allard, 2005: 864), rather than 'a source of learning' (Santoro and Allard, 2005: 872). The danger of deficit thinking is that:

> … accounts based on student deficits or character flaws are not likely to generate pedagogical problem-solving, since teachers constructing these accounts may believe the deficits and flaws to be outside their influence and control. (Greenleaf *et al.*, 1994: 531)

Unfortunately, this may result in a 'misguided liberal attitude' that allows Pasifika students, for example, to underachieve and to 'float by without any expectations or demands on them' (Samu, 2006: 41). And to the contrary, many Pasifika students respect the teachers who justifiably discipline them (Hill and Hawk, 2000).

Megan, an experienced secondary teacher interviewed for this research, indicated her growing awareness of deficit theorising. For example:

> ... it's supposed to be about forty per cent Māori students at [X] College but sometimes it seems a lot more than that. And within that particular group – well, Māori and Pacifika – there do seem to be quite a few behavioural problems. Now, I've done a wee bit of reading around the behavioural issues and I guess really a number of those issues arise because of the cultural differences – we teach in a European culture, from that kind of perspective. [Megan]
>
> [Somali students] they would be from the Muslim culture, and I had never experienced this before, they were always not so bright, lacked a lot of literacy skills, quite happy to sit at the back of the classroom and not really kind of push themselves forward, and I kind of felt that was just a cultural thing, and that was ... ok. And you just sort of accepted it. But [then] I had this very, very intelligent [Somali] student ... [Megan]

Another way to theorise diversity and the disparity of educational outcomes is to use sociocultural and discursive theorising (Lim and Renshaw, 2001) in which learning is not seen as the accumulation of knowledge but as the increasing competence to engage in communications, activities and practices within a community. Teaching and learning in a multicultural situation is seen as reciprocal, with both teacher and students learning to communicate and act within each other's communities. When using this theorising, teachers view students as being embedded in their culture, which needs to be ascertained and taken into account in the teaching and learning. Such sociocultural theorising asserts that the student cannot be separated from her or his culture and is seen as a person-with-culture, not as a person-solo. In sociocultural theorising, the differential power between teacher and student may be used to explain the disparity of achievement between students of different ethnicities. Teachers are positioned to have power, authority and privilege – all of which are used in deciding whose cultural knowledge, cultural identity, cultural contexts, expectations, ways of forming relationships, for example, showing respect, ways of communication are valued and rewarded in the classroom (Swartz, 2009).

However, dismissing deficit thinking has been critiqued as being dismissive of influence of the class and the socioeconomic identity of the students (Openshaw, 2007; Thrupp, 2010), although some authors do acknowledge that both culture and class are predictors of educational success (Santoro and Allard, 2005).

In summary, whilst deficit theorising expects the student to be the site for responsibility for change, sociocultural theorising sees the teacher as the site for responsibility for change in student achievement.

3 Culturally responsive teaching includes having high expectations of students, not expectations based on stereotypes

One key aspect of culturally responsive teaching is that of having high expectations of students, and taking pedagogical actions based on those expectations, not based on deficit thinking. Teaching with assumptions that high achievement is a goal for all students, removes the explanations of cultural mismatches between teacher and student, and home and school, and stereotypes for low achievement. One experienced teacher noted:

... it's hugely about, from my experience, what's it's about is also having high expectations – sometimes kids have low expectations coming in ... Māori and Pasifika, they're
not having not any success. The *Te Kotahitanga* programme teaches us not to blame
the students, but to look at your own teaching, and while that's obviously not everyone
necessarily agrees wholeheartedly with that, I think that there's been a bit of a shift for
a lot of our teachers. For me, I've always – I don't see so much of a shift – I think I've
always done it the *Te Kotahitanga* way, but I didn't know that's what it was. [Harry]

Beginning teacher Katie also mentioned low expectations but, as indicated in her earlier
comment, chose not to differentiate students culturally:

Some of the time those kids are actually living into the expectations of them not
achieving, and so by not highlighting the fact that Māori students are underachieving
within my classroom setting ... I don't let them slip into that. Or try and minimise it.
[Katie]

4 Culturally responsive teaching involves forming relationships based on professional caring and a commitment that the student will achieve academically

The relationship formed between teacher and student is a key aspect of culturally responsive
teaching. Indeed, learning may not take place until an appropriate relationship is established
and student engagement achieved (Bishop and Berryman, 2006). As we saw in Chapter 2,
teaching may be viewed as a relational practice, with an emphasis on relationships based on
trust, respect and caring by both the teacher and the student (Richards *et al.*, 2006; Hill and
Hawk, 2000; Bishop and Berryman, 2006). This includes the teacher creating a culturally-
safe environment in the classroom (that is, classrooms which are inclusive culturally, not
exclusive, of students of a specific ethnicity (Macfarlane *et al.*, 2007).

A teacher is able to find out what is seen as respectful and caring by a student whose
culture is different from their own, through their interactions and communications with the
student and members of their community. Caring is often perceived by students as occurring
when a teacher cares that they learn and achieve, and shows a commitment to keep on being
pedagogically engaged with the students when the going gets tough (Bishop and Berryman,
2006). That is, the teacher continues to focus on learning and achieving, not slipping back
to interactions solely on behaviour management and absenteeism. One experienced teacher
commented in interview that forming positive relationships with students was the basis of
his pedagogy:

The diversity of students: how do I address these aspects? We've got 48 different
nationalities in our school so we focus on that every day in our classrooms [at this
high school] ... Māori and Pacifika hugely are attracted to the type of CooLA[4] type of
approach, working in groups. And we've got *Te Kotahitanga*[5] PD (professional development) going on in the school, which has been quite useful for us in terms of looking

---

4 CooLA is the Co-Operative Learning and Assessment work (CooLA) developed by Dr Paul Lowe, Morrinsville
   College. See Lowe, 2004.
5 *Te Kotahitanga* is a research and development project to raise the achievement of Maori students in mainstream
   New Zealand schools. See Bishop *et al.*, 2009.

at Māori and Pasifika students as well. At the end of the day, my experience is that what works for a student will work for any student, regardless of race, colour, creed. It's the relationship and if you can get relationships with all the different diversities of students, then you're forward and you're into it, I think. [Harry]

Knowing a student as the person-with-culture, rather than seeing them as the person-solo, without their culture being considered, is seen as a key to forming healthy relationships. Relationships in the classroom also include student–student relationships, and culturally responsive teaching is seen to include teachers helping students to learn and interact with people of different cultures, with mutual respect and equity (Richards *et al.*, 2006). For example, in their research in multicultural secondary schools in low socioeconomic areas in Auckland, New Zealand, with predominantly Pasifika students, Hill and Hawk (2000) found that respect and trust were seen by the students and teachers as being very important in the student–teacher relationship. For students, being treated like people and adults, not students and children, was important. The teachers communicated respect for students in their talk of valuing the contributions of students. Some of the reasons students gave for not respecting a teacher were: 'they ignore you, they don't get to know you, hurt your feelings, put you down, growl at you for laughing, make "facials", they don't believe you can do it' (Hill and Hawk, 2000: section 4.2). 'Giving of themselves' was another aspect seen as important by these students in teacher–student relationships. By this was meant that the teacher shared with students some of their family life: for example, their holidays, their feelings, apologising when wrong. Caring for them was also seen by these students as important: for example, 'giving extra personal time, listening to their ideas, supporting them with personal problems, following up after a difficult time, driving them to or from an event' (Hill and Hawk, 2000: section 4.2), but they still saw these teachers as justifiably disciplining them when need be. Reciprocity was also seen as important by these students: if the teacher respected them, they would respect the teacher. Other aspects of relationships seen as important by these students included: fairness, participation with students in classroom activities, patience, perseverance and not giving up on students, keeping their word.

5 Culturally responsive teaching includes teachers knowing and relating to students as culturally located human beings

Sociocultural theorising asserts that students do not leave their culture at the school gates; culturally responsive teachers use multiple ways to find out what worldviews, values, practices and cultural knowledge are being brought with students into the classroom. Without this it is not possible for the teacher to effectively teach students (Swartz, 2009). A Samoan saying goes:

> O tu, aganu'u, ma agaifanua a le tamaititi o le a le mafia ona ulufale atu i le potuaoga sei vagana ua fa'atauaina ma faaulufaleina muamua i le loto ma le loto ma le agaga o le faiaoga. (The culture of the child cannot enter the classroom until it has first entered the consciousness of the teacher.) (Allen *et al.*, 2009: 49)

Such teaching requires a disposition to want to find out and know about a student's cultural world (Giles, 2008b), when there is the acceptance that 'students and their teachers may *live* in different worlds' (Gay, 2010: 144; italics in original). Being socioculturally conscious is defined as:

... the awareness that a person's worldview is not universal but is profoundly influenced by life experiences, as mediated by a variety of factors, including race, ethnicity, gender and social class. Teachers who lack sociocultural awareness will unconsciously and inevitably rely on their own personal experiences to make sense of students' lives (Villegas and Lucas, 2007: 31).

For example, one beginning teacher spoke of his valuing of different cultures in the classroom:

A lot of the reason for coming up to the North Island [of New Zealand] was that I was trying to immerse myself in the more cultural side of it. ... because I've worked in different cultures, I really enjoy it, I think it's definitely beneficial to the class, I think bringing as many cultures to the class is always a help. I think this school really puts it [to] the forefront, they really put it up in front, they show all their cards, they definitely want the improvement there.

[Okay, and how well prepared do you feel in terms of teaching Pasifika students?]
Same, yeah, try and bring it into the fold. And not try and bring it into the fold [as if it's] an extension of the Māori culture. But it is [about] ... keeping the originality, keeping the distinction ... [James]

By knowing students as cultural beings, teachers get to know their students, not just as members of an ethnic group, but also as individuals, to avoid stereotypic explanations of student behaviour (Richards *et al.*, 2006; Weinstein *et al.*, 2004). For example, in Māori culture it is offensive to look an elder, or a person in a position of responsibility, in the eye. When a student has their eyes downward, 'they are not being defiant but practicing their culture' (Richards *et al.*, 2006: 8). On the other hand, most Māori are bicultural (Māori-Pākehā), as Māori are immersed in non-Māori culture in the media for example, and a student may choose to engage in direct eye contact when talking with a Pākehā teacher, in what they consider to be a Pākehā cultural situation. Knowing a student and their cultural identity(s) may help a teacher make sense of student behaviour, such as when eye contact is or is not made. In another example, an instance is recorded of a group of Pasifika boys leaving a health education class on sexuality, not because they were misbehaving, but because their female cousins – close family members – are in the class, and it would be culturally inappropriate for them to be there when sexuality is being discussed (Samu, 2006).

An experienced secondary teacher talked about how she saw her students' actions, being late to class, not as misbehaviour, but as practising their culture:

There are things like the students who leave school [to go to the mosque] on a Friday, so they're late coming back, that's just a reality of the place, and we don't have anything [such as a prayer room] onsite so they do have to go – it's not very far away – but they do have to go up the road so they are quite often late back. [Mary]

She also mentioned her need to know students well enough to ensure cultural safety in the classroom:

If you look at the evidence around, and the things that have been published about the *Te Kotahitanga* research, about what makes students feel that they have an identity and they are safe … I'm sure we challenge a lot of our students in that sense. However, there are the basics: like, our students are known by their birth name more often than not, unless they have – we have a few international students that come in, who want to anglicise their name, but more often than not students are known by their birth name and … teachers make a real genuine effort to make sure that that name is used correctly and respectfully. And you manage to get your tongue around them because some of them are real tongue twisters. So for things as basic as names, to respecting or communicating with them in a way that they find respectful … [Mary]

The ability of the teacher to elicit cultural understandings and practices from the students, rather than prior learning about a broad range of cultural, ethnic and linguistic groups from books, etc., is considered important in teaching for diversity (Greenleaf *et al.*, 1994).

The beginning teachers interviewed indicated the ways in which they had begun to know students as culturally embedded people, and what they needed to continue. One beginning teacher mentioned that she needed more than a theoretical knowledge of the cultures of her students:

> *[And (learning about) Pasifika students (in your initial teacher education)?]*
> Probably not so much, I don't recall doing an awful lot. I remember having some like largely theoretical discussions … there was some things I think I knew before hand, because [of] – some of the experiences I've had outside teaching. … I think the discussions we had on Pasifika [students] was probably too theoretical. [Sylvia]

As did beginning teacher Sandy:

> The teacher education programme here was sort of a very generic introduction to Māori culture. I didn't feel it was adequate to prepare teachers for what are the issues facing Māori students … which is much more than to say 'Okay how do we connect?' So it comes back to the 'what' and the 'how' … what strategies do we use with students, with Māori students, what strategies are more successful? [Sandy]

Beginning teacher Stephanie commented on her learning about students' cultural identities:

> I guess I was guilty of lumping what I thought as Pacific culture and Māori culture as one entity and really they're quite different. … Prior to that I would have just made assumptions that because the students looked Samoan then they must be from the same background, but yeah I've definitely learnt to separate out the cultures there. [Stephanie]

Initial teacher education for culturally responsive teaching is a starting point for many beginning teachers, and a first-hand working knowledge and experiences are seen as crucial (Kana, 2003), for culture cannot be understood solely in the abstract (Allen *et al.*, 2009). For example, Kana and Aitken (2007) used drama 'as a tool for student teachers to encounter social justice issues in a meaningful way' based on a fictional story of 'a beginning teacher (of European descent) [who] unwittingly diminishes the experiences of Māori and other non-European children in her class' (Kana and Aitken, 2007: 697). The goal was to promote empathy by 'walking in someone else's shoes' and to resolve tensions in ways that maintained the complexity of the issues and teaching.

Aitken and Kana (2010) also explored culturally responsive drama teaching in the initial teacher education setting and in a drama 'methods' classes for pre-service teachers, to engage Māori student teachers. Previously, only the Eurocentric story of Goldilocks had been used as a model, for the pre-service teachers' later use on practicum, the teacher-in-role strategy and the drama convention of 'hot-seating' – that is, the interviewing of story characters in role. The Pied Piper of Hamelin was also used in the creative aspect of drama education. As they commented:

> [Before] Viv [Aitken] had always simply covered the same content and used the same teaching strategies as in other mainstream classes. This was based on her assumptions that offering the same content was being equitable, and therefore the 'right' thing to do. In spite of there being no negative feedback in student appraisal from the group, Viv remembers a feeling that something was not quite right with her teaching–learning relationship and this was sometimes reflected in students' level of participation and their overall achievement in the paper. (Aitken and Kana, 2010: 10)

In moving towards a culturally responsive pedagogy, Aitken, supported by Kana, used Māori rituals to start the lesson; Māori language and terms were used as appropriate; and the students were invited to 'keep [your] eyes open for ways [you] can bring in indigenous connections' (p. 13). They stated: 'we were constantly aware of a delicate interplay between the knowledge the students brought with them and the knowledge embedded in the curriculum learning area being explored' (Aitken and Kana, 2010: 13). Eventually, they replaced the Eurocentric stories with Māori legends around Maui, 'a multitalented demigod figure central to many Polynesian stories' (Aitken and Kana, 2010: 20), for these Māori language immersion student teachers, then all first-year mainstream classes, and finally for the practicum component of teaching schoolchildren as well. The cultural experiences and knowledge of the students were being validated, and the tutors' 'rethinking has expanded beyond the "what" of content, to look at the "how", "where" and the "when" of the delivery' (Aitken and Kana, 2010: 23).

Learning from their students, rather than from books and lecturers, can continue the learning of beginning teachers. One pedagogy that can be used to elicit cultural understandings, values and practices from students is that of formative assessment, also called assessment for learning (Bell, 2000). It is formative assessment that gives teachers the knowledge to teach in a culturally responsive manner, no matter which culture the student is bringing to the classroom. How formative assessment is undertaken may vary with the culture of the student, for example by using written responses with students in Samoa (Lee Hang, 2011) and cooperative learning activities with students in Vietnam (Nguyen *et al.*, 2009). But the goal is the same – to elicit student thinking. The use of formative assessment is highlighted as an effective teaching strategy for raising achievement (Black and Wiliam, 1998) and the mainstream classrooms in the *Te Kotahitanga* programme (Bishop and Glynn, 1999). Other pedagogies that can be used to find out about students' cultures are: co-construction of shared understandings, mediation and scaffolding (see Chapter 3).

Learning from other teachers and staff in the school was mentioned in the interviews:

[Did your ITE course prepare you for) teaching Māori students?]
Pretty well, [the school has] got quite a few Māori students, so it has prepared me quite well. ... Just some of the cultural things that you learnt and ... just little things, like last

year I picked up the habit of not letting kids [sit][6] on desks, and now it really bothers me because it's just a habit – 'Get off the desk.' And just like some pronunciation things and just being willing to give things a go too. [The tutor] always said to us, even if you get it wrong just try it, try and use the language. ... I grew up in Pakuranga [a predominantly Pakeha area], so ... I didn't really have a lot of exposure to it [Māori culture] at all, so I found it was quite good actually and just being willing to be more open to it and just give it a go, although you might say it wrong, or you might do something wrong initially, at least you've show a willingness of being more accepting of the Māori perspective I guess. [Sylvia]

Total immersion in a cultural context which the teacher wishes to learn about is another strategy (Kana, 2003; Allen *et al.*, 2009). In New Zealand, Delia Baskerville (2009) examined through reflective narration a 'three month full-immersion teacher professional development experience in Māori cultural protocols and practices that changed my consciousness and voice, enabled me to address my deficit thinking and find ways to manage cultural difference in the classroom' (Baskerville 2009: 462). For example, in living on the *marae*, she learnt about the importance of:

> ... time to set the tone, to give clear explanations of the process, to ensure we all knew each other, understood the intention of the *korero* (shared talking), and validate everyone in their right to express their opinion and be listened to. This process was never rushed. Time was allocated to question, challenge, and to explicitly ensure all developed a shared understanding of the agenda. High expectations were set. I realised the importance of *korero*. I viewed inclusion through a new lens informed by these insights. ...
>
> I became familiar and at ease with: a *kaupapa* (agenda) that was agreed and reinforced; *karakia*, waiting and ensuring circumstances for all to be ready and willing to learn; *powhiri* (welcome) that developed my sense of belonging to *Aotearoa* New Zealand; *hui* (meeting) that privileged my voice in negotiating shared understandings with the group of facilitators; safe disclosure; the value of supervision; *marae* (Māori meeting place) justice in restoring relationships and *poroporoaki* (goodbye) in terms of closure. I learnt how different living in a Māori cultural and community context was from school and our mainstream community. (Baskerville 2009: 464–5)

Baskerville noted that her pedagogy had changed as a result of this experience, listing these changes among many:

> ... in the classroom, I now strategise to privilege the silent voices in the classroom and provide opportunities for them to speak by foreshadowing the question I am about to pose (Baskerville 2009: 466).

Likewise, in the Pasifika context, travelling to Samoa and living with a Samoan family, as part of an in-service professional development, was a way for Palagi (non-Pasifika) teachers to know Samoan students and the culture they bring to the classroom (Allen *et al.*, 2009). In their study, one of the teachers commented:

---

6 Placing the buttocks on a table where food is eaten is very offensive to Māori.

Seeing how much is shared – the food ... The way the babies are held. The way they talk to each other so much ... This has been quite a profound thing. As a teacher, I know that Pasifika children need to work together, but now I know why and I've seen how deep that need is. (Allen *et al.*, 2009: 55)

Video websites are also helpful: for example, the gallery of video clips from the New Zealand Ministry of Education (2010) on effective teaching for Pasifika students.[7]

Home visits and interaction with families (along with other learning experiences) are further experiences that help teachers to teach diverse students. In a study by Kidd *et al.* (2008), the initial teacher education teachers involved realised how much there was to learn from families about the students' individual needs, which helped them teach the students better.

Finally, Gay (2010) cautions us that obtaining an awareness of the students' cultural embeddedness is not a substitute for action; it is the start, not the end. And this awareness can only come about if teachers build trusting relationships with students so that they will self-disclose. A part of building a relationship with students of ethnicities not our own is to give something of ourselves to the relationship: sharing our own culture with the students, for example, our language, traditions, foods, rituals; letting students into our world, for example, in an appropriate way, telling students what we did on the weekend; and spending some of our precious time to build the relationship.

6 Culturally responsive teaching includes building relationships and communication with the families and communities of students

Learning by teachers about their students being people 'embedded in a culture' may necessitate visiting the families of students, at home and at community gatherings; participating in community events; inviting family members to contribute to the teaching and learning in the classroom (Richards *et al.*, 2006). However, such communications need to be culturally responsive ones (Ibrahim *et al.*, 2009). A beginning teacher commented on this aspect of being a culturally responsive teacher:

It's been a lot of learning and respect and understanding and learning about how the families operate and it's been fascinating and important. We also have some other ethnicities now coming into the school with [the] refugee population so we are getting even more variance. We have children from African countries and South East Asia, so it's changing all the time. I wouldn't say I've ever thought this is too hard, because it was a choice to go [here].

[So how have you been supported to learn about your students' family and communities?] Once again probably because the school is so predominately Pacific Island families and there was quite a lot of Pacific Island teachers on the staff that we learn through discussion in an informal way and discussion about individual students, that's how I learn really. Discussing through the various other student services staff who are there as well ... [Ellie]

7 Available at http://pasifika.tki.org.nz/Media-gallery/Effective-teaching-for-Pasifika-students/ (accessed 4. July 2011).

An experienced teacher also mentioned that her learning journey had been helped by a member of the students' community:

> We ... did for a long time have an advisor here from the Somalian community. ... And he was quite useful because not only could you ... ask about a particular student in terms of family or having communication with family because his parents didn't speak English and those sorts of things, but you could quiz him up and say, 'what is the custom around this?' or 'what do we need to be mindful of?' or 'I think I've offended someone because I've done such and such, what have I done that wasn't right?' Or, when a student has said 'you can't do that, that doesn't fit with my culture', you could check it out and so you know if they're pulling the wool over your eyes ... so you could actually sound off from somebody who was on staff and whose role was that. But I'm not quite sure where the funding came from for that but we don't have that position anymore. ... But it was really useful; and he wasn't full-time ... so he was sometimes in classrooms with students and he was in the staff room ... in the lunch breaks and things, and you could actually sidle over to him and say, 'I need to know ...'; 'What about ...?' ... [Mary]

Building relationships with students' families and communities may involve having an open-door policy for parents and family members at the school; welcoming parents, caregivers and families with a cup of tea; inviting them in if you see them walking around outside the school buildings, having the students greet them and inviting them to contribute to a lesson.

7 *Culturally responsive teaching involves using the cultural and ethnic knowledge, language, values and practices of the students as a resource to inform teaching decision-making about curriculum and pedagogy*

Having found out from students (as well as from books, colleagues, initial teacher education, and the school community) about the cultural knowledge, values, practices and experiences students bring to the classroom, what does a culturally responsive teacher do next? How do teachers use this information to inform their teaching as requested by students (Bishop *et al.*, 2003; Macfarlane, 2004)? In New Zealand, these questions are embedded in Durie's three goals for Māori education: that Māori students will be able to live as Māori; be both national and international citizens; and benefit from a high standard of living (Durie, 2001). To achieve this requires the use of student cultural knowledge in teacher decision-making on what to teach and, just as importantly, what not to teach; and how and how not to teach. The following are suggested ways to use a student's cultural knowledge in teaching decision-making.

One way is to use the languages of the students. Although many graduating initial teacher education students do not feel as prepared as they would like to be to teach Māori and Pasifika students (Kane and Fontaine, 2008; Anthony *et al.*, 2008), beginning teacher Katie indicated her use of *Te Reo Māori* (the Māori language and one of New Zealand's official languages) in the classroom:

> Because it's all very well saying that you can study Māori myths and legends in English, but how really can you do that in science, how can you actually bring in other cultures into teaching science? I was having the same discussion with the home ec[onomics]

teacher who's doing that course ... she is doing that similar assignment, looking at how you can bring culture into your subject. And so she said 'well with cooking ... it's so easy to bring in all these other cultural influences'. So she goes 'How do you do it in science?' and I said 'I don't, I've got names on the wall, the Māori names for the different bones in the body and the different planets and a Māori motif and maybe a Māori proverb and that's it, it's all on the wall. There's nothing I really feel like I can do and I know it's part of my job ... [Katie]

While there are resources and research available for Māori science education (New Zealand Ministry of Education, 2010), the key point is to note that Katie was incorporating Māori language and its connected cultural knowledge into the classroom, thus validating it as worthwhile knowledge to learn. Using and learning Māori language in the school setting was mentioned by another beginning teacher:

[What about teaching of Māori students, did you feel it [the ITE course] prepared you to do that?]
Probably because of my practicum, I went down to X [about an hour's drive away], and some of my classes were – half the children there were Māori, and in that respect, I guess, for actual teaching and for the actual culture down at that school ... I was as prepared as any ... The actual Māori component at university – I was glad I had that, that was necessary for me ... because it had been a while since I was involved in anything like that, and even straightforward things like singing the national anthem in Māori, because I wasn't brought up with that version, and it's something that all the school children here take for granted and even my own children do. My children know a lot more than I do, so it's been great to have been brought up to speed because prior to last year I was ... old school taught ... and didn't have that background. [Stephanie]

A second way to use the cultural knowledge of students in teaching decision-making is to teach the content in meaningful contexts for the students. Teaching science (or any other subject) within meaningful contexts for the students, as suggested in the New Zealand curriculum (New Zealand Ministry of Education, 2007) was mentioned by two of the experienced teachers:

Try within the context ... in which we're teaching the science, is to make sure that we include examples of obvious living examples of where these kids are at in their own worlds. [Harry]
   So the whole idea about putting more environmental education ... slant on things would be to embrace some of the Māori and Pacific cultures. So if we managed to get out there in the environment, let's look at some of the old cultural practices, even let's see how we can bring Māori culture into teaching Science. And I think if we can do that, it's about making the connections and those students being able to connect with you, with the reasons why they're learning the Science, and then I think you get the whole engagement thing happening after that and then once we've got a wee bit of success then success breeds success ... [Megan]

Hence, teachers may be inclusive with students, with the use of their cultural contexts to embed the learning and make links between their world and the world of science or mathematics, etc. Aspects of their cultural knowledge, such as dance, music, food, artwork, in the content of the curriculum may also be used. For example, science teachers in New Zealand have used the *hangi* (a Māori earth oven, using river stones) to teach the scientific concept of heat capacity, and have included Māori myths and legends on mountain formation in units of work on volcanoes and earthquakes (not necessarily as examples of scientific knowledge in Western science but as a way of knowing and making sense) (Bell, 2005a). This integration of cultural aspects in high-status subjects such as science and mathematics is important (Gay, 2002). And while this use of cultural contexts and aspects is a start, it has been called 'additive multiculturalism' (Swartz, 2009), as the dominant worldview of the teacher and schooling (and associated power positioning) has not been modified, just added to (Santoro and Allard, 2005).

Another strategy to use the cultural knowledge of students is the inclusion of specific cultural celebrations and practices. This was mentioned by beginning teacher Katie:

> Sometimes it can just be very simple things … [like] acknowledging *Matairiki* [Māori new year in the southern mid-winter] or just small things … I think we also have to be very careful not to sort of force it, so trying to make every lesson a five minute component. … We did have an opportunity, we talked about burials and we talked about *tangi* because one of the boys asked where other people bury their people, did they have them at home or … So sometimes, you know, the students provide the opportunity for the cultural awareness even if you haven't planned it. [Katie]

None of the beginning or experienced teachers interviewed (and they were all non-Māori) suggested other ways of including the non-Eurocentric cultures of student in the classroom. Their comments were suggestive of teachers beginning their journeys towards culturally responsive teaching, through their inclusion of language, meaningful contexts and celebrations as part of their pedagogy.

However, Sleeter (2010) suggests that culturally responsive teaching goes beyond the conceptions of cultural celebration, which does not equate with academic achievement; trivialisation, which results in culturally responsive pedagogy being reduced to 10 or so best steps, rather than this pedagogy being a mindset of seeking input from students; and essentialising culture, which creates a homogeneous picture of a group of students, who then do not need to be engaged in order to obtain input on culture from the students themselves. In addition, the above aspects of culturally responsive pedagogy, of themselves, are not seen as sufficient, for they do not address key issues of unequal distribution of power and resources, through racism, social injustice and other forms of oppression, including colonisation (May and Sleeter, 2010b). Sleeter (2010) argues that culturally responsive teaching goes further to both remove the silence of oppression and inequity in the classroom, and to take political action, as discussed in the next section.

8 Culturally responsive teaching is emancipatory and transformative, and hence political

An important aspect of culturally responsive teaching is seen as that of challenging and disrupting the wider discourses, which maintain the inequity of educational outcomes (Swartz, 2009). To do so is to give priority to political analysis (May and Sleeter, 2010a) and to see that 'culturally responsive pedagogy is not only about teaching, but is also a political endeavor' (Sleeter, 2010: 20). The political aspect includes questioning and challenging the discourses of deficit, entitlement and privilege, and structural and institutional racism in society; and a concern for social justice, especially for equity of schooling outcomes.

Ladson-Billings (1995) outlined a theory for culturally relevant teaching, comprised of three criteria: academic success, cultural competence, and sociopolitical consciousness. In this section, the third of these components is discussed: sociopolitical consciousness, defined as 'developing critical perspectives that challenge inequities that schools (and other institutions) perpetuate' (Ladson-Billings, 1995: 469). According to Young, Ladson-Billings's point was not 'to prescribe elements that would make a lesson culturally relevant but rather to emphasize that a culturally relevant pedagogue is always conscious of all three components when planning elements' (Young, 2010: 249), not just the first one or two. A pedagogy with only one or two of the components is seen as incomplete (Young, 2010). Some teachers may deliberately choose to work in culturally diverse contexts as part of their social justice work (Strachan, 2005).

Culturally responsive teaching that is emancipatory, transformative and political may start with the teacher being an advocate for the students, in professional situations where the students are not present (Villegas and Lucas, 2007) – for example, ensuring that appropriate book resources, reflecting the cultures of students, are bought by the school; that communication with caregivers and parents is in the child's home language; that a teacher speaks out and intervenes if the child's cultural practices are misinterpreted as misbehaviour by another teacher; that becoming a culturally responsive teacher is a topic for professional development in the school; that there is a commitment for extra tuition to be given to help a student achieve; and that the 'rules of the game' are explicitly explained to the student who is struggling to comprehend the dominant culture.

Being an advocate for a student may require us to speak out to identify and challenge racism, despite disrupting 'white comfort' and 'niceness' (Galman *et al.*, 2010). It may include supporting students to succeed by allaying fears and concerns, when no one in their family has gone on to tertiary education and forged a path to walk down *(Hale et al.*, 2008). It may include supporting a student, when talking about his former teachers, to change the words 'The teachers did not notice my being Pasifika' to 'The teachers ignored my being Pasifika', thereby replacing description with critical thinking. It may include classroom curricula, which make visible critiques of taken-for-granted knowledge. New Zealand examples of this include challenging the notions that New Zealand's social history began with European settlement/colonisation, by considering the arrival of Māori *waka* (canoes) between 1100 and 1300 AD; and that Māori *waka* arrived by chance, by the reporting of the highly skilled celestial navigation the Māori used (Bishop and Glynn, 1999). It may mean including social issues relating to, for example, Māori and Pasifika students (Young, 2010). For example, Donn Ratana is an art educator who encourages initial teacher education students to express their political activism in their artwork.

It may include contributing to national/state educational policy-making. For example, at the national level in Aotearoa New Zealand, Māori (and some Pākehā: Metge, 2008) educationalists have been proactive in ensuring that national educational policy is inclusive of culturally responsive teaching (New Zealand Ministry of Education, 2007; New Zealand Teachers Council, 2007) and researching pedagogy from a Māori perspective – for example, in Māori settings (Smith, 1997; Pere, 1982; Hohepa *et al.*, 1996; Hemara, 2000), and mainstream settings (Bishop and Glynn, 1999). Māori educationalists have questioned the existing assumptions, values and practices regarding Māori underachievement and power-relationships in schools. The New Zealand Ministry of Education now lists as a priority 'Māori enjoying education success as Māori' (New Zealand Ministry of Education, 2009).

Examples of Culturally Responsive Teaching in Aotearoa New Zealand

Two examples of culturally responsive secondary pedagogies in the Aotearoa New Zealand setting are now given. In the first example, Russell Bishop and colleagues (Bishop *et al.*, 2003: 95–6) have outlined an effective teaching profile, in the context of Māori education:

> Effective teachers of Māori students create a culturally appropriate and responsive context for learning in their classroom. In doing so they demonstrate the following understandings:
> a) they positively and vehemently reject deficit theorising as a means of explaining Māori students' educational achievement levels (and professional development projects need to ensure that this happens); and
> b) they know and understand how to bring about change in Māori students' educational achievement and are professionally committed to doing so (and professional development projects need to ensure that this happens); in the following observable ways:
>   1) *Manaakitanga*: They care for the students as culturally-located human beings above all else. (*Mana* refers to authority and *aki*, the task of urging some one to act. It refers to the task of building and nurturing a supportive and loving environment.)
>   2) *Mana motuhake*: They care for the performance of their students. (In modern times *mana* has taken on various meanings such as legitimation and authority, and can also relate to an individual's or a group's ability to participate at the local and global level. *Mana motuhake* involves the development of personal or group identity and independence.)
>   3) *Ngā tūrango takitahi me ngā mana whakahaere*: They are able to create a secure, well-managed learning environment. (*Ngā tūranga takitahi me nga mana whaka-haere* involves specific individual roles and responsibilities that are required in order to achieve individual and group outcomes.)
>   4) *Wānanga*: They are able to engage in effective teaching interactions with Māori students as Māori. (As well as being known as Māori centres of learning, *wānanga* as a learning forum involves a rich and dynamic sharing of knowledge. With this exchange of views, ideas are given life and spirit through dialogue, debate and careful consideration in order to reshape and accommodate new knowledge.)
>   5) *Ako*: They can use strategies that promote effective teaching interactions and relationships with their learners. (*Ako* means to learn as well as to teach. It is both the acquisition of knowledge and the processing and imparting of knowledge. More importantly *ako* is a teaching–learning practice that is culturally specific and appropriate to Māori pedagogy.)
>   6) *Kōtahitanga*: They promote, monitor and reflect on outcomes that in turn lead to improvements in educational achievement for Mäori students. (*Kōtahitanga* is a collaborative response towards a commonly held vision, goal or other such purpose or outcome).

The Effective Teaching Profile is based on the concept of culturally responsive teaching, and is structured on Māori knowledge, values and customs. Evidence of the effectiveness of this pedagogy with Māori students attending school more regularly, engaging as learners and achieving in national qualifications has been researched and documented (Bishop and

Berryman, 2010). Of interest is that similar gains were also made by Pasifika students in the *Te Kotahitanga* schools (Bishop and Berryman, 2010).

Another culturally responsive secondary pedagogy is that of the Hikairo Rationale (Macfarlane, 2000) and the Educultural Wheel (Macfarlane, 2004). Although the Hikairo Rationale was initially developed as a series of guidelines for classroom behaviour management, it has a synergy with other pedagogies. 'The Hikairo approach is appropriate for working with both Māori and non-Māori students and teachers, even though its guiding values and metaphors come from within a Māori world view' (Macfarlane, 2004: 76). The seven key principles spell out the name of Hikairo – a Māori chief of great standing:

Step 1: *Huakina Mai* (Opening doorways). '[F]rom the outset, it is crucial that the teacher gets to know the students' experiences, attitudes and emotional states, and the students get to know the teacher's expectations' (Macfarlane, 2004: 76).

Step 2: *Ihi* (Assertiveness). The teacher expresses him or herself in an assertive manner – '... to act in their own best interests, to stand up for themselves without undue anxiety, to express honest feelings comfortably, or to exercise personal rights without denying the rights of others ... ' (Macfarlane, 2000: 24).

Step 3: *Kotahitanga* (Unity). This refers to the process by which students, teachers and *whanau* members together negotiate behaviour rules and behaviour management strategies' (Macfarlane, 2000: 24).

Step 4: *Awhinata* (The helping process interventions). These strategies 'attempt to change behaviour through altering both the antecedents and the consequences of behaviour' (Macfarlane, 2000: 24). For example, a small, culturally appropriate non-verbal message may be used to stop unacceptable behaviour escalating. For example, cultural appropriate and responsive feedback, such as Māori metaphors and icons, is given.

Step 5: *I Runga I te Manaaki* (Pastoral care). Within the context of violations of *tapu* (sacredness), 'serious behaviours need to be addressed through Maori concepts such as tika, pono, and aroha, all essential elements of a caring and healing process. Tika relates to fairness, pono to integrity, and aroha to inclusion' (Macfarlane, 2000: 24).

Step 6: *Raranga* (The weaving process). A *hui* (a meeting conducted with Māori protocol) 'encourages diverse and multiple participation' (Macfarlane, 2000: 25) to discuss the educational goals and needs of a student. Family members such as parents, siblings, aunts and uncles and grandparents are included in the *hui* with non-Māori professionals to reach negotiated and collaborative decisions.

Step 7: *Oranga* (Wellbeing). Here the notion of the wellbeing of the individual is deeply embedded in the wellbeing of the group, with success on the four dimensions of '... giving and receiving love; achieving a sense of worth in one's own eyes and in the eyes of others; having fun; and becoming self-disciplined' (Macfarlane, 2000: 25).

The effectiveness of this pedagogy in the context of schooling for at-risk youth has been documented by Angus Macfarlane (2000).

In addition, in the Educultural Wheel, Macfarlane (2004) asks teachers to consider: *Whanaungatanga*: building relationships; *Manaakitanga*: the ethic of caring; *Rangatiratanga*: teacher effectiveness; *Kotahitanga*: the ethic of bounding; and *Pumanawatanga*: morale, tone, pulse.

Likewise, a Pasifika culturally-responsive pedagogy is outlined by Samu (2006), but it is not a list of specific strategies or approaches to use, but rather a framework of principles, similar to the list given in this chapter and beginning on page 42.

Concluding comment

In many Western countries, the dominance of neo-liberal discourses in education has meant that governments have made policies that ignore the central importance of context, culture and the need to challenge racism in considerations of education and teaching (Sleeter, 2010). In New Zealand, while neo-liberal discourses are evident (Thrupp, 2010), the educational policies in the national curriculum, and in major research and development initiatives in Māori education, still promote culturally responsive pedagogies, largely due to the energy and political work of Māori and Pasifika educators.

Study and discussion

- Explain why using the cultural knowledge of either an indigenous or an immigrant student as part of the taught curriculum in the classroom is considered to be culturally responsive teaching.
- Can you give an example from your own teaching?

5   Teaching as an emotion practice

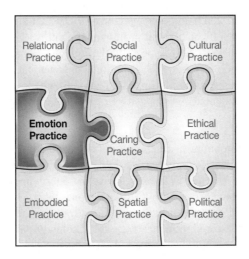

Introduction

Teachers are not just knowledge and skills workers, they are emotion workers as well:

> [A]s an occupation teaching is highly charged with feeling, aroused by and directed towards not just people but also values and ideals. (Nias, 1996: 293]

A teacher may be joyful at the end of a lesson which had the students engaged, talking on task and learning; happy for the student who is awarded a scholarship to study at a university; sad with a student whose mother has died; despairing of the student who is able but chooses not to learn; annoyed with a colleague who does not do his share of the team work; excited for a student winning a place in the final of the Science Fair; frustrated with a statement in the curriculum; fearful of the response of a student to disciplinary measures; guilty at not being able to help a student obtain the national standard; enthusiastic to trial a new teaching approach; relieved at the list of teacher criteria for registration; and upset by the comments of parents.

The emotional practice of teaching (Hargreaves, 1998) is a sociocultural term which emphasises the complex relationship inextricably linking emotion and teaching (Zembylas, 2004b), as well as linking emotion and cognition, without equating emotional and irrational (Zembylas, 2004a); and linking emotion and the social, cultural and historical contexts in which teachers work (Nias, 1996). In this chapter, I am using the term 'emotion practice', rather than 'emotional practice', to avoid any connotations with the irrational. I have, however, used 'emotional practice' when other authors have used it in their writing.

We as teachers feel emotions with respect to our students, colleagues, the parents and caregivers of students, and our own professional practices, beliefs and values (Nias, 1996). Each of these is discussed in turn.

Teachers have emotions linked to their *interaction with people*

There are emotions discursively constructed in our relationships with people at school. The emotions may be strongly felt, as teachers are responsible for the quality of relationships between ourselves and students, and for the conduct and progress of students (Nias, 1996; Naring et al., 2006). These relationships with students, which are a part of teaching, are a large part of a teacher's self-esteem and professional identity – and therefore also of their vulnerability (Kelchtermans, 1996), especially during educational reforms (Kelchtermans, 2005). Demetriou et al. (2009) argue that emotional engagement with students can engage students more in learning, resulting in increased learning outcomes.

Liking and loving the students was a positive expression about teaching by one beginning teacher. For example:

> Oh, the kids [are important in teaching], it's always the kids. Even [the] ratbags. Oh, they're cheeky and there's no way I would have said half the things they say to me to any of my teachers, but they're wicked. I love the ones who, you know, will sit down, know the expectations, get on with it. I like the ones who get on with it but are cheeky as well, and I actually, I like trying to get the best out of the ones who really can't be bothered. And some are nightmares, they are absolutely pains ... because they don't want to work at all ... it's always the kids. The kids make it more than the staff I've got to say, [they are] what you come to school for basically. ... another thing I love about this job is that they make every day different ... It's great that you don't know what you're going to get [from them] ... there's routine but there's, you know, fun and excitement in the meantime sort of thing, so yeah. [Samantha]

Pride in the students was expressed. For example:

> I was so proud of them [a tourism class on a field trip] and I told them that when we got back as well, before I let them off the bus and I said 'Look you were a credit to the school, you are a credit to yourselves' ... Apart from anything else, it was relief on my part, because it was a bit of a gamble taking them over there [to a rally car practice venue], never having done it [before]. ... They were very much, not only representative of the school, [they] were representative of me, if they made a terrible impression it would have really gutted me, and also I just wouldn't have considered taking anybody back next year. ... They've set a nice pathway for me to take some more kids next year, and, yeah, that was a really nice feeling I've got to say. ... They were real stars, I was really proud of them. So yeah, that's probably the best day [of teaching for me]. [Samantha]

However, one beginning teacher mentioned the feeling of being scared in relation to the management of students:

Classroom management. … because it's such a nuts and bolts [need], at the beginning of the year. If that's not in place, the teaching is just pushed to the back for a while and it can be quite scary. It's fine here, but if you encounter a school that has complete classroom management issues throughout the school, that's a scary, scary thing and I can see how so many teachers tuck tail and run after the first year if that's not in place. … [Stephanie]

Beginning teacher Samantha discussed her feelings of tiredness about the constant inter-action with people which is required in teaching:

… the thing that I found very difficult, well not difficult, it was just something I had to get used to, was the fact that … my last boss, if he had a bad day he would just hide behind his computer, he didn't have to pick up the phone, he would just be at a desk, not really answering to anybody. Whereas here you're constantly on show and that's been almost more tiring than anything, because it's not just managing behaviour, it's thinking ahead and being on your toes all the time. [Samantha]

Colleagues were talked about positively, usually about giving support. For example:

[What has sustained you in your first 18 months?]
… the excellent support of my colleagues, [it] has been incredibly supportive. You know if you have had a bad day or a problem, they have been there done that, and laugh about it, those things have kept me going. There have been some low points, 'I'm in the wrong job', 'I can't do this anymore' or that type of thing. I don't know if you really truly believe that, it's just the nature of teaching, you just want to drive out the school gates and keep going sometimes, but not often. It's more an exceptional thing [that's got you low], but you just simply don't go. Every day isn't joy and fun, wonderful. And yet I do hear some teachers saying that they do feel that, but I don't know whether they are telling the truth or whether they are just in a different type of school. But it's quite tough and you do need the support of colleagues and family as well, that is what has kept me going. And also believing that, yes, you can do it in the end, that you are contributing in some way. [Ellie]

[Have there been any rewarding experiences for you while you've been here?]
I think one of the rewarding experiences is working with my mentor, who is a classroom specialist [teacher]. And he's told me a lot of ways of dealing with kids, like … they're different kinds of kids than you would find in another school, so doing things in the class like … fun activities and lots of experiments and dealing with their misbehaviour and stuff. I've been able to raise the achievement levels a bit so that is like a personal success for me. I've been able to develop quite a good rapport with them, but it is not that great, but I've been able to talk to them. …

[In what areas would you like to have more support …?]
Discipline. … it's nice to have someone, who you could talk to about the problems you have in the school. And know that it's going to stay there, and it's not going to come back and bite you. [Sarika]

Experienced teacher Harry expressed his positive feelings about the skills of some of the younger staff:

'ICT'. .... probably until about four years ago, I was a bit of a [late starter] in this sense. And I got my first data projector and then I also employed some wonderful young year 1 and year 2 and 3 teachers, who have mostly come out from Waikato [University] and their ability to incorporate stuff off the net and ...[it] has been absolutely sensational. [Harry]

However, beginning teacher Samantha expressed negative feelings about working with one colleague in particular:

... I had a very good, I mean, she was [an] excellent tutor teacher in French and very industrious. But I felt constantly under pressure that I wasn't doing as well as she would have liked me to. There seemed to be a real negative undertone, it was nothing explicit, she was always very supportive, always giving me advice, always giving me ... some sort of emotional bump up like 'don't worry about it'. The first class I taught was in Spanish and it was a Year 9 class and I'd never taught before, she pointed all this out, 'you've never taught before', 'you're teaching a language you don't know', 'you've done great, don't worry about it, alright?', but I always felt that I wasn't quite good enough for her. [Samantha]

One beginning teacher said he felt daunted when interacting with senior management in schools:

At times it ... all the other stuff, the admin and bureaucracy stuff together ... can feel daunting, you feel, I revert back to feeling like a student, I feel that I'm back in that little high school [that I went too]. [James]

As teachers, our emotions are linked to our own *professional beliefs, practices and values*

When our practices are not perceived by us to match our own expectations or those of others, we may feel negative emotions. Understandably, as teachers we may have negative feelings if we are being judged by ourselves or others as not performing at the required standards. We may have positive feelings when we are acting in a way which is consistent with our beliefs and values. What we understand, believe and value as teaching and what it means to be a teacher, may also be at odds with the understandings, beliefs and values of others, giving rise to negative emotions – for example, when there is a loss of professional respect, reputation and autonomy as a result of educational policy (Nias, 1996).

One beginning teacher was asked about her prior beliefs about teaching, and what she believed now. She replied in terms of her teaching practices and expressed feelings of being under stress:

Yeah I have found it [teaching] hard, I will be honest, I had fantastic ... expectations of how I was going to teach before I got here, but the reality of being faced with marking, behaviour management in particular ... All those elements combine to be so time consuming, that your focus goes from how can I address every single individual learner, how can I can assess how they are learning, and what I need to teach towards, and get the best out of them. You become completely consumed with their behaviour, how do I get them quiet, how do I get them learning? [Samantha]

She also talked of receiving feedback on her teaching, a process she had found exhausting, stressful and nerve-wracking:

> I had three observations back-to-back basically in about a week and a half, which was good, but also exhausting and also quite nerve-wracking because I hadn't been observed for so long. I have been left alone to do what I want here basically and that was one worry I had, that I could be going completely wrong ... with the class ... and nobody from administration would know... [Samantha]

Another beginning teacher mentioned her feelings of frustration with classroom management:

> *[this first six months of teaching?]*
> It's tough. ... It's hard work.
>
> *[Is there anything that's been particularly frustrating for you?]*
> I think just frustration with the classroom management bit. That is the biggest problem I'm facing that I'm not being able to control, take control over the classroom and I'm working on it. [Sarika]

The belief of giving or making a difference was a positive aspect of teaching mentioned by beginning teacher Sarika, giving her a good feeling about herself as a teacher:

> *[When I'm teaching at my best I am like a ...]*
> It's [a] low flow of energy, probably I feel very good about myself and be able to create a difference. Yeah so ... you know making a difference. [Sarika]

Beginning teacher Ellie discussed her feelings of stress with her changed beliefs and expectations in her second year of teaching:

> *[What is it like being a second-year teacher?]*
> Well, it's interesting, because in some ways I find it quite a lot harder, not just because of the increased hours, but just because ... you kind of have a higher expectation of yourself now ... Last year was more survival, whereas this year is different in that you are trying to perfect things more, I think. So in some ways harder, I think I've found it quite hard this year. And it's not just about the [extra] time because that is not really that noticeable. But then a lot of things are much easier because you know all the systems and you know your colleagues, and all that sort of thing. It hasn't been easier this year, put it that way. [Ellie]

In summary, teachers feel emotions with respect to the people we work with, and with our own beliefs, values and practice.

Theorising emotions

There are two main ways that emotions are theorised. First, emotions can be theorised as a part of a person's biological being (Sutton and Wheatley, 2003), or as psychological competence or disposition (Hargreaves, 2005). They are viewed as the emotional mind, connected but separate from the rational, cognitive mind (Hargreaves, 2000). For example, Goleman

(1996) lists eight families of emotions: anger, sadness, fear, enjoyment, love, surprise, disgust, and shame. And five emotion competencies: emotional self-awareness, managing emotions, harnessing emotions productively, reading emotions, and handling relationships.

Second, we can view emotions as discursive, social constructs within relationships (Harré, 1986; Harré and Parrott, 1996). Emotions are seen to exist between people more than within them, and are an important form of communication between individuals. Teaching and emotion are interwoven and connected through teaching being a social, cultural and political practice:

> [T]he emotions that teachers experience and express, for example, are not just matters of personal dispositions but are constructed in social relationships and systems of values in their families, cultures and school situations. These relationships and values profoundly influence how and when particular emotions are constructed, expressed and communicated (Zembylas, 2004b: 186).

If we view them thus, we are indicating that we view emotions as linked to power, culture and the social in relationships (Zembylas, 2005: 937):

> In general my conception of emotion in this paper rests on two important assumptions:
> 1. Emotions are not private or universal and are not impulses that simply happen to passive sufferers (the Aristotelian view). Instead, emotions are constituted through language and refer to a wider social life. This view challenges any sharp distinction between the 'private' domain (the existentialist and the psychoanalytic concern) and the 'public' domain (the structuralist concern).
> 2. Power relations are inherent in 'emotion talk' and shape the expression of emotions by permitting us to feel some emotions while prohibiting others (for example, through moral norms and explicit social values, e.g. efficiency, objectivity, neutrality). Unavoidably, then, resistance is a part and power is productive ...

In this view, emotion talking and discourses are bound by social rules and norms and may differ from context to context. These emotion rules reflect power relations and, as such, there are appropriate and inappropriate emotions, deviant and normal, permitted and non-permitted emotion talk and practices. These emotional rules police teachers as to how to express, use, manage and control emotions linked with teaching (Zembylas, 2002a, 2002b, 2003). Feelings of anger, anxiety and vulnerability are often not expressed to students nor shared with colleagues. Feelings of empathy, calmness, and kindness are more likely to be expressed and shared. Teachers may also feel anger and anxiety in their relationships with colleagues. They may feel satisfaction and meaningfulness when their students learn or grow.

Aspects of teaching as an emotion practice

In this section, key concepts relating to teaching as an emotion practice are discussed.

Emotional identity

Emotional identity is a term used to refer to that part of a teacher's professional identity constructed by the emotions (and values, beliefs) that are central to a teacher in the relational practices of teaching (Shapiro, 2009). It is argued that emotion plays a major part in the construction of our identity as a teacher (Shapiro, 2009). Part of a teacher's identity is that which is constructed on feelings, such as: guilt when we have not given as much written feedback on assignments as we feel we should; a secret fear of not being in control of classroom behaviour; fear of failing and not doing it right; ethical caring when we do not bad-mouth another teacher in front of students; dislike of conflict with colleagues; and a feeling of powerlessness when our actual practices aren't those we want to put into action.

The emotional identity of some of the beginning teachers included the positive feelings – the passion, amazement and buzz – associated with being a teacher. For example:

> *[When I am teaching at my best, I am like...]*
> I'm passionate about what I am teaching. [Katie]
>> That's what gets me up in the morning, it's seeing some of the [talented] students and I think good art should always make you jealous. And I see some students' their work and you're sitting there, like, what was I doing when I was that age? It's phenomenal. [James]
>> Like I'm on fire. ... Yeah that's how you feel it gives you a real, real buzz, yeah definitely, didn't happen very often ... [Samantha]

Beginning teacher Samantha expressed her positive feelings about being a teacher:

> *[What helps you stay in teaching?]*
> Money. ... also I'm enjoying it. ... I hated being a secretary, absolutely loathed it, and I hated going in every day, and I knew it wasn't taking me anywhere, and I knew I was wasting my life, and now I have a life. I'm doing something I love, even when you have little brats firing off at you, it's still so much more fun than ever being a secretary was. Yeah, it's definitely a love of it, it's a passion for it, every day being different, short manageable sort of time spans to do things in. [Samantha]
>> But if you get into a school like this, where you are looked after and you have good systems, then I would say 'yes it's the best career in the world' to be completely honest. [Samantha]

For some beginning teachers, being confident was seen as a part of their emotional identity. For example:

> *[In what way did your practicum experiences contribute to your professional learning as a teacher?]*
> It did give me the confidence to come and get a job, standing in front [of] so many students ... that confidence I was able to get, that confidence. [Sarika]
>> [Chemistry] theory is no problem at all, [the] practical was just a matter of going through ... various practical things in chemistry, which you don't encounter anywhere else, so yeah, we've been through everything now, so [I am] reasonably confident. [Stephanie]

The beginning teachers mentioned feeling more confident in their second year. For example:

> *[What is it like being a second-year teacher?]*
> Absolutely heaps better. Increased confidence, increased consistency big-time, knowing the systems in the school, knowing what sort of discipline to meet for what reason, for

what level, that kind of thing. ... I am planning far less ... and I just jump in and take it, which makes a huge difference. So I have a life this year, much more than I did last year ... I am not a slave to teaching, which I felt a little bit like last year and just vastly increased confidence of one's own abilities and ... I am sort of concentrating more on actual teaching rather than behaviour management which really helps ... rather than having to fight fires all the time and 'sit down' and 'don't do this' and 'don't do that'. [Samantha]

Teaching was talked about as a challenge, with positive feelings being expressed. For example:

> *[Is there anything else you want to tell us about your experiences of teaching and learning to teach?]*
> There is a lot more to it than I thought, it's like an onion, every layer you peel off there is another layer underneath so there is always more and more layers. I love researching, I love lesson planning, maybe sometimes too much, but I think there is just so much because you are dealing with learning, psychology, tools, people, everyday is different, the weather affects the kids, it affects the teachers, you've got technology, there is just so many different facets and different ways of doing and learning that I don't think I could ever get bored with it really. [Sandy]

One experienced teacher described her emotional identity as a teacher by discussing her positive feelings towards being a teacher through making a contribution to the students' educational experiences and through enjoying teaching:

> And ... education for me is something very positive anyway; my personal educational experience was pretty positive and I'd like to be part of making other people's educational experience very positive ... I know that's not easy, I mean we're dealing with teenagers and we're dealing with people and we've got large bureaucratic organisations and there's government policies that require changes and there's money – there's all sorts of things and barriers, but at the end of the day, I can do what I can do and I'm enjoying doing it, so I'm going to keep doing it. [Mary]

One experienced teacher discussed what made him feel 'rapt' as a teacher:

> I've got ... at the moment a level 3 Science class, an NCEA [National Certificate in Educational Achievement] level 3 Science class, and this is a subject that I've ... introduced to the school ... [in] 2002, 2003 and having great success with them, with the Sciences, with quite a few scholarships from our Science students, so I'm pretty rapt, yeah. [Harry]

He also talked about feeling comfortable and loving teaching:

> I'd just say for me that probably 95% of my days are good days of teaching, I love teaching; sometimes the kids don't have such good days. ... I think it's ... for me it's just feeling very comfortable with what I'm teaching, feeling very comfortable [Harry]

Beginning teacher Samantha talked of teaching involving a feeling of being courageous, of having the courage to try out new things in the classroom, as a part of her emotional identity:

*[During the first six months what areas of your teaching or working in the school have
you sought advice on?]*
   ... primarily I have asked a lot about behaviour management from a lot of people, 'what
tips have you got?', various things have been, you know, fed my way. Actually it's
funny because it sounds so straightforward, you just hear it and implement it, but yeah,
it takes, it does take a bit of courage to do it, because you're not sure and it's quite easy
to procrastinate on it, which I don't normally do ... [Samantha]

Emotional work

Emotional work refers to 'efforts made to understand others, to have empathy with their
situation, to feel their feelings as part of one's own' (England and Farkas, 1986: 91). In
addition, 'emotional work refers to the intention as well as the actions to improve how
others (e.g. students) feel' (Isenbarger and Zembylas, 2006: 123). Hence, emotional work is
an aspect of caring as a teaching practice (Noddings, 1992) (see Chapter 6). The expression
of caring – either words or actions – to students, colleagues or family may be termed
support. Of concern is when changes in educational policy may result in changes to what
is valued as a part of teacher competency. For example, Hebson *et al.* (2007) argued that in
recent education reforms in the United Kingdom there has been a reconstruction of teacher
competency from building relationships with students using emotional work, to teacher
competency focusing on more of the technical competencies in planning, organisation and
behaviour management. That is, competency has changed to a view in which caring and
emotional work are not valued as a part of competent teaching, because an observer cannot
easily measure it.
   Emotional work includes *emotional understanding* which is a term used by Hargreaves
(2000) to refer to the ways teachers and students read each others' emotions. Moreover,
emotional understanding requires a strong, continuous relationship between teacher and
student so that they can do so. Working with colleagues (Hargreaves, 2001b), school
managers, competency inspectors (Hebson *et al.*, 2007) and parents (Lasky, 2000) also
involves relationships and therefore emotion understanding. 'Successful teaching ...
depends on teachers establishing close bonds with key people around them, colleagues as
well as students, and on creating working conditions that make emotional understanding
possible' (Hargreaves, 2001b). The notion of *emotional genealogy* has been used to describe
'accounts of the strategies and tactics that have taken place in various emotional practices
at different moments in relation to one's teaching' (Zembylas, 2005: 936).
   Beginning teacher Katie expressed her way of managing her emotions, as part of emotion
work, in her second year of teaching:

   ... the main thing that I've learnt this year [is] not to sweat the small stuff. [Katie]

Emotional labour

Emotional labour is a term used to describe how individuals control and manage their
emotions to make sure that they are expressed in a way that is consistent with social norms
or expectations. The term is also defined thus:

   I use the term *emotional labor* to mean the management of feelings to create a publicly
   observable facial and bodily display; emotional ... This labor requires one to induce or

suppress feeling in order to sustain the outward countenance that produces the proper state of mind in others. (Hochschild, 1983: 7; italics in original)

When emotions are faked, suppressed, underplayed, overplayed, neutralised or changed according to specific emotional rules and in order to advance educational goals, teachers perform emotional labour, which may be viewed as positive or negative by the teacher (Isenbarger and Zembylas, 2006). For example, beginning teacher Ellie discussed behaviour management:

> ... behavioural management and it's incredibly difficult you know ... there's are big behavioural management issues. ... so those are the areas that I find the least rewarding sometimes, but then on the other hand sometimes they can actually be quite rewarding if you work at those areas too. But those [the frustrating ones] are the ones that wake me up at 4 o'clock in the morning sort of thing, which I'm trying to stop doing. [Ellie]

Ellie also discussed putting on a professional face:

> *[If you were asked to describe teaching as a metaphor, how you would complete this sentence, 'When I'm teaching at my best I am like ...'?]*
> ... I'm like a – mmm – I think [I] might change the sentence slightly but I guess it's good acting or something, it's like a successful actor. ... because every lesson is like a performance and when it's going well I'm like a good actor in a way, because you have to always have that professional face, and also you have to be ... positive as well, always, that is a challenge. So when it's going well, I always know that I've acted really well and I've been myself, but I've also ... been positive. That's when it's going well. [Ellie]

Hochschild (1983) argued that there are two components to emotional labour – surface acting and deep acting. Surface acting involves masking emotions and faking emotions. Deep acting involves attempts to actually feel the emotion and so deceive oneself as well as others (Zhang and Zhu, 2008).

Too much negative emotional labour may result in teacher burnout (Zembylas, 2004a; Isenbarger and Zembylas, 2006; Naring et al., 2006; Brouwers and Tomic, 2000; Hargreaves, 2000), with burnout being defined as:

> '... a psychological syndrome of emotional exhaustion, depersonalization, and reduced personal accomplishment that can occur among individuals who work with other people in some capacity. Emotional exhaustion refers to feelings of being emotionally overextended and depleted of one's emotional resources. Depersonalization refers to a negative, callous, or excessively detached response to other people, who are usually the recipients of one's services or care.' ... Reduced personal accomplishment is described as 'a person's negative self-evaluation in relation to his or her job performance' ... (Brouwers and Tomic, 2000: 239; quoting Maslach and Schaufeli, Maslach and Marek)

Burnout is linked to self-efficacy in classroom management. High self-efficacy in classroom management can lead to a sense of personal accomplishment, while low self-efficacy in classroom management can contribute to the depersonalisation aspect of burnout (Brouwers and Tomic, 2000). However, teachers may be willing to do emotional labour, even if it involves suffering – for example, in the teaching of science, which is seen to value reason over emotion, which in turn may be viewed as irrational (Zembylas, 2004a).

Some of the beginning teachers discussed their teaching in a way as to suggest the negative effects of emotion labour:

> *[So at this point in time ... halfway through your first year, what would you say was the most important thing for you as a teacher?]*
> Surviving the rest of the year ... I mean that sounds bizarre, but just keeping your head up, because [in the] middle of last term, I just really hit some very low moments and wondered what on earth I was doing. Just because I didn't think I could do all the things required, it just seemed so crowded ... and [I] worried about my ... energy levels and all that sort of thing. So yeah, I think that's how I felt probably about the middle of the first term, but as the term was ending I felt less like that, so I want to go, I do want to go on. I feel very strongly inclined to want to get my registration, that's ... a goal, I decided I must set sort of short term goals, so I'm over half way through the first year and that means I've got ... two terms left and then I've got the same thing again next year and then ... I just hope that I will be registered then. That's my goal I suppose, so that's where I am at. But yeah, there were still some low moments last term. Low moments, yes. [Ellie]

> *[What's it like being a beginning teacher?]*
> I actually am not enjoying it much. It's getting better for me ... like I said a couple of times I sort of wanted to leave the job, just couldn't handle the stress, the amount of mental stress, but it's getting better it's because I'm changing my attitude about things. Rather than the school changing ... I've come to a compromise [with the] help I can get and work with that. So, I'm actually not enjoying it at the moment, I cannot be creative ... because I'm very creative with everything. But because of all the mental stress and everything ... I cant put in [as] much of the work that I want to, [to] make things. [Sarika]

Using emotions evaluatively

Emotions can be used evaluatively in relationships, in that emotions, as perceived by the teacher, provide evidence for what she or he values (Zembylas, 2004a). Negative emotions may indicate to a teacher when their values have been crossed, while positive emotions may indicate to the teacher when they are acting in a way consistent with their beliefs and values. For example, beginning teacher Samantha expressed her sense of guilt when she had not taught as she would have liked to:

> [There has been a] very big shift in my approach to be[ing] a form class teacher. Whereas last year it ... was an extra burden, just something that used up a lot of my time chasing up absences and all that sort of thing ... so much more is second nature now with my teaching, and my content knowledge is that much greater, and I am more relaxed about what I am teaching. Yeah, I have much more time to target my form class and I really have done since the beginning. It's been really something I wanted to focus on, because I felt quite guilty last year that I didn't do a good enough job in my view. [Samantha]

Emotional geographies

Emotional geographies of schooling and human interaction is a term used by Hargreaves to refer to 'the spatial and experiential patterns of closeness and/or distance in human interactions and relationships' (Hargreaves, 2000: 815). He lists five forms of emotional geographies to describe the distance or closeness that disrupt emotional understanding in schools. Sociocultural geographies are described by Hargraves (2000) as the emotional distance or closeness between teachers, students and parents, due to cultural differences and similarities. Moral geographies is the term used to describe the emotional distance or closeness in relationships with respect to the match of the teacher's purposes and those of others in the school community; professional geographies describes the emotional distance or closeness constructed with respect to the teacher's view of what it means to be a professional, with gender differences noted; political geographies describes how hierarchical power relationships disrupt the emotional distances in relationships; and physical geographies describes the abundance or lack of opportunities for communication within the school community, with resulting emotional closeness or distance (Hargreaves, 2000). It is through participating in the community of teachers in a school that pre-service and beginning teachers learn the ways in which emotional geographies are an aspect of their teaching (Goldstein and Lake, 2000).

The notion of emotional geographies is further used by Zembylas (in press) to emphasise the spatial and political aspects of emotions as constructed in relationships between students. He explores how emotional geographies work as spaces of exclusion for Turkish-speaking students in a majority Greek Cypriot/multicultural school, by the segregation of and emotional distance between the two groups of students, with resulting 'real and uneven material outcomes' (Zembylas, in press: 2).

In summary, teaching can be viewed as an emotion practice, highlighting the construction and use of emotions in the relationships, which are a part of teaching.

Study and discussion

- Can you give an example of when you did emotional work – that is, empathising with students?
- Can you give an example of when you did emotional labour (managed rather than immediately expressed your feeling)?
- In what ways have your emotions helped you clarify who you are as a teacher – that is, what emotions have helped you form your identity as a teacher?

6 Teaching as a caring practice

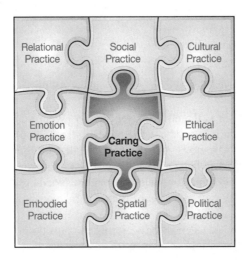

In theorising teaching as a caring practice, we are focusing on the caring done by teachers within the relationships between teacher and student, which are in turn embedded in the social, institutional and cultural contexts of schooling and education. Caring is seen as a fundamental aspect both of being human (Noddings, 1992) and of being a teacher. It is a crucial part of a teacher's professional identity (Vogt, 2002).

What is caring?

Caring is a concern for the welfare and wellbeing of the cared-for – for example, of the students we teach. Caring is 'not based on love as we do not need love in order to care' (Perez, 2000: 102). Nor is it just about being kind and supportive and giving 'gentle smiles and warm hugs' (Goldstein, 1998; Goldstein and Lake, 2000). In caring for a secondary student, we may show empathy when their grandmother dies and grant them an extension for their assignment; we may be concerned when they fail a test, and go over the test results with them individually to see where additional help is needed to improve their learning; we may greet them in the corridor and ask how their rugby game went at the weekend; and we may notice their lack of engagement with the learning in a lesson, and afterwards ask them if they are okay.

In its widest sense, caring implies moral and social responsibilities (Gilligan, 1982; Hargreaves and Tucker, 1991), and as such may be viewed as different from a morality of rights (Gilligan, 1982). Caring as responsibility is a part of the ethics of care (Noddings, 1992; Gilligan, 1982), which is described as 'a morality based on the recognition of needs, relation and response' (Noddings, 1992: 21). In using an ethic of care, moral decisions are made based on ways of sustaining relationships and connections (Gilligan, 1982). Ethics of care need not be viewed in opposition to ethics of rights, justice and fairness, which are seen to be governed by moral reasoning, universality, impartiality, principles and rules, but can co-exist with them (Katz *et al.*, 1999). As Noddings argued:

> Justice draws to our attention the unfairness of a situation in which large numbers of children are deprived of the potential material benefits of schooling. Care cautions us to look at individual children before we recommend a remedy and to listen to those whose aspirations, interest, talents, and legitimate values may differ from our own. (Noddings, 1999: 15)

and summarised:

> Care picks up where justice leaves off. (Noddings, 1999: 16)

Hence, caring can be seen as the ethical use of power (Weinstein, 1998), and therefore the abuse of power is not caring, as it is not ethical (Larson, 2006). Caring can 'expand our notion of the "ethical" ' (Tronto, 1998: 15), and include social justice from the perspective of gender, cultural (including language) and social class (Gomez *et al.*, 2004).

An important aspect of caring is its relational nature. Noddings (1992) defines caring, not as an inherent personality trait, but as constructed in relationships:

> A caring relation is, in its most basic form, a connection or encounter between two human beings – a carer and a recipient of care, or cared-for. In order for the relation to be properly called caring, both parties must contribute to it in characteristic ways (Noddings, 1992: 15).

There are two people in a caring relationship: the carer and the cared-for.

Two characteristics of the carer are engrossment and motivational displacement (Noddings, 1992). Engrossment is likened to attention, described as 'the open, non-selective receptivity to the cared-for' (Noddings, 1992: 15), and 'when I care, I really hear, see or feel what the other tries to convey' (Noddings, 1992: 16). It allows the carer to include the cared-for (White, 2003). Motivational displacement is seen as 'the sense that our motive energy is flowing towards others and their projects' (Noddings, 1992: 16), putting aside momentarily our own. 'Engrossment and motivational displacement do not tell us what to do; they merely characterize our consciousness when we care.' (Noddings, 1992: 16). Nor do the characteristics indicate depth of feeling (Goldstein, 1998). The action based on the carer's attentiveness is towards the welfare and wellbeing of the cared-for.

The characteristics of the cared-for are 'reception, recognition and response' (Noddings, 1992: 16). When the cared-for receives the caring, and shows that it has been received, the caring is complete. Hence, an action is only caring if the cared-for responds that she or he sees it as caring. This reciprocity is an important aspect of Noddings's definition of caring as a relation. The need for reciprocity in the definition has been critiqued by researchers working in the area of social justice, who claim that minority students' sense of alienation and powerlessness, or very young children's lack of understanding of the situation, may prevent them from responding or showing their responsiveness to the teacher (White, 2003; Goldstein, 1998). To continue to be caring in the face of lack of reciprocity may result in emotional labour and burnout, unless the teacher has faith in and commitment to the students (White, 2003).

And lastly, a carer is seen as *being* in the relational: caring is not a set of specific behaviours or virtues or principles:

> There are no absolute principles to guide one's caring in their interactions with others. Rooted in attentive behaviour, receptive engrossment with a specific human being in a specific context, caring encounters are, by their very nature, variable, situated and unique. (Goldstein, 1998: 246)

Caring as a part of teaching

Teaching as a caring practice can be seen as a teacher's responsibility and concern for the welfare and wellbeing of students. It is not just about displaying kindly emotions towards the students. We as teachers do use our emotions in caring about and caring for students (Ashley and Lee, 2003) but we also use our knowledge and skills for the betterment of students, including having high expectations and the attainment of learning goals (Goldstein, 1998). We care that students succeed, sometimes in the face of much adversity, and enact our caring in our curriculum, pedagogy and classroom management (Weinstein, 1998). Hence, teaching as a caring practice is important, not only in the teaching of early childhood and primary pupils, but also in secondary and tertiary teaching (Gomez *et al.*, 2004).

There are many ways in which we as teachers enact our caring in the school setting. For example, by using formative assessment (see Chapter 3), a teacher can ascertain the needs of a specific student and not have to rely on stereotypes or generalisations to make teaching and curriculum decisions in the classroom (Garza, 2009). During such activities as small group discussions, cooperative learning activities and brainstorming, a teacher can get to know the prior thinking, experiences and values of students as a part of formative assessment (assessment for learning) as part of teaching the content to be learnt. Teachers enact their caring when they have high expectations for all students, not expectations based on stereotypes of gender, economic status and ethnicity. Indeed, caring by a teacher is positively linked in the literature to improved student commitment to school and engagement to learning (Perez, 2000).

Caring also involves a caring for and valuing of knowledge, caring that what the students learn is useful, reliable and worth knowing (Nash, 2003; Noddings, 1992). A caring teacher teaches students in a way that communicates the nature of the discipline and criteria for judging the truth of new knowledge and evidence (Nash, 2003). Caring is not an extra add-on to the work of a teaching in teaching the content to be learnt (Gomez *et al.*, 2004), but an integral part of pedagogy and curriculum.

Student voices and perceptions of caring

While we as teachers may intend to be caring, our students may not always see our teaching as such. Listening to students' voices is one way to find out what students experience as caring (Garza, 2009; Gomez *et al.*, 2004), and having a dialogue with students is essential for the establishment of a caring teacher–student relationship (Gomez *et al.*, 2004; Goldstein and Freedman, 2003; Noddings, 1992).

In his study of Latino and White [sic] high school students, Garza (2009) found that both groups of students perceived the following as indicative of the teacher caring: '(a) provid[e] scaffolding during a teaching episode, (b) reflect a kind disposition through actions, (c) are always available to the student, (d) show a personal interest in students' well-being inside and outside the classroom, and (e) provide affective academic support in the classroom setting' (Garza 2009: 14). Providing scaffolding during a teaching episode included the teacher explaining, giving information, re-teaching, making formative assessment and other instructional help for student success, indicating that they have expectations of the students. Reflecting a kind disposition through actions included having a sense of humour and a caring demeanour, and using kind words. Always being available to the students referred to the teacher being accessible when the student needed him or her, and not solely at a prescribed time, such as after school on Wednesdays (Garza, 2009). That is, the teacher addressed the student's needs when it was convenient to the student, not themselves. Showing a personal interest referred to a teacher's genuine interest in getting to know students as individuals – their interests, experiences, backgrounds – through dialogue with them. Providing affective academic support referred to the teacher who expresses concern for students when they are failing and who also does whatever teaching is necessary to help them pass (Garza, 2009). This may include flexibility with deadlines, giving second chances, and multiple opportunities for success. While each group of students perceived the same five categories of caring, the priority giving to each of the five was different (Garza, 2009). The Latino students valued most caring which 'provides scaffolding during a teaching episode', and they least valued 'actions reflect a kind disposition', whereas the White [sic] students most valued caring through 'actions reflect a kind disposition' and least valued 'provides affective academic support'.

In a study of primary and secondary students' perceptions of caring in physical education (Larson, 2006), the students reported 11 clusters of teaching practices that were considered by them to be caring: 'showed me how to do a skill, honored my request, gave me a compliment, confronted my behavior, inquired about my health, attended to me when I was injured, allowed me to re-do my test, motivated me, played/practiced with me during class, persuaded me, showed concern for my health' (Larson, 2006: 337). Further analysis of the clusters gave rise to three subcategories of showing caring: that the teacher recognised me, helped me learn, and trusted/respected me, with a main category of caring that the teacher paid attention to me (Larson, 2006: 337).

Tertiary students' perceptions of caring, as part of effective teaching, were researched (by Teven, 2001), with a focus on teacher behaviours that the students saw as caring. The findings indicated the students' perceptions of caring were 'positively related to their perceptions of their teachers' immediacy, responsiveness, and assertiveness while negatively related to teacher verbal aggressiveness' (Teven, 2001: 159).

Caring as a culturally situated practice

Recent research on caring in education has focused on caring as a culturally situated practice (Gomez *et al.*, 2004), meaning that what care looks like and how it is given and received varies between cultures (Gomez *et al.*, 2004; Noddings, 2001). What is seen as caring in one culture may not be seen as caring in another. For example:

> In the early 1990s, I was supervising an international doctoral student who generated data about Asian secondary science students' experience of schooling in New Zealand.

One of her interviewees said 'the teachers here don't care, they do not hit us'. Given that corporal punishment is illegal in New Zealand I needed considerable help to understand this statement from the student's perspective. [Beverley]

In focusing on caring, we develop meaningful relationships with students, in which communication of respect can occur. Such respect would include validation of the student's language, cultural identity, and cultural ways of showing trust and respect (Garza, 2009). If a student perceives the school does not care about his or her achievement and welfare, he or she is unlikely to care about school and schooling, and underachieve and disengage (Nash, 2003).

One pre-service secondary teacher's understanding of care in teaching was researched (Gomez *et al.*, 2004), with the findings indicating that this teacher used the overarching theme of fostering students to take responsibility for themselves as her cultural model of care. Seeing caring as helping the students to 'take responsibility for themselves' located her caring in a view where responsibility for educational or economic success is in the hands of individuals (Gomez *et al.*, 2004). Such a view 'does not acknowledge structural inequities in schools and society, caused by, for example, institutional racism, or gendered distributions of labor' (Gomez *et al.*, 2004: 481), against which an individual may have little power. 'It is only by understanding the ways that youth are differentially located in sociocultural worlds that we as educators can effectively understand and respond to their "needs"' (Gomez *et al.*, 2004: 487). In caring for students of different cultures, ethnicities, gender and economic status, a teacher cannot rely on caring based on her or his own culture, but instead needs to elicit from the students what they think caring is, and what their needs are.

Teaching as a caring practice may also be viewed as gendered. The prototypical notion of caring is one of mothering and female, as in the mother–child relationship, where women 'look after' children. This view is more prevalent in the primary school but is also present in the secondary school in terms of teachers' responsibility with respect to '*parentis loci*' (Forrester, 2005; Gomez *et al.*, 2004). Vogt's (2002) study with Swiss and English primary teachers indicated no gender difference in the teachers' views of themselves as caring teachers. Vogt (2002) concluded that caring as a teacher did not have to perpetuate patriarchal discourses linking caring to femininity but could be a part of the professional identity of teachers, with teachers' views of caring being described as a continuum from:

- caring as a commitment to teaching and to students; to:
- caring as relatedness, i.e., caring about building good relationships with their students and caring about their personal circumstances, and establishing trust and respect in the relationship; to:
- caring as physical care, e.g., caring about safety in the school laboratory; to:
- caring as expressing affection, such as the physical contact in a cuddle or hand on the shoulder; to:
- caring as parenting and mothering.

Caring and dilemmas

Teaching as a caring practice gives rise to dilemmas and conflicts, as there is no such thing as the perfect caring: 'there are more needs for care than can ever be met' (Tronto, 1998: 17). Dilemmas and conflicts may arise, for example, over whom to care for. Do we attend to student needs and neglect our own, resulting in burnout? Pre-service teachers may have unrealistic expectations that they will and can care for all students all the time (Goldstein and Freedman, 2003). Having such unrealistic high expectations may give rise to feelings of guilt in not being able to protect students from harm or neglect (Hargreaves and Tucker, 1991). On the other hand, caring for only the personal needs of students may lead to less care in total, neglecting care, for example, of academic achievement (Hargreaves and Tucker, 1991).

Another dilemma faced by pre-service and beginning teachers is that of whether to be caring (being nice) or manage behaviour (being mean) (Weinstein, 1998). Beginning teachers tend to perceive this situation as a dilemma and an either/or situation (Weinstein, 1998). More experienced teachers may see behaviour management (so that the students engage with the learning) as a caring act. In addition, behaviour management may be more readily achieved if a caring relationship between teacher and students exists.

Another dilemma is that teaching as a caring practice may become devalued, squeezed out and surpassed in teachers' daily work with the imposition of the new managerial discourses of governments. Caring for students may have a low status in performance monitoring and appraisals, which focus on the measurable outcomes such as technical competencies in planning, organisation and behaviour management. Caring may be displaced in overloaded curricula, which can lead to teacher-centred pedagogies and rote learning, and in national standards that may lead to 'teaching to the test'. Caring may also be displaced due to auditing and inspection and mandated pedagogies, as in the United Kingdom, (Hebson *et al.*, 2007; Forrester, 2005; Larson, 2006; Hargreaves and Tucker, 1991). In a climate of performativity rather than professionalism, the school and institutional context may make it harder for teachers to build caring relationships with students, and teachers may find that 'what they are asked to do sometimes conflicts with or neglects the caring activities associated with teaching and learning' (Forrester, 2005: 285). It may also make it difficult for a teacher to do formative assessment to modify the curriculum and pedagogy for individual needs (Larson, 2006). There is, however, a need for more causal and correlational research in this area. A distinction can be made between 'performing (doing your best for the inspection regime) and caring (doing your very best for the children)' (Forrester, 2005: 274) and, given that these may exist side-by-side, the demands on teachers are considerable. A time when these two demands may sit side-by-side is when a teacher cares that his or her students achieve on state or national standards and qualifications. But in general, it is the drive for efficiency, increased accountability and outcomes-based teaching that is seen to have changed teaching to 'performance' at the expense of other practices such as caring (Forrester, 2005; O'Connor, 2008), resulting in teachers' feelings of guilt that they are not meeting their own expectations based on their values, ethics and morals (Hargreaves and Tucker, 1991). As Noddings wrote, at times 'the structures of schooling work against care' (Noddings, 1992: 20).

The teachers talking caring

In interviews, seven of the nine beginning teachers and two of the experienced teachers talked about caring for different aspects in their teaching: caring for students per se, students' achievement, the whole student, their own career, their own self-care and their colleagues.

Caring about the students themselves

The beginning teachers talked in general about caring for students as being a central part of their teaching. For example:

> [I]t's a personal thing [teaching to individual learners] for me, I want to make sure I'm addressing everybody, and getting the best out of them that I can do, because that's [why] I'm here, I'm not here for me, I'm here for them. [Samantha]

In talking about caring for special needs students, beginning teacher Samantha related caring to mothering:

> So even when you're explaining it ... they [special needs learners] still don't take it in, and you know, it's just little things as well, like getting them to write things into their books ... it's hard because you have to be a little bit like a mum ... [Samantha]

Samantha also talked about caring in terms of responsibility:

> *[What helps you stay in teaching?]*
> ... The kids, they keep me coming in, sense of responsibility. I don't want to let people down ... but also just generally responsibility to the kids, responsibility to other staff members, I don't want to let people down, also I'm enjoying it. [Samantha]

Caring about students' achievement

Four of the beginning teachers indicated that they cared about their students' achievement. For example:

> *[Has your view of a 'good' teacher changed since you began teaching?]*
> I think certainly my view of good teachers has been built upon ... for me, teaching is more than just standing in a classroom teaching. You've got relationships to build with the kids. I think that's almost more important to me than actual teaching. I care deeply that they do well and not just at school but that we're basically moulding young adults here. ... I enjoy the responsibility and I do want to see them do well, and I tell them that, and if they start going off the rails, I don't come on all heavy but I do get involved. Whereas I do see some teachers not care, they are there for the hour and that is it. [Samantha]

Beginning teacher Sylvia indicated that she cared about a student achieving and, when he did, it was a very good experience for her as a teacher:

> *[Can you tell me about your best day or best experience as a teacher over the year?]*
> I'm struggling to think of one ... It probably goes way back to Term 1 when I had a boy in a fairly difficult class, [who is] ... quite a capable boy, but [he] just gets himself caught up in the wrong crowd. And he did an assignment, and he did really well, and he was really pleased, and he was really happy, and I think that was probably one of the highlights of the year for me. I can't think of a particular day but on that particular day that would have been one of the best days that I can recall.

[And so what made it a good day for you, this boy achieving a good assignment?]
I think because he was really happy and was really satisfied, and that makes you feel like you have made a difference in terms of their learning and their level of achievement. He had done a practice [assignment] prior to that, where he hadn't got it and he had actually made the changes that I had suggested. They were satisfying steps.

[Did he stay on at school for the whole year?]
Yeah. [Sylvia]

Beginning teacher Stephanie, in a boys' school, talked of her caring for students who had difficulty writing:

[How would you cater ... in a classroom ... [for] students who are learning quickly and those who are struggling a bit?]
I don't know if lowering my expectations is probably the word for it, because I have a couple in my class who are not able, their writing is very slow and they have great difficulty with writing, so I guess I have a different way of assessing that they've done the work for the day. I mean I have different judgement criteria for the different boys and nobody's said 'oh that's not fair miss, he hasn't done as much work as us, or he hasn't written as much as us'. [Stephanie]

Beginning teacher Katie cared that her students reached their potential and understood the science being taught:

[Okay so what's the most important thing to you at the moment about being a teacher?]
Extending my kids to their potential ... [Katie]

[What has sustained you in your first 18 months?]
Seeing that my kids understand it [science]. Having them ask questions, which are not necessarily directly on track, but showing that they are actually thinking about things. ... Having the kids being able to feel comfortable enough to ask questions that they obviously haven't really thought about before but that can have so much impact on them, and being able to answer them honestly. That is what has sustained me. The tricky little ones that aren't just run-of-the-mill questions, where the kids take you a bit outside your comfort zone and keep you thinking about it as well ... and seeing the students enjoy themselves. [Katie]

Caring about the whole student

Two of the beginning teachers also talked about caring for all aspects of the students, rather than just focusing only on achievement. For example:

I've got to know the [students] over time ... there's one in particular who has come to me for advice on his subject options for next year, and has asked if I could maybe back him up a little bit, because he was being slightly directed into really non-academic subjects, when he'd actually got quite a good brain. He had just been a real pain that's all, and I suddenly realised that he's actually really matured in the past couple of terms and he's really focusing on his future and he's been so much easier to sort of control and get to be quiet or to sit down ... [This] doesn't mean he'll do it 'til the end of term. He might go completely off the wall again like this lesson coming up, but that's been a pleasure to see people ... really starting to make the best of themselves and growing up a little bit ... it is almost counselling, advice. [Samantha]

Samantha repeated her talk of caring of the whole student in a later interview:

[When I am teaching at my best, I am like ...]
I am there to give them an education but I am also there to round them into whole human beings, who are going to go off and be successful and fly the nest, which is effectively what they are, little fledglings about to fly off. So that is very much a part of me and my teaching in general, sort of, like, looking after them. [Samantha]

Beginning teacher Sylvia talked about her caring to 'turn kids around':

[So what would you say would be the most rewarding experiences?]
Rewarding? Probably just when you can get a kid to turn around, like there's been a few ... in mainly the Year 9 ... it's their first experience of high school, and when you have them [at] the start of the year – appallingly, like, just all over the place, and can't focus, they can't produce anything because they just can't sit still long enough to do anything. That's quite rewarding, when you can get them to turn around. ... But yeah that's quite satisfying. It is good, I do like having a relationship with the kids [Sylvia]

Caring about their career

One beginning teacher who was struggling with classroom management in a low socio-economic level school, commented:

I really care about my job you know, I changed a career, a good career for coming into teaching. [Sarika]

Self-care

Self-care was also discussed in terms of managing stress, fatigue and possible burnout in the first two years of beginning teaching. For example, beginning teacher Katie discussed not working at the weekends:

... and I made a point after the first two terms of having much more of a life on the weekends because I wasn't having a single weekend. There was always something happening. ... and now I've realised how much I can already do, much more is second nature and ... I've got my weekends back. [Samantha]

Beginning teacher Sandy commented on not being able to care for all students all the time:

I know it's not very PC, but to say to yourself that maybe you're not in a position to help every single student in your class, but you can help [most] of them and maybe [you] just have to be a bit selective sometimes to help your own energy. [Sandy]

Sandy also talked of self-care when she commented on not always offering to do tasks outside of her teaching, in her first year of teaching:

> [So do you get involved in any extra curricular activities at the school?]
> I help out [in] various things. But I must admit I have stayed in the background because I have family and there are only so many hours in the day. I'm very wary of jumping in with boots on, I've seen a few people do that and get burnt. So I sort of think, well maybe for your first [year] just to breath through your nose, as somebody once told me. [Sandy]

Beginning teacher Katie discussed her need to use her non-contact time during the day for rest:

> I probably haven't used it [the 0.2 non-teaching time[1]] as effectively as I could have. Like sometimes you just need that down time, just mentally need a break as opposed to actually needing to do something in those breaks, it still vanishes very quickly. [Katie]

Even experienced teachers take time during the day as down time, as experienced teacher Mary, who was also a Dean, explained:

> I don't have the load of five consecutive teaching classes, because that's very hard. ... if you're teaching five classes [in a five-lesson day] and you've got things to pack up at breaktime and stuff to get out for period three, and you can have the same [at] lunch too if you're not careful then, ... you don't get a lot of down time yourself and that is quite challenging. So one, I'm more experienced and ... two, I also do have the luxury of having those breaks in between that student interaction. ... [also] you need one lesson at least where you've got plans for those students to be doing the major portion of the lesson, interactively in groups, individually or however but that requires less of that teacher energy to keep it driving through. [Mary]

Caring for colleagues

Caring for colleagues is also a part of teaching as a caring practice. Experienced teacher Harry explained how he cared for beginning teachers in his science department by reducing their workload:

> I ... provide everything for my year 1 and 2 teachers, so they can teach – paint by numbers – for the first two years, so they get to know what it is they're teaching, and they can work on their classroom management strategies, and then they put the icing on the cake and they start doing it their way. And as long as they [the students] meet the [learning] outcomes, I don't care ... [so long as] they're enjoying their teaching – if they're enjoying their teaching the kids will be enjoying being taught by them. [Harry]

---

1 All first-year teachers have a non-contact time allowance in their workload amounting to 0.2, or 20 per cent, of the working week, giving them more time for preparation and planning.

Summary

In summary, teaching as a caring practice is described as requiring commitment and taking responsibility; caring about and caring for the protection, welfare, nurturance, personal and social growth and development of the student as well their educational outcomes; attentiveness to the needs of students; responsiveness to the needs of the students by taking actions which will be meaningful for the cared-for – for the students; and meaningful connectedness with the students for the development of trusting interpersonal relationships, in which communication is possible (Garza, 2009; Gomez *et al.*, 2004; Perez, 2000; Larson, 2006; Tronto, 1998; Hargreaves and Tucker, 1991; Vogt, 2002). Teaching as a caring practice involves a teacher's thinking, talking, feelings, dispositions and enacting their caring (Gomez *et al.*, 2004). It also involves a knowledge of the context in which the caring relationship is being developed, and validating who the student is: 'their cultural, social and linguistic assets' (Garza, 2009: 5). And, last but not least, it is the teacher who needs to initiate care in the relationship (Gomez *et al.*, 2004).

Study and discussion

- Can you give examples from your own teaching of times when you were caring for your students?
- How is the caring of teachers different from the caring of parents?

7 Teaching as an ethical practice

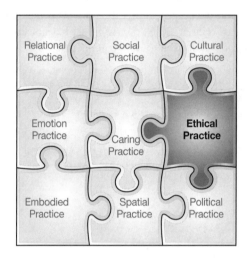

Teaching may be viewed as an inherently and fundamentally ethical and moral practice (Tate, 2007; Buzzelli and Johnston, 2001; Campbell, 2003; Hall, 2001). Here, the term 'ethics' is used to mean a philosophy or way of thinking about the moral principals of right and wrong, good and bad, virtue and vice, and caring and non-caring. This chapter discusses some aspects of teaching as an ethical practice, taking into account a sociocultural perspective.

First, teaching as an ethical practice has a knowledge base, including dispositions and values, which can be learnt by teachers as part of their initial education and ongoing professional development. The ethical and moral knowledge base of teachers includes an understanding of procedural justice of due process, universality, impartiality and fairness (Strike, 1990); social justice and the responsibilities of teachers (Noddings, 1992); respect for the autonomy and reason of students (Snook, 2003); truthfulness (Tate, 2007); consequences of actions (Husu and Tirri, 2003) and commitment (Sanger and Osguthorpe, 2011). Much of this knowledge base is in the contents of relevant Codes of Ethics, which are developed by the professional teaching community as a documentation of 'the collectively agreed-to ethical standards for the practice of teaching' (Strike, 1990: 48). The codes of ethics are important as teachers work within both the contractual nature of teacher employment and the limits of public trust (Hall, 2008). Teachers' work differs from that of parents (Katz, 1980) – for example, in the levels of attachment, intensity of affect, bias and impartiality; and teachers' work has boundaries not to be crossed (Campbell, 2008). The New Zealand Teachers Council Code of Ethics states that:

> The professional interactions of teachers are governed by four fundamental principles:
>
> - Autonomy to treat people with rights that are to be honoured and defended,
> - Justice to share power and prevent the abuse of power,
> - Responsible care to do good and minimise harm to others,
> - Truth to be honest with others and self,
>
> with commitments to learners, parents and care-givers, society, and the profession. (New Zealand Teachers Council, 2010)

Such a code as a set of guidelines may not be all encompassing (Campbell, 2008). It is not a set of rules to be blindly adhered to, but is a guide to teacher decision-making, taking into account contextual factors.

The basic ethical dilemma for teachers, according to Snook (2003), is that as teachers we must respect the autonomy of the students to have their own beliefs, behaviour, values and lifeplan, but at the same time we have an obligation to change the students' beliefs, behaviour and values as part of our teaching and the mandated curriculum. In addition, we as teachers are obliged to foster the development of students' own reasoning – that is, that the student can give his or her own reasons for their beliefs, behaviour and values. Thinking for oneself means one does not have to rely forever on the views of others. These two aspects of teaching as an ethical practice, at least in New Zealand as a democracy, are a requirement of an ethical teacher–student relationship. Ethical teaching practices are seen as a guard against the abuse of power and authority in the teacher–student relationship.

A second aspect of teaching as an ethical practice is the protection of the welfare of the students and doing no harm to them, given the students' dependency, vulnerability and powerlessness. This aspect of ethical practice is related to teaching as a caring practice and the ethics of care, which is based on relationships and responsibilities (Noddings, 1992), as discussed in Chapter 6. In using an ethics of care, moral decisions are made based on ways of sustaining relationships and connections (Gilligan, 1982). Ethics of care need not be viewed in opposition to ethics of rights, justice and fairness, which are seen to be governed by moral reasoning, universality, impartiality, principles and rules, but can co-exist with them (Katz *et al.*, 1999). As noted previously, Noddings argued:

> Justice draws to our attention the unfairness of a situation in which large numbers of children are deprived of the potential material benefits of schooling. Care cautions us to look at individual children before we recommend a remedy and to listen to those whose aspirations, interest, talents, and legitimate values may differ from our own. (Noddings, 1999: 15)

For example, beginning teacher Sarika discussed how uncomfortable she felt with the behaviour management systems in the school, with respect to keeping herself and the students safe:

> *[So what's it like being a beginning teacher in your school here?]*
> I actually am not enjoying it much. … It's the disciplinary side basically, the backup … support for discipline, because this school is pretty tough to work in.

[Yes I noticed the security guard on the [gate]]
There are four security guards. ... I've just found out that I don't actually agree totally with the philosophy of the school, which is quite difficult. ... Schools have different ways of dealing with discipline and [in] this school everything tends to be kept on a very low profile. If someone misbehaves they don't ... the disciplinary side is very soft ... they tend to mollycoddle the kids to make them stay in the school, rather than dealing with them and then the teachers have to take the ownership of everything that happens. So that is a big mental stress ...

[I noticed there were big security cameras and so you're being filmed?]
[I]f you go out of this classroom, there's huge cameras everywhere and every-thing that gets done here, gets picked up. The whole school is fitted with security cameras. Drugs, gangsters, yeah it's very tough in [name of city] to work in. Very few beginning teachers choose to work here. I took it as a challenge, which I think I won't be able to fulfill it because at the end of the year I'm looking to move on ... [Sarika]

Another aspect of ethical practice that was mentioned is that of ensuring that the employment of teachers meets legal requirements for the protection of students:

... one of the things that was really quite, caused a lot of problems for me in the first term this year was the fact that ... for some of us who had lived overseas for a while, we had to get security clearances again and I'd lived in England and that took quite a long time to get that. And it was all a bit of a panic and this school was very exceptional in assisting me with that. But ... it could rub the school up the wrong way, and it's terribly frustrating because the headmaster has to get legal permission to actually have [me] ... teaching in his school. ... Only the end of last term now have I started actually being paid properly ... [Ellie]

A third aspect of teaching as an ethical practice is using social justice or distributive justice in ethical decision-making to inform teaching practices in the classroom (Beyer, 1997; Hall and Bishop, 2001; Snook, 2003). The social justice aspect of ethical practice is the notion of justice and fairness to ensure equity of opportunity and outcomes of all students (Campbell, 2008; Strike, 1990; van Houtte, 2007). The distributive justice aspect is covered by the universal rules of fair treatment, due process and impartiality for all (Campbell, 2003; Katz *et al.*, 1999). This moral and ethical complexity is highlighted when teachers are asked to decide if ethical and moral 'good' is discharged by being fair and impartial or by being caring – for example, when the teacher needs to decide whether to spend time helping one student, who has been absent for five school days attending a *tangi* (a Maori funeral which is typically longer than a European one, lasting for days not hours), to revise for an assessment, but not other students. Will the other students view the extra help as favouritism? Within a discussion of multicultural education, Endres (2002) explores the notion of generalised respect as a part of ethical practice, as well as the respect for cultural differences in the multicultural classroom. He argues that teachers need to 'balance attention to difference and commonality among their students' (Endres, 2002: 172), and that 'both forms of respect (generalised moral respect and cultural respect) are logically dependant on one another and have a mutually supportive place in the practice of teaching' (Endres, 2002: 173).

Both the beginning and the experienced teachers discussed aspects of caring as an aspect of ethics. For example, as noted previously beginning teacher Stephanie, in a boys' school, talked of her caring for students who had difficulty writing:

> *[How would you cater ... in a classroom ... [for] students who are learning quickly and those who are struggling a bit?]*
> I don't know if lowering my expectations is probably the word for it, because I have a couple in my class who are not able, their writing is very slow and they have great difficulty with writing, so I guess I have a different way of assessing that they've done the work for the day. I mean I have different judgement criteria for the different boys and nobody's said 'oh that's not fair miss, he hasn't done as much work as us, or he hasn't written as much as us'. [Stephanie]

A fourth aspect of teaching as an ethical practice deals with the ways in which a teacher relates with the students in the class, during teaching and learning. These relationships need to be appropriate ones for a teacher and a student, a minor, and not inappropriate ones such as the parental relationship one has with one's own children (Webb and Blond, 1995) or sexual relationships. Within the teacher–student relationship, a teacher communicates ethical and moral messages when they are seen by the students as being 'fair', 'just', 'kind', giving', 'caring', 'considerate', 'loving', 'responsible', 'committed', 'professional', 'having integrity', 'having high standards', 'honest', 'trustworthy', 'courageous', 'patient', 'thoughtful', 'civil', 'constant', 'respectful', 'honourable', 'tolerant', 'polite' and not 'cruel', 'dehumanising', 'irresponsible', 'abusive', 'exploiting' or doing physical, psychological, emotional, spiritual harm. Tate (2007) discusses good teachers (for example, those nominated for teaching excellence awards) as being described by students, colleagues and parents as being 'committed', 'dedicated' and 'devoted', showing 'consistent, persistent, personal actions of caring teachers', who 'live by asymmetrical ideals of service', 'have no favourites', are prepared to 'go beyond the call of duty' or 'go to great lengths to serve as advocates for children who have no one else to fight for them', and to 'take action for their students' sakes' (Tate, 2007: 10–13). Teachers practice an attentiveness to the social, emotional and moral environments of their classrooms for trust, respect and confidence (Tate, 2007; Elbaz, 1992). A distinction to be made here is between 'lessons in morality' (moral, values and character education being taught as part of the curriculum) and the daily communication of modelling being professionally ethical ('moral lessons') in what teachers do and say in the classroom (Campbell, 2003; Strike, 1990). In modelling ethical practices, teachers are reflecting society's and culture's expectations, norms, values, and mores –, for example, social justice, democratic rights and human rights. 'Teachers' actions inevitably transmit messages about what is considered good and bad, right and wrong' (Campbell, 2003: 46). These teachers' actions are often unplanned and tacit, and the teachers themselves may be unaware or conscious of them (Campbell, 1997).

Beginning teacher Katie commented on her views of the appropriate teacher–student relationship:

> *[Has your view of a 'good' teacher changed since you began teaching?]*
> No I don't think so. ... a good teacher is ... not someone that needs to be your friend and ... new teachers [may have] the perspective that they need to be friends with the students and that is definitely not the case, but I've never felt that I needed to be. Someone that they, students, respect, I think is a real big part. [Katie]

Experienced teacher Harry also discussed trust in the teacher–student relationship:

> For me ... you build up when you first come to any class, you build up your respect ... you don't get respect just because you're a teacher anymore. I think maybe you did in the past a lot more. You build up a respect for them and they respect you. And once they establish that, the worst experiences don't often happen that much, it's something out of the blue I think. ... So it's a matter of getting that trust and respect with the kids, they know their boundaries, where they are, where they can [go] and stuff. [Harry]

A fifth aspect of teaching as an ethical practice is that of teachers using their authority and power in ethical ways (Tate, 2007; Buzzelli and Johnston, 2001), which is especially important as teaching nearly always involves unequal power relationships (Buzzelli and Johnston, 2001). An important reason for ethical practice is that teachers are caretakers of public trust concerning their children (Lumpkin, 2007). Teachers have authority due to their role '*in loco parentis*' (in place of the parent), 'whereby the parent (under laws passed by the state) delegates to the school and its teachers certain quite limited responsibilities and in the exercise of these responsibilities teachers need a degree of power over the child' (Snook, 2003: 32). Teachers also have authority in terms of being an authority on the subject matter being taught. As Buzzelli and Johnston (2001) argue, 'the authority of the teacher is a constant in education. ... [T]he way the teacher's authority is enacted in the classroom is a profoundly moral matter' (Buzzelli and Johnston, 2001: 874). The authority of teachers may also give them power which is constructed and enacted in the relationship between teacher and student, and student and student.

Experienced teacher Megan expressed her awareness of the authority and power she had to influence a student's life:

> I've been teaching for thirteen years, I've gone through a lot of phases where I've felt I'm just going to have to pack this job in because I just can't see the point to it ... it was quite a battle. ... I think people don't realise how important a job it is, you stand in front of the same people for a number of years, you have a really big impact on their lives and if you're not doing it right ... you've got a service you're supposed to be giving, so if you're not enthusiastic about doing this, a few years down the track there the student could be stuck in a factory, it could really affect their lifestyle so I see it as really important. [Megan]

A sixth aspect of teaching as an ethical practice may include the explicit teaching of values, especially when itemised in a national or state curriculum. The *New Zealand Curriculum* (New Zealand Ministry of Education, 2007; available online at http://nzcurriculum.tki.org.nz/Curriculum-documents/The-New-Zealand-Curriculum/Values/ accessed 5 July 2011) states:

> **Values: To be encouraged, modelled, and explored**
> Values are deeply held beliefs about what is important or desirable. They are expressed through the ways in which people think and act.
>
> Every decision relating to curriculum and every interaction that takes place in a school reflects the values of the individuals involved and the collective values of the institution.

The values on the list below enjoy widespread support because it is by holding these values and acting on them that we are able to live together and thrive. The list is neither exhaustive nor exclusive. Students will be encouraged to value:

excellence, *by aiming high and by persevering in the face of difficulties*

innovation, inquiry, and curiosity, *by thinking critically, creatively, and reflectively*

diversity, *as found in our different cultures, languages, and heritages*

equity, *through fairness and social justice*

community and participation *for the common good*

ecological sustainability, *which includes care for the environment*

integrity, *which involves being honest, responsible, and accountable and acting ethically*

and to **respect** themselves, others, and human rights.

The beginning teachers discussed teaching students morals and values, including a work ethic, and socially appropriate ways of behaving:

> *[… so what's the most important thing to you at this time about being a teacher?]*
> [S]chool is [not just] about … the kind of academic learning, it's also the social stuff … [the] social learning and morals and values … I think if we can teach them some important values, we'll get them into some sort of structural work ethic before they leave here, then that's probably the most important contribution they'll have to their lives, because for some of the kids that we teach, we are probably the only structure they have in their lives, so yeah, I think here for me that's the most important thing. [Sylvia]
>
> A frustration [is having to say] 'no chewing gum, no swearing'. And they don't realise they're swearing until their mouth is already open and it's halfway out. Those are frustrating for me because it just distracts from the learning, I want to say 'just come and sit down and get on with it'. [Samantha]
>
> … we've got to really make a concerted effort as a school to breed manners into them, 'please', 'thank-you's' and all the rest of it. And respect. [Samantha]

Experienced teacher Megan also discussed including values in the curriculum:

> One of the big drives to do, this particular year, was to actually think about how I can deliver a really good values-based education or curriculum in my classroom. … So I've had three or four years now … looking at doing this and in a low decile school, how can I make a change in these students' learning, how can I motivate them to learn. And one of the answers I've … come up with is well … try and get them to value education a lot more and it's just a … huge, huge task. So one of the ways I thought we might try and look at values education a bit more was introducing a little bit of environmental education. So trying to look more around [at] the beauty of what's outside you, and how we can use it rather than … would I really value education, being stuck in this dump of a classroom with graffiti all over the walls and … that sort of thing? It's very much an environment sort of basis there. [Megan]

Another aspect of teaching as an ethical practice is being competent in the curriculum, especially curriculum content, pedagogically competent and appropriately qualified as teachers (Campbell, 2003; Strike, 1990). Ethical teachers are said to be both academically, intellectually and morally honest (Tate, 2007). Tate describes the 'good' teacher as being one who pursues and disseminates what is thought to be true. Such teachers 'know their stuff', 'love the truth', 'have a passion for learning', 'live the truth and do not cheat', and teach the critical thinking skills of being 'open-minded, curious, skeptical, thorough, and careful' (Tate, 2007: 5–7).

Beginning teacher Katie discussed what she thought a competent teacher was:

> Someone that is actively wanting to improve their course, and improve their execution of their lessons, to make it most efficient and worthwhile, both in terms of the learning content, but also the learning experiences for the students, for their life skills. [Katie]

The last aspect of teaching as an ethical practice is ethical decision-making by teachers. Given the school and classroom dilemmas, issues and challenges which teachers face, there are moral and ethical complexities and nuances in teachers' work (Campbell, 2008; Tippins *et al.*, 1993; Campbell, 1997, 2003; Shapira-Lishchinsky, 2011; Bullough, 2011; Snook, 2003). These dilemmas and conflicts require teachers to use their critical thinking, ethical sensitivities, justifiable judgements and knowledge of the sociocultural contexts in ethical decision-making (Beyer, 1997). Such ethical decision-making is used in response to such situations as these:

- a beginning teacher sees a colleague physically punch a student in the back (Hall, 2008);
- a teacher talks about a student's academic progress in the staffroom with another teacher, in earshot of a parent-helper (Hall, 2008);
- a teacher drinking alcohol after the students' 'lights-out' on an overnight school camp (Hall, 2001);
- disciplining students whose culture is not one's own (Hall, 2001).

As Hall states:

> If teachers do a public job, then the clients of teachers should expect ethical decisions not to be based on the private taste or morality of the teacher. Decisions should stand up to scrutiny in the light of publicly acknowledged criteria such as client autonomy, justice, responsible care, truth, and being honorable – but recognise that in some circumstances these principles may pull against one another (Hall, 2008: 236).

Study and discussion

- In what ways is teaching as an ethical practice exemplified by: 'Justice to share power and prevent the abuse of power, Responsible care to do good and minimise harm to others' (New Zealand Teachers Council Code of Ethics: New Zealand Teachers Council, 2010)?
- Can you give an example from your own teaching of each of these two ways of being ethical as a teacher?

8   Teaching as an embodied practice

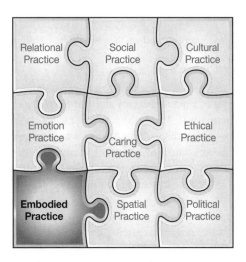

Teaching may be said to be an embodied practice when we view teaching not just as a practice of the mind but also as a practice of the body (Shapiro, 1999). In viewing teaching as an embodied practice, we are saying that teaching is shaped by our lived, bodily experiences and we are giving the body primacy in the construction of knowledge and consciousness, with the body being seen as 'an agent of knowledge production' (Wilcox, 2009: 104).

In this view, both teachers and students are viewed as embodied knowers, constructing knowledge grounded in bodily existence (Shapiro, 1999; Thompson, 2000), and therefore, both teaching and learning are seen as starting from lived experiences. Teachers and students are seen as 'thinking through their bodies' (Thompson, 2000: 165), with the body seen as the 'primary site for lived experiences ... The body is always speaking to us' (Anderson, 2006: 369–70). For example, Hoi (in Shahjahan, 2009) used an exercise with her students of experiencing raisins. She asked them what they knew about raisins, with responses generally that they are dry and a health food. Then she asked them to observe and feel a raisin in their hands; then experience the raisin in their mouths, and then during and after swallowing. Hoi summed up that these embodied experiences of knowing a raisin (typically as moist) tended to leave a more powerful impression than the cognitive knowing of raisins. This is a good example of how teachers and students do not need to rely on mind-privileging pedagogies in the classroom. Teaching as an embodied practice aims for students to learn from experiences, with their bodies as well as their minds. Hence the body has a voice, to which teachers and students listen. As well, the teacher's body is on stage (Estola and Elbaz-Luwisch, 2003). For example, the body tells us that we are tired at the end of the day, or that we are ill. Beginning teacher Samantha referred to the effect that her tired or ill body had on her teaching:

> The only time it's difficult is when you're ill because you are up there in front of everybody and you've still got to manage them. It's also when you're tired as well, it's so much harder to teach because the last thing you want to be doing actually is standing up there and teaching. And [the] kids pick up on that so they starting behaving even worse than they would normally. [Samantha]

Beginning teacher Stephanie commented on her teaching being affected by tiredness and sickness:

> *[What about the worst day or experiences since we last talked?]*
> I've been sick a couple of times this term and last term. I haven't taken any sick days off but you know when you feel under the weather ... and I'm just tired and run down and it's just hard work getting through the lesson, well just sort of physically hard work, more than anything, where you just, you feel yourself, you've spent the whole hour asking them to be quiet ... probably just combined with the tiredness, because when I'm feeling healthy, nothing seems to be too much of a problem. It's just when I get sick it's a bit of a grind. [Stephanie]

Stephanie also mentioned the strain of balancing her work and home lives:

> There's definitely not a dull moment during the day ... but in saying that I can normally contain all my after-school work to the weekend. Because you just get too tired otherwise, you can't do it, you've got to get home, I have got three young children, got a farm to organise, food to cook ... [Stephanie]

Attending to bodily energy levels during the school day relies on teachers listening to their bodies, as was discussed in Chapter 7 in the section on caring for the self. More importantly, as teachers we listen to our own bodies and, in doing so, become aware of ourselves as teachers – of our identity as teachers and what it means to be a teacher (Macintyre Latta and Buck, 2008).

Eight aspects of teaching as an embodied practice are now discussed in turn. First, by considering teaching as an embodied practice, we are viewing the body and mind in a relational way, and no longer ignoring the body as in the Cartesian body–mind split. Centrality is given to situated knowledge that is inscribed in the flesh, with no 'separation of mind and body, thought and feeling, creativity and existence' (Shapiro, 1999: xiii). The body/subject can be seen as a means for producing pedagogical knowledge and practices through an engagement with our own body experiences and memories (Shapiro, 1999). In this view, we are constructing the knowing mind, the knowing heart (emotions) and the knowing body as one. For example, experienced teacher Megan discussed teaching as an embodied practice when talking about how her non-verbal (bodily) behaviour communicated to students:

... one of the key things to change my classroom management was somebody said to me, 'you know, you go in here and you look like you're expecting trouble. And therefore you're going to get it.' [Megan]

Megan was bringing her mind, and its links to action and her sociocultural context, with her into the classroom. She was remembering past experiences of being in the classroom and basing her expectations for new teaching episodes on these experiences. These expectations were not just constructed in her mind but in her body as well. As Barbour (Barbour, 2004, 2006) notes in discussing embodiment:

> Embodiment is a holistic experience, as distinct from the 'body' (which remains differentiated from the 'mind'). I argue that embodiment encompasses an individual person's biological (somatic), intellectual, emotional, social, gendered, artistic and spiritual experience, within their cultural, historical and geographical location. Embodiment is not a random or arbitrary set of genetic material – it recognises the material conditions of race, gender, sexuality, ability, history and culture. Embodiment therefore indicates a holistic experiencing individual (Barbour 2006: 87).

Hence, bodies can be seen as a 'social, cultural, and historical construction as well as physical and personal phenomena' (Estola and Elbaz-Luwisch, 2003: 703). For example, in communicating with Māori students, teachers do not touch them on the head, which is considered sacred. The teaching body is simultaneously both concrete and culturally bound, and teachers' bodies as cultural constructions are moral and emotional (Estola and Elbaz-Luwisch, 2003). Barbour (2004) also discusses the notion of embodied ways of knowing, and construes teaching as an embodied way of knowing.

A second aspect of teaching as an embodied practice is that our sexuality is engraved in our bodies. Teachers' bodies and sexualities are shaped and disciplined through language and socially constructed knowledge (Middleton, 1998), with what it means to be a female or male teacher being socially constructed and engraved on our bodies. In being aware of and attentive to our bodies (bodily functions such as menstruation, emotions and senses), we can construct an 'embodied, gendered reality beyond what has been defined for us by society' (Thompson, 2000: 165). 'The teacher with a body marked different (disabled, gay, pregnant) is keenly aware of embodiment in the classroom' (Anderson, 2006: 374). Beginning teacher Samantha discussed her experiences of being sexually harassed by a junior high school boy. The sexual attention was initiated by the student and, as the teacher could not remove the sexuality engraved in her body, the student had to learn appropriate behaviour:

> I've not had any physical assault, [but] I've had quite a bit of, too much I would say, sort of sexual innuendos, either at me or just in general and it's the sexual attention of [one] 14-year-old boy that really quite concerns me, because you're ... not used to it, but you've come to expect it almost of someone much older, but to find it in someone so young, cracking on to their teachers, which is just ridiculous ... little boys love to flirt, that's not a problem and you know to some degree I'm seen as both the mother figure or a big sister or something like that, that doesn't bother me. But it's the overly sexual nature of some of them that really does concern me because it's way out of order. I don't want to deal with it, I don't want to hear it, I don't want to see it, but I have to say I'm unsure as to exactly what I'm supposed to do about it because ... it's a suggestive thing, it's not [actually] put into words so I can go and report it type thing.

I've found with a couple of people, [to whom] I have mentioned it … who are senior and could deal with it, have slightly laughed it off. And they were male and I thought, well you probably don't really know what it feels like, even if [the boy] is only 14, it's not really relevant, it's not the age, it's the behaviour that's being exhibited … I was shocked, so I spoke to the dean of that year and he was like 'ho ho, sort of thing, how ridiculous …', but I don't think he ever followed anything up. So it makes you slightly wary of reporting it again and as I say it was kind of, it was [a] suggestive comment. [Samantha]

Experienced teacher Beverley recorded her experiences of being a woman science teacher, when her body was taken into account by colleagues:

I started teaching in the 1970s when women teachers were not permitted to wear trousers as it was thought to be inappropriate for women. As was the fashion, I often wore a very short mini-skirt, which I thought was probably more inappropriate than trousers. I inquired and when it was eventually permitted, I tended to wear trousers most of the time as I taught in the science laboratory, and it was more practical. Another time was when as a young and married teacher, I requested to go on an in-service course on teaching physics to Year 9 and 10 students as I had majored in biology, the head of department replied that he did not see the point as I would probably be pregnant soon and leave the profession. I asked again to go on the course and eventually he approved the funding for me to go. [Beverley]

In summary, our embodied sexuality is socially constructed by students and colleagues, sometimes positioning us in ways we do not wish.

Third, notions of race, ethnicity and culture are socially constructed knowledge, which we experience as embodied knowers. Teachers experience as embodied knowers what it means to have a body with, for example, skin colour and facial features which may or may not be the same as those of our students (Thompson, 2000). Teachers know in an embodied way through experiences, and this embodied knowledge informs our teaching practices. Of importance here are the teachers' and students' experiences of their bodies. Bishop (2005), in discussing ways of knowing and being Māori, noted that the act of knowing is understood as participation, which includes somatic, psychic and emotional involvement.

Fourth, teaching with disability is highlighted when we view teaching as an embodied practice (Anderson, 2006). A teacher may live, experience and know disability in the classroom in an embodied way, as experienced teacher Beverley noted:

As a teacher with partial hearing, I am aware of my body in the classroom. For example, I will stand in the middle of the classroom, not at the front, to speak to the whole class. If a student is answering a question in a whole-class discussion, I will walk towards them to hear them better. I can lip read students who are talking when I am talking, and who feel inaudible as they are in the back row. I experience tiredness when I have concentrated to listen against the background noise of the classroom all day. [Beverley]

Beverley is aware of her teaching in an embodied practice.

In her second interview, beginning teacher Sally discussed the time when she hurt her ankle and had trouble walking:

[The next question is about your best day or experience, so ...]
That was easy, that was an unplanned lesson. ... I'm usually very organised, it's only ever happened once. It was only several weeks ago. It was a Year 9 class and for some reason – I have a locked cabinet – I left my key at home, and I'd left my planning book in the staff room, and my ankle was sore. I walked into the classroom, and I thought, 'Oh' ... and I thought about my sore ankle and I thought about the locked cupboard and away I went. And we had a fabulous lesson and the kids were really [engaged). ... it was a great confidence booster because I knew then, that if all I had was a white board marker and I knew my class, I would be okay. ... [But it was also my worst experience] managing the three lots of stairs with a sprained ankle and trying not to get grumpy by Period 6 in the afternoon. ... I was just tired, and the ankle [was] sore and so I didn't have the concentration or the energy or enthusiasm level. [Sally]

A further example is found in the writing of Anderson (2006) who described his own experiences and embodied ways of knowing as a teacher in a wheelchair.

A fifth aspect of teaching as an embodied practice is that of the presence or absence of teachers' bodies (Estola and Elbaz-Luwisch, 2003). For example, the absence or presence of Māori and Pasifika bodies as teachers in many New Zealand schools communicates to students messages about whose knowledge and culture are seen as having worth and authority in New Zealand society. The presence of the teacher is also written about in terms of teaching as a spiritual practice (Shahjahan, 2009) (see also Chapter 2), with the teacher being fully present for the student – not just in body, but in mind and spirit too.

Another aspect of teaching as an embodied practice is the way in which we teachers use our bodies in the classroom. Teachers use gestures when talking to students. For example, Hwang and Roth (2010) discuss the embodied nature of physics lectures, emphasising that there is 'more to lectures than the talk plus the notes' (Hwang and Roth, 2010: 1). They argue that the 'more' they refer to is the use of gestures, body movements, body positions, drawing diagrams, writing equations on the board/screen and moving around the classroom – the embodied performance of the teacher (or in this case the lecturer). Hwang and Roth (2010) argue that it is the embodied performance that explains the phenomenon of students understanding the lecture, better than reading the textbook or, for example, notes online. Teachers use different body positions for control – for example, walking around the room to monitor and control student behaviour, talking to the whole class from the front of the classroom, maintaining or not maintaining eye contact with different cultural groups, and standing beside a student who is distracted easily to keep him or her on task. We can use a particular gaze to get a student to stop talking, we can shake our head to tell a student to stop doing something, or we can raise our eyebrows to acknowledge a Pasifika student.

The physical appearance of teachers' and students' bodies is taken into account by each other. For example, Shaunessy and Alvarez McHatton (2009) reported that students felt that teachers stereoptyped them based upon their appearance, especially upon the way they dressed.

And lastly, the notion of teaching as an embodied practice can inform our pedagogies. A common activity in teaching as an embodied practice is for teachers, visitors from the community and students to share their experiences of culture, gender, sexuality and disability, because 'personal encounters engage the minds and bodies of people in the classroom' (Anderson, 2006: 372). With ethical and confidentiality considerations met first, a teacher can promote 'personal authenticity that promotes deepening levels of trust' (Anderson, 2006: 375). Teachers can use embodied theories and practices to raise critical consciousness of, and foster activism to disrupt embodied, oppressive, socially constructed power relationships in the classroom based on gender, culture, sexuality and disability, being mindful that humans embody multiple identities of gender, race and disability simultaneously (Thompson, 2000). Teaching as an embodied practice may involve a teacher positioning the body at the 'front and centre of knowledge production' (Wilcox, 2009: 107), using dance, theatre and music as a way of knowledge production and validation (Barbour, 2004). This invokes Gardner's notion of multiple intelligences, and in particular, of bodily intelligence (Gardner, 1983). For example, science students studying populations in ecology studies were asked to 'get inside a wolf and think like a wolf' while using a computer model simulation of prey–predator population dynamics (Wilensky and Reisman, 2006). Likewise, drama has been used in secondary science classrooms to promote learning (Dorion, 2009), with the dialogic discourses, the multimodal characteristics and the visualisation and imagination highlighting the embodied knowledge of teacher and student.

In summary, teaching as an embodied practice focuses on the way that teachers use, position and regulate their bodies in the classroom (Watkins, 2007).

Study and discussion

- Describe a time when you recall using your body to illustrate what you were teaching.
- In what ways do our sick and disabled bodies influence our teaching practices?

9 Teaching as a spatial practice

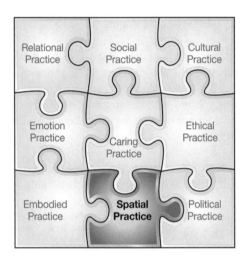

To theorise teaching as a spatial practice is to view teaching as inherently spatial and temporal. That is, in thinking about teaching as a spatial practice, we are viewing the social relationships of teaching as existing in space and time. The ways in which space and time are conceptualised in teaching include the physical working spaces in a classroom and school: spaces constructed within relationships, for example, in the teacher–student relationship, and the virtual teaching spaces in e-learning. These are all spaces (and times) which enable, shape and constrain teaching. For example, classrooms don't enable the teaching of dance, and dance rooms don't enable students to do research using information and communication technology (Ovens, 2008). As teachers, spatial metaphors permeate much of our thinking (Hirst and Cooper, 2008). For example, in previous chapters we have discussed the notion of space in discussing Vygotsky's zone of proximal development, emotional distance in relationships, and social distances in relationships. This chapter explores teaching as a spatial practice.

Location of the school

The geographical location of a school may be a factor in a teacher's decision to apply for a job in a particular school. For example, two of the beginning teachers interviewed mentioned that they had applied for teaching positions in specific schools located within a commuting distance of their home. Samantha had applied to schools within a commute of where she was living, even though the commuting distance was bigger than she would have liked:

> ... I had to try from Pukekohe [in the north] round in a huge circle via Paeroa, Te Aroha, down to Otorohanga and back into Hamilton, dropping off, I think it was 25 CVs in a day, and then I got the call next day from here would I like an interview in the afternoon? [Samantha]
>
> The only thing is the blooming commute, which is really quite long. But that aside, no I wouldn't want to go anywhere else. [Samantha]

Beginning teacher Ellie commented on her chosen school as being a close commute from home, and therefore a part of her own community:

> I do actually live quite close to here, which is a factor, not a key factor, but I did draw a circle around where I would like to commute to, commuting distance, so it was a factor. [Ellie]
>
> ... it's my community, I live in the community that is important for me. I feel like I am contributing to the community. You get a good sense of reward because you are part of the community. [Ellie]

Its geographical location may also mean that a school has a designated title. Beginning teacher Katie was aware of the rural location of her school, but:

> ... I always have issues with calling themselves a rural school when there's a MacDonald's just up the road. [Katie]

The geographical location of a school will have cultural, economic and social implications in terms of the community that the school is a part of.

Physical spaces

The physical spaces teachers teach in can 'either encourage or discourage interaction and communication between people' (Jordon, 2001: 98). Noisy, crowded, oddly shaped rooms, poorly ventilated rooms and drab rooms are avoided, if possible, by most teachers. The pedagogies which teachers use are enabled or hindered by the physical environment and architecture of the classroom and its furniture. Or, in other words, the pedagogy dictates the spaces for learning – for example, teachers may be consulted about their preference in the design of new or renovated classrooms. For example, a studio-designed classroom, rather than a traditional classroom, was found by two tertiary teachers and most of the students in a study to be more supportive of inquiry learning, formative assessment, problem solving, collaboration, students walking around to talk with other students, information literacy, printing out writing, and communication between students (Taylor, 2009). The two teachers in the study reported that the shape of the room and the furniture design facilitated a change in their teaching pedagogy from traditional transmission lecturing to inquiry-based, student-centred teaching. The studio used in the study was a classroom characterised by a 'combination of moveable furniture, tables that group students in learning teams, a centrally located or moveable teacher's station that does not create a "front" of the room, wireless laptops and computer projection, and wall spaces for writing or posting ideas' (Taylor, 2009: 218). A key aspect of the classroom design was that the studio classroom was a flexible space, which did not rule out a teacher talking to the whole class if need be, but which enabled the students to initiate moving between learning teams and rearranging the furniture as necessary. The studio included an interactive whiteboard, rolling chairs and small tables, and plenty of space not occupied by furniture. Studio design has also been researched by Lynch *et al.*, (2002) and Moore and Lackney (1995).

In a descriptive, not causal, study, the relationship between the physical school environment and student academic achievement was explored (Tanner, 2008). Four sets of design patterns were selected (Tanner, 2008: 445):

- 'movement and circulation (e.g., adequate personal space and efficient movement patterns throughout the school)'. The density of students was seen as an important consideration;
- 'large group meeting spaces (e.g., social gathering places)'. These are spaces where students can meet formally and informally and which can create a sense of welcome and belonging;
- 'day lighting and views (e.g., windows with natural light)'. Natural lighting, colour and views overlooking life were considered.
- 'instructional neighborhoods (e.g., large and small group areas that accommodate wet and dry activities)'. The configuration of the teaching and learning spaces was considered important.

The findings reported were that each of the four design variables was positively related to student achievement, 'even after controlling for school SES' (Tanner, 2008: 445). The author noted that the design of the research did not allow for causal or co-relational relationships to be concluded, only an association.

Other aspects of architecture and furniture reported to be linked to pedagogy, and in particular to promote inquiry-based and interdependent teaching and learning, include:

- larger learning areas than a traditional classroom, for space for leaving displays, and project works in progress, and for movement and collaboration of students (Behrenbruch and Bolger, 2006);
- communication-friendly spaces (Jarman and Worton, 2008);
- interaction between library and classroom staff and spaces (Dracoulas, 2007);
- spaces suitable for the professional development of staff (Jenlink and Jenlink, 2008).

Physical space was a topic mentioned by many of the interviewed teachers. A beginning teacher discussed how she did not feel she could meet the learning needs of all her students as she was teaching in many classrooms:

> ... when you're not in the same classroom all the time ... I can't carry everything around with me on a big trolley or something, [but] ... if we were in the same classroom it would be an awful lot easier to set the place up to have ... a reading corner or something like that if they want to go and read. [Samantha]

One beginning teacher was teaching in a newly-opened school:

[W]e are kind of short of classrooms at the moment, because the buildings aren't ready, so we're having to move around and share classrooms … so some of those frustrations … [Sylvia]

Beginning teacher Katie, a teacher of science, also expressed concern about the rooms she taught in, with respect to safety and configuration for both whole-class teaching and small group work during practicals, which often involve the use of water and electricity:

… and one thing I do struggle with is the practical execution of practicals in a science class especially when you have 35 kids in one science lab and the safety thing. And I guess that comes from [having been a physiotherapist] … knowing the legal responsibilities and all that side of things, [I am] very aware when it comes to safety in the lab and I don't do practicals if I think there is going to be some risk … something I wanted to work on was how to set up my classroom to be the most effective way for theory and practical, and when you have got large numbers it's very limiting and … I don't know whether there is a perfect set up – I haven't found it yet, so maybe there isn't one and that's [why] I'm so dissatisfied. [Katie]

Social spaces

Another way of thinking about space and time in a sociocultural view of teaching is that of the social spaces – the spaces within which teachers and students communicate with each other. A teacher may configure the social spaces in the classroom for communication. For example, a study with three primary teachers concluded that 'there are some differences in the teachers' decision making about the classroom environment which seems to relate to pedagogic style' (Pointon and Kershner, 2000: 125). The three teachers made decisions on arranging the classroom, taking into account the grouping of the students, whether based on friendships, ability or gender. Seating arrangements were based on behaviour management, social factors, security and comfort, cognitive learning, and developing student autonomy.

Being close to colleagues for ease of communication and building collegial relationships was mentioned by the beginning teachers, who also discussed how being physically close to a colleague helped develop social spaces for professional development:

I was in a lab next door to my mentor teacher last year, which was fantastic. I also had an adjoining classroom to where the technician lived so that was equally as fantastic. [Katie]

There is a science teacher who has been around for a number of years at the same school [a new school for Katie]; she is in the adjacent lab to me so we share stuff all the time, we catch up morning teas and all the rest of it. [Katie]

[And the other meetings were with your supervisor [or] mentor?]
Yeah. They weren't always formal, like we … have the same office space so she would just ask me how things were going and just come up with suggestions and things like that. If I've had specific problems we'd come up with a plan to how to approach things. [Sylvia]

The teachers mentioned the hierarchies that exist in the social spaces in schools. For example, beginning teacher Sally discussed not having her own teaching room. She had commented that it was unfair that the senior, more experienced teachers had their own rooms, but not the beginning teachers. A hierarchical distribution of power via the allocation of teaching spaces was implied:

> ... a lot of the senior teachers [are] teaching senior classes of 16 to a class, and they might have 3 classes because they have other responsibilities [and they are teaching] in their own room. And junior teachers, meaning junior in experience, not in age, have 5 or 6 classes of 30 junior students each and they are moving around. To me that seems totally unfair because 1) they [the senior teachers] are better managers, 2) they have half the students and 3) they have all that experience. ... I don't agree with it. I don't think it's right. [Sally]

In her second year, she was expected to move around 11 classrooms, so she negotiated with her principal for her own teaching room:

> ... if I'm moving all the time as a new teacher and I haven't got my resources with me, because I can't carry boxes of dictionaries and boxes of reading material and stuff like that, it must affect my students. ... And in fact it would have made it impossible to teach my Unit Standards girls the way I do, because I have all my Units running concurrently and they can pick whatever they want. ... So it would have changed my teaching practice, it would have been terribly detrimental to it. [Sally]

The use of the chairs in staffroom was mentioned by one beginning teacher, when talking about her experiences on practicum:

> We were very much student teachers, we sat in the wrong place to start with. Absolutely [a] cardinal sin, nobody said [anything]. It's not like people had place names [on the chairs] ... but we were very much made to feel desperately inferior and actually quite a pain for being there, and strangely enough, that's very off-putting when you're coming into a new career. [Samantha]

The hierarchy in the social spaces was also mentioned with respect to position and time in the social spaces:

> There's a shifting of focus from being a student teacher, who is there temporarily and very much bottom of the rung ... at least [in your first year of teaching, you are a] provisional teacher, but you are a teacher. There's much more of a sort of equality of status this year than there was on practicum. I'm still bottom of the rung but I feel less inferior than I did being a student. [Samantha]

Another beginning teacher felt keenly how she was positioned as a new teacher, despite the skills she brought with her into teaching, and she spoke about 'doing the time':

> I find that really hard because ... my last ... full time role was as manager of my own business. I'm not used to being told what to do all the time and ... I can see that things don't work, but you can't do anything, like you can sort of gently, well you can't even really do that, because schools are really hierarchical, this [school] probably less so than other places, but you know it's quite difficult [when I see] where things don't

work, but not actually being able to do anything about it. And you are used to having more clout, you know a bit more responsibility, more authority, it's quite difficult to go back down and start again and teaching unfortunately is one of those professions where you just do the time really. But yeah, yeah that's probably the most frustrating thing for me. [Sylvia]

Interpersonal space is an important aspect to consider in thinking about social spaces. Some cultures accept a very small interpersonal space, while others operate on a much larger interpersonal space. In the classroom, some pedagogies – for example, lecturing to the whole class – work on a large interpersonal space, and others – for example, giving feedback to an individual student – work with a shorter interpersonal distance. But it is not just the physical distance being referred to but also the power-distance in the relationship (Phuong-Mai *et al.*, 2009; Ho, 2009).

The notion of emotional geographies (Hargreaves, 2001a, 2001b) is another way of talking of the distance and closeness in relationships. Hargreaves wrote of:

> ... personal geographies that delineate how close to or distant from one another people become in the personal aspects of their relationships; cultural geographies where differences of race, culture, gender and disability, including different ways of experiencing and expressing emotion, can create distance between people, and lead them to be treated as stereotypes; moral geographies where people pursue common purposes and feel senses of accomplishment together, or where they are more distant being defensive about their own purposes and unconcerned or in disagreement about the purposes of others; professional geographies where definitions and norms of professionalism either set professionals apart from their colleagues and clients, or open them up to exploring professional issues together; political geographies where differences of power and status can distort interpersonal communication, or where such differences can be used not to protect people's own interests but to empower others; and, physical geographies of time and space which can bring and keep people in proximity over long periods so that relationships might develop, or which can reduce these relationships to strings of episodic interactions. (Hargreaves, 2001b: 509)

Teachers may distance themselves from their students or build close relationships. Kramer Schlosser (1992) reported on a study exploring the school lives of 31 culturally diverse students in a school in the USA, and in particular those of the teachers who were considered by the students as most successful in helping them learn. Teachers perceived by the students to be low-impact teachers were those who considered it professionally appropriate to maintain a distance between themselves and students. They distanced themselves from the students and were perceived as uncaring and unfair, contributing to the sense of disengagement with learning and school by the students. Conversely, high-impact teachers were those seen by the students as building close, caring and warm relationships with students, connecting with their out-of-school lives, and resulting in more student engagement and higher achievement.

The social spaces can also be viewed as discursively constructed in the social relationships in schools (Jenlink and Jenlink, 2008; Hirst and Cooper, 2008) and university (Jenlink and Jenlink, 2008; Jewson, 2007; Middleton and McKinley, 2010). The social space is seen as discursively constructed when:

Rather than being an arena where social relationships just take place, space is made through the social – it is enacted and so continually created and recreated ... [The discourses and practices that define the work of educators and students] originate from within the social space of school as well as the discursive, normative practices imposed upon the social space of the school from the outside. (Jenlink and Jenlink, 2008: 313)

For example, teaching as an embodied practice, as discussed in the previous chapter, can be defined as 'building relationships between self, others, and subject matter; living in-between these entities' (Macintyre Latta and Buck, 2008: 317). Hence, the learning community is seen as discursively constructed within the classroom and the school walls (Jenlink and Jenlink, 2008) as well as within the pedagogical spaces (Hirst and Cooper, 2008), as are learning spaces for teachers (Clandinin, 2008).

Time and space in teaching

If we consider teaching as a spatial practice, as discussed in the previous chapter, we are also considering the temporal component of teaching. Teachers are mindful of time and the time-spaces in which they work: of their teaching timetable which structures the time-spaces in their day; of the time the lesson starts, the proportion of time through the lesson; whether the lesson objectives are being met within the timeframe of each lesson; and whether the curriculum will be 'covered' before the exam.

The interviewed teachers were mindful of the time that shaped their work into temporal spaces. The beginning teachers were asked about how they used the 0.2 time allocation of additional non-teaching time for beginning teachers in their weekly timetable:

> *[Can you tell me about how the 0.2 time allocation is working for you?]*
> It's working well, I mean, mine is predominantly on one day which makes it quite difficult. It's nice today [the day of non-teaching time] but towards the end of the week it makes it quite difficult but that's just timetabling. [Sylvia]
>
> It was really good and I will definitely miss it [the 0.2 allocation] next year, but that's the way it goes. But I think, as time got on, I did get better at utilising my time better and getting things done quicker. So it was good, it was a valuable time to have. [Sylvia]

Some of the beginning teachers talked about working in a 'smarter' way to manage their time better:

> ... just getting more into a routine and finding that I'm spending a lot less time at home working. Getting a bit better at utilising your time better and creating resources quickly and just working smarter rather than harder, I've found that to be the biggest change in the second half of the year. [Sylvia]
>
> Just the whole process of how to do it quicker or better, whatever subject you're teaching ... as often as possible, if I'm doing anything in class, I try and get the kids to do their own marking, but that can sometimes take longer than doing it yourself. [Sandy]

Routines were also mentioned:

> [Now, after 6 months of teaching,] probably for me a bit more settled, more into the routine ... [what] really comes home to haunt you when you don't do it properly, is the

whole routine, the importance of routine, especially in the junior school; they just can't really cope at all. [Sylvia]

Managing time for family and home life was mentioned:

... time, ... I have a family and have commitments too, time and I think the need to not try and allow school work to take up too much of your time otherwise you never get a break. [Sandy]

Managing the curriculum to be learnt for senior assessments, in the time available, was discussed, in this case, in managing the behaviour of a class:

Unfortunately, because it was at the end of the term, there was also that need to keep pushing because we need to finish the unit standard before the end of the year ... [Sandy]

Experienced teacher Harry also discussed time:

And occasionally when you're in senior management, you don't get as much time to do that [preparation and planning], so you're kind of – you're winging it a bit from time to time. [Harry]

In summary, the teachers interviewed discussed the ways in which time segments, organises and creates spaces for their teaching.

A discursive view of time and space may be used to theorise how time and space are constructed within different cultures, as distinct from the objective view in Western and scientific thinking. Massey (2005) argued for a relational view of space in which space and time are seen as discursively co-constructed during interactions, in a constant and ongoing process, and in which plurality or multiple views are enabled. In such a relational view, the relationship refers to the relationship between people, the environment and the spiritual. For example, *va* is a word common to many Pacific nations, and its meaning in the Samoan language and culture has been defined by Wendt (1996, cited in Lee Hang, 2011: 310) as:

'... the space between, the between-ness, not empty space, not space that separates but space that relates, that holds separate entities and things together in the unity-in-all, the space that is context giving meaning to things. The meanings change as the relation-ships/the contexts change.'

Lee Hang explained *va* as a cultural, social, relational and sacred space:

Albert Wendt's definition of *va* brings to the fore the importance of relationships. This of course is not unique to Samoa as Thaman ... has identified it as a common value in many Pacific island nations. Mila-Schaaf and Ka'ili ... have also identified *va* as a Tongan value. *Va-fealoa'i* or *va fealoaloa'i* on the other hand, refers to the protocols of mutual respect that governs the exchanges made within these sacred spaces ... in terms of relational space Le Tagaloa ... has identified nine specific human relations as *tapu* (sacred) or as *va tapuia* and these include: the relation between brother and sister; parents and their children; opposite genders; same genders; host and guest;

matai with another matai; the living and the dead; humans and their environment; and finally between the humans and God. ... The importance of the concept of *va* [is] as a relational, social and sacred space. (Lee Hang, 2011: 310–11)

Likewise Kalavite (2010) also discussed *va* with respect to Tongan culture and articulated the way in which the *tā–vā* (time–space) relationships that Tongan tertiary students in New Zealand have with government and university administration, with family, the church, God and communities, may be different to the time–space relationships in the non-Pasifika world. For example, whereas the non-Pasifika lecturers and students understood that evenings were for study, the Tongan students had many family and church obligations to fulfil.

In a relational view of space, space becomes a place when it becomes 'socially relevant and meaningful to a person' (Al-Mahmood, 2006: 44). Place-based pedagogies are those which aim for a student's learning to be directly connected to the 'well-being of the social and ecological places that people inhabit' and which are 'concerned with context and the value of learning from and nurturing specific places, communities or regions' (Gruenewald, 2003), which include social, cultural and political spaces. But how is 'place' viewed if we have a discursive and relational view of time and space? Such a discursive view is articulated by Van Eijck and Roth (2010) when discussing place-based education on Victoria Island, British Columbia, Canada, where indigenous First Nation peoples live with Canadians of mainly European and Asian descent. Van Eijck and Roth (2010), drawing on Bakhtin's work, wrote of understanding ...

> ... place as the result of dialectical and dialogical relation of the material world and its chronotopic (time–space) nature in the various conversations (discourses) in which it is constituted as *this* place (Van Eijck and Roth, 2010: 869; italics in original).

This definition emphasises the narrative, the interaction (both dialectic and dialogic), and the relational. In speaking about the Tod Inlet Marine Park on Victoria Island, which is on the Pacific coast of Canada, they used scientific and English language to discuss the geography and the flora and fauna of the park. In both languages, Tod Inlet is constructed as separate from the knowers – an objective view. But in describing Tod Inlet using the language of the local indigenous Saanich people, the inlet is constructed as a sacred place for gathering food and water, for training warriors in survival and as a place for 'absolution, prayer and renewal' (Van Eijck and Roth, 2010: 875). The knower and the knowledge are inseparable. The narrative form of the language means that a time–space dimension is inherently present. The language speaks of the indigenous people, living in the area for over 2000 years, as belonging to the land, and as caretakers of the land. The authors argue:

> Place as a social construct, is defined by the perspectives people attribute to it and, in turn, these attributions collectively become the voice by which people are bound up with the places represented (Van Eijck and Roth, 2010: 879).

As there are as many constructions as there are people, place is 'a multitude of voices that tell places rather than a single voice' (Van Eijck and Roth, 2010: 880). Hence the voices that speak through the English names for aspects of Tod Inlet are different from the voices that speak through Saanich names. The Saanich names give voice to a place that 'comes into existence by virtue of the role it plays in the life of the Saanich people ... in the annually repeating life world practices' (Van Eijck and Roth, 2010: 886), a life with emotions and values. In summary, space as place is viewed as a narrated and 'lived entity rather than a point in space and time' (Van Eijck and Roth, 2010: 882). For teachers, the use of (in this case, Saanich) names teaches not just the knowledge and ways of knowing of the (Saanich) people, but also that they are valued enough to be included in the curriculum.

E-learning spaces

E-learning teaching spaces are the virtual or cyber-spaces/places in which teachers and students interact through the internet, and other educational media – for example, telephone, Skype, email, Twitter and Facebook (Palloff and Pratt, 2003, 2005; Earl and Forbes, 2008; Wright, 2010). A key aspect of online teaching is the separation of teacher and student in space and time. They are separated in space, as they are usually not in the same physical space but are in another room, building, city or country, or on the other side of the world. These e-spaces intersect with the physical spaces in which teachers and student work at their keyboards and screens (Al-Mahmood, 2006; Kling and Courtright, 2004). These working spaces may be in an office, bedroom, living area, garage, school or café.

Online classes are to varying degrees interactive between teacher and student, so there is an element of time as well as space (Bender, 2003). The teacher and student are not separated by time in synchronous or real-time discussions, when teacher and students are all online at the same moment. Asynchronous discussions, in which discussions are not in real time, are defined as belonging to:

> A text-based computer-mediated communication environment that allows individuals to interact with one another without the constraint of time and place. (Hew *et al.*, 2009)

An e-learning web site is available to teachers and students to log into and contribute at a convenient time during the week that the module is accessible:

> Whilst I log on to teach online in the morning at work, students tend to log on during the day if they are full-time students, after school if they are using a school computer for their studies, or late in the evening when children are asleep. [Beverley]

A key feature of asynchronous discussion is that a written record is kept of student and teacher contributions in the cyber-space. Asynchronous discussion is seen as giving students the opportunity to reflect on previous contributions before they contribute, and to use higher-order thinking skills in their own contributions and replies (Hew *et al.*, 2009; Hara *et al.*, 2000), although the increased use of higher-order skills cannot be automatically assumed (Tallent-Runnels *et al.*, 2006; Hammond, 2005; Hew *et al.*, 2009). The asynchronous discussions give the students time and space for thinking. Ways to promote discussion online are a recurring theme in the literature (Hew *et al.*, 2009), in terms of both the number of contributions and the quality of thinking in the contributions. For example, Hara *et al.* (2000) suggest the starter-wrapper pedagogy in which students are assigned roles to start the discussion or 'wrap up' (summarise) the discussion, as a way to increase both quantity and quality. Participation in online discussions is seen as important, as they are seen to promote learning outcomes (Tallent-Runnels *et al.*, 2006; Hew *et al.*, 2009b), especially those interactions in which students are engaged or on-task with respect to the content (Tallent-Runnels *et al.*, 2006; Hew *et al.*, 2009).

As discussed earlier, 'relational' space as the emotional and social distance between the teacher and student is seen as important in teaching and learning, as in the commonly used terms to describe people: 'cold, detached and remote', 'warm, caring and friendly.

A key aspect of online teaching is the distinction between physical distance and relational distance (Bender, 2003). As the online teacher is usually separated in time and space from students, especially in asynchronous communication, the relational distance between teacher and student becomes highlighted and in need of attention. Of importance in online teaching and learning is whether the students feel like 'insiders' or outsiders' – that is, whether they belong to the community of practice that is the online class (Bender, 2003). Hence, a key role of the online teacher becomes that of personalising the educational approach and minimising the relational distance (Bender, 2003). The task is to make the cyber-space a place where students feel they belong and are keen to log on to see what other students have contributed to discussions since they last looked. As online teachers, we use a variety of tools to create an online, interactive community of practice: management systems – for example Moodle – which enable interaction; emoticons; online discussions; chat rooms, personal introduction forums; posting announcements; using other ICT media as well – for example, Twitter, Facebook, Skype and video clips; and, if need be; asking students to recount a personal experience related to the content as part of their learning activities; the use of formative assessment feedback and feedforward to give a reply to specific students; politeness strategies (Locke and Daly, 2007); and the use of collaborative, cooperative learning tasks (Roberts, 2003; De Laat *et al.*, 2007).

Hence, the notion of 'community' and 'collaboration' is seen as an important aspect of e-teaching and learning (Stuckey and Barab, 2007; Roberts and Lund, 2007; Palloff and Pratt, 2005). The distinction is made between a community of learners and a group of students working collaboratively (Barab *et al.*, 2004a), so that 'community' is defined as 'a persistent, sustained [socio-technical] network of individuals who share and develop an overlapping knowledge base, set of beliefs, values, history and experiences focused on a common practice and/or mutual enterprise' (Barab *et al.*, 2004b: 55).

The importance of community in e-teaching is part of a sociocultural view of teaching, with e-teaching being undertaken in a sociocultural space, and e-teaching and learning being viewed as social practices (Garner and Gillingham, 1996; Khoo, 2010). Deliberate strategies on the part of the e-teacher are needed to build a community from a collection or group of e-learners: for example, trust building through 'social communication … communication of enthusiasm …coping with technical uncertainty … individual initiative … predictable communication … substantial and timely responses' (Jarvenpaa and Leidner, 1998: 30; Kling and Courtright, 2004. Campbell and Yates (2005) summarise aspects which students contribute to a sense of community and belonging in the 4-Rs of e-learning: relationships, reflection on learning, resourcefulness (and information location skills) and resilience (motivation to succeed).

The development of a sense of community is seen as crucial in e-teaching to enable collaborative activity (Palloff and Pratt, 2003) to promote the 'development of critical thinking skills, co-creation of knowledge and meaning, reflection and transformative learning (Palloff and Pratt, 2005: 4). Such collaborative activities include 'small group assignments, research assignments asking students to seek out and present additional resource material to their peers, group work on case studies, simulations, shared facilitation, homework forums, asynchronous discussion of the reading and discussion questions, and papers posted to the course site with mutual feedback provided' (Palloff and Pratt, 2005: 10).

The e-space may also be seen as a 'rhetorical space' (Locke, 2007; Locke and Daly, 2007) in which the 'speaker is always, as Bakhtin noted, a respondent' (Locke and Daly, 2007: 180), with the speaker taking into account the listener in their utterance. Hence, in theorising the e-space as rhetorical, we are making the distinction between talking and communication:

> A second pattern that emerges in our cases is the highly social nature of Internet communication. The students and teachers who sit at computers pecking out stories of events in their lives are quite obviously intent on telling the stories to others in the global village, not on storing them in the recesses of the machine. ... Humans talk to accomplish social purposes (e.g., to impart or seek information, to amuse or be amused, to persuade or to be persuaded) ... From these perspectives, the Internet conversations are like other forms of communication in their socialness ... (Garner and Gillingham, 1996: 130)

And '... if the space is rhetorical, then it can also be thought of as epistemic' (Garner and Gillingham, 1996: 180), that is, as having its own socially produced knowledge, with its own rules of behaving and values. For example, turns are taken at being the speaker (writer) and listener (reader). But the rules of communication in e-teaching spaces differ from those in the physical classroom (Cazden, 2001; Gardener, 2008; Garner and Gillingham, 1996). As Locke and Daly (2007) argue:

> ... a rhetorical space is inevitably reshaped or reconfigured by its attendant technologies. In addition, as Walter Ong ... argues in respect of writing, technology has the power, directly and indirectly, to shape human thought processes (consciousness). A technology, then, is more than just an aid to learning. It shapes the cognitive processes that underpin learning. (Locke and Daly 2007: 121)

A further aspect of e-spaces as rhetorical spaces is the constraint on the use of the non-verbal communication that is available in face-to-face communication, as Locke and Daly (2007: 122; quoting Locke, 2004) discuss:

> ... written talk constrains participants' use of prosodic features of spoken language (variations in pitch, loudness, tempo, emphasis and rhythm), paralinguistics effects (pauses, gaps, certain vocal effects such as 'giggling') and kinesic signals (body movements, gestures, facial expressions).

Instead, online students and teachers have available to them other communication tools, positive politeness strategies and texted signals such as emoticons. The former include the use of the inclusive 'we', hedging (for example: 'for me personally'), agreement (for example: 'I agree with you'), intensification of interest (for example: 'I am really interested in how ...'), in-group address (for example, an invitation to use a shortened form of the first name, or referring to the class as a group or team), assertion of common ground (for example: 'I share your concern') and compliments (Locke and Daly, 2007). The use of emoticons also communicates non-verbal language online, (e.g., the smile :-), grin :->, confused :-/ and sheepish :-}) (Locke and Daly, 2007).

Constructivist and sociocultural views of learning (Bell, 2005a; Holmes and Gardner, 2006; Salomon and Perkins, 1998), including distributed learning (Salomon, 1993) are helpful in thinking about teaching the e-learner (Palloff and Pratt, 2003). In developing a community and collaboration, e-teaching is able to be learner-centred, with a sharing of power to negotiate the curriculum to meet both the teacher's goals of the course and the prior experiences, learning needs and interests of the students (Stephenson, 2001b; Stacey and Wiesenberg, 2007; Forbes, in press; Forbes, in preparation), with the establishment of safety and trust a priority (Gulati, 2008). A key activity for the teacher is to be present in the online space (Forbes, in preparation). The teacher's presence can be communicated to the students, for example, by the teacher's contribution to subject matter debates, asking questions, pacing discussions, and by answering student questions; but also by explicitly stating that they are present but just 'listening'. The teacher's presence is also communicated if the teacher is perceived by the students to be 'listening' to their online contributions, reading them for meaning and critique.

Cyber-spaces promote different pedagogies (Stephenson, 2001a) from those used in the traditional classrooms (De Laat *et al.*, 2007), with a corresponding change in teacher roles (Holmes and Gardner, 2006). Rather than using the computer, the Internet, and interactive smart boards as variations of the whiteboard, overhead projector, video, textbook or tasksheet, online teaching involves new pedagogies and roles for the teacher (Sharma and Juwah, 2006). New pedagogical roles and activities for e-teachers abound in the literature – see, for example: Sharma and Juwah (2006); Stephenson (2001a); Gonzalez (2009); Mayes (2001); Roberts (2003); De Laat *et al.* (2007); Bonk *et al.* (2001). However, Tallent-Runnels *et al.* (2006) argue that, in a review of the relevant research, they found 'no comprehensive theory or model that informed studies of online instruction' (Tallent-Runnels *et al.* 2006: 115), although research based on a sociocultural view of e-teaching and learning is emerging (Khoo, 2010; Forbes, in preparation). As Thompson (2007) notes:

> Unfortunately, much of the recent e-learning discourse has in effect relegated teachers to a minor role. Naming their activity 'e-learning' obscures their professional contribution (i.e. teaching or educating) ... (Thompson, 2007: 165)

However, Palloff and Pratt (2003) addressed the active role of the e-teacher:

> We have often discussed the need for the instructor to move out of the middle, vacating the 'sage on the stage' role and becoming the 'guide on the side'. Does this mean that instructors also need to vacate their role as content experts? The answer to that question is a resounding *no*. (Palloff and Pratt, 2003: 125; italics in original)

Knowing what to do as an e-teacher starts with knowing how to be present online:

> The teacher, or if you wish, facilitator, plays a key role throughout the e-learning experience – even when the discourse and activities are controlled by the students. The teacher is an ever present and key person, managing and monitoring the process. We suggest that teacher presence is a necessary part ... (Al-Mahmood and McLoughlin, 2004: 42)

Key aspects of e-teaching include:

- expectations of participation and achievement made visible by both students and teacher (Roberts and Lund, 2007; Palloff and Pratt, 2005; Dykman and Davis, 2008);
- presence of the teacher: social presence, cognitive presence, teaching presence, managerial presence (Garrison and Anderson, 2003; Palloff and Pratt, 2005; Al-Mahmood and McLoughlin, 2004; Bonk *et al.*, 2001; Forbes, in preparation);

- interaction as dialogic communication in the e-discussions between teacher and student, and between students (Roberts and Lund, 2007; Palloff and Pratt, 2005; Hew *et al.*, 2009), with interactivity through the inclusion of material that helps to create 'interaction with *concepts*, *tasks* and *people*' (Mayes, 2006: 9; italics in original);
- feedback and feedforward (formative assessment or assessment for learning) from the teacher for feedback on learning achieved and feedforward for further learning if the success criteria for the learning have not been met (Roberts and Lund, 2007; Forbes, 2005);
- facilitation for e-safety (Roberts and Lund, 2007; Butterworth, 2005) and the discussion for acknowledgement and participation encouragement (Roberts and Lund 2007);
- sense of belonging to a learning community of teachers and students (Palloff and Pratt, 2005) and not just a sense of being in an e-classroom.

In the first series of interviews, which were undertaken in June 2006, the beginning teachers were asked about how prepared they felt for using ICT as part of their pedagogy. Most said they felt prepared to varying degrees but that their school did not have the resources for them to use. For example, beginning teacher Sandy said:

> I feel fairly confident in ICT anyway ... many schools just don't have ICT resources, so it's all very well, [knowing how to use] a smart board. But [you] get out to a school like ours and the smart board is in one person's room and you don't get to use ... [Sandy]

Experienced teacher Megan mentioned developing her online teaching:

> I'm planning on turning the [new] course to be partly online, so that it doesn't require quite so many teacher face-to-face teaching hours, and I'm just kind of hoping that this will be a good platform to launch it on, because I know that every time you want to do a new programme that people, the timetabler, always says, 'oh there's not enough space in this timetable' or whatever.
>   ... so I do spend a bit of time thinking about how we can use ICT to enhance our learning, but yeah, catching ... keeping up with it, is quite difficult and also there's the financial aspect of it as well, yeah so ... [Megan]

> *[Do you have any Smart Boards in the schools that you're teaching in?]*
> We don't. ... because they cost a little bit of money. [Megan]

Experienced teacher Harry talked about learning to use new pedagogies based on ICT:

> And, you know, just ... and more recently ... just the power of teaching through ICT has really opened up some doors for me as well. [Harry]

In summary, theorising teaching as a spatial practice highlights the use in teaching of physical spaces, social spaces and e-spaces.

Study and discussion

- Can you give an example of the way the physical spaces you teach in have influenced your teaching practices?
- Using an example from your own teaching, discuss how relational spaces (the spaces in the relationship between teacher and student) influence your teaching practices.

10 Teaching as a political practice

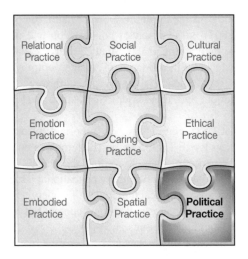

Teaching may be viewed as a political practice, as teachers address the discourses of power in schools, especially those of inequality and social injustice. Teachers use their power in their relationships with students, colleagues and others involved in education for transformation. Teachers may be political when they use their own informal and life experiences and beliefs in governmental and political parties, unions, social movements such as the women's and indigenous movements, and environmental movements, such as sustainability and permaculture, as a pedagogical resource to inform their teaching (Myers, 2009; Bar-Tal and Harel, 2002). But there are many more subtle and complex ways that teachers challenge the 'taken-for-granted' and normative assumptions about teachers and teaching (Myers, 2009). In this chapter, the notion of teaching as a political practice is discussed under the headings of social justice; the curriculum; government policy; teachers' unions and politics of the school.

Social justice

Teachers are able to promote and enable social justice in their work (Ayers, 2004, 2009), even though they may not be aware of it. While not supporting indoctrination, teachers in democracies are able, to varying degrees, to disrupt socially unjust discourses in curriculum, government policy and their employment. Rather than endorse and perpetuate the social injustices, teachers, in their teaching practices, may challenge and disrupt social injustices. I use the word 'may' here deliberately, because to be overtly political is not a universal experience of teachers (Myers, 2009). Teaching as a political practice is evident in making visible in the classroom curriculum the voices of, for example, women, indigenous peoples, minority cultural groups, disabled people and gays and lesbians. In making their voices visible, different knowledges and ways of knowing become a part of the taught and learnt curricula and gain the status that comes with this (Pinar *et al.*, 1995; Apple, 1982).

Curriculum

A national or state curriculum is contested and negotiated by the shareholders or stakeholders. The curriculum (national, state and classroom) is a site for struggle and representation (Rodriguez, 2006). For example, in New Zealand, the curriculum (New Zealand Ministry of Education, 2007) is the result of consultation and negotiation between such groups as: teachers, including both the professional teacher associations and teacher unions; parents, often through the local School Boards of Trustees; employers; trade unions; professional groups such as the Royal Society; the government through the Minister of Education and the Ministry of Education; and, to a lesser extent, students (Bell and Baker, 1997; Bell *et al.*, 1995).

It is not just about what knowledge is seen as important to include in a curriculum but also about how a society sees itself. Therefore, curriculum development and identity politics are related (Mao, 2008). When one changes, so does the other. 'What curriculum includes or excludes and what forms it takes are not merely educational issues concerning educators. They are also identity questions tied to each member of society' (Mao, 2008: 590). What is in a curriculum is not just a collection or collation of content but has embedded in it power and hierarchies of culture, social, economics and politics.

Teaching as a political practice means teachers asking the questions 'whose knowledge counts?' when enacting the intended curriculum in the classroom, and 'who is invisible in the classroom by not being in the curriculum?'. These questions need to be asked by teachers involved in national and state curriculum development as well as teachers planning the classroom curriculum, during lesson planning. Teachers make many choices and decisions at many stages in the planning and teaching of the classroom curriculum:

> Teachers make choices about how to depict the subject matter in their classrooms and what counts as knowledge. They select themes, emphasising some while ignoring others, and introduce curricular materials that collectively embody an understanding of their discipline and a reflection of their life experiences. Teachers also manage the range of topics that are allowed for discussion in the classroom. While some researchers have emphasised the influence of the official curriculum, especially textbooks, it is widely acknowledged that teachers play an important part role in curriculum decisions. (Myers, 2009: 32)

During the career of a teacher, there may be changes in what society deems as appropriate for classroom learning. For example, while in the 1980s it was safe to talk about girls' exclusion from science education, it was not okay to talk about sexual abuse or homosexuality (Leathwood, 2004).

Teachers may co-construct or negotiate the curriculum with students in the classroom, asking students to decide what they wish to learn (the content of the curriculum) and the learning activities within the parameters of the official or national curriculum (Mansell, 2009; Boomer *et al.*, 1992; Bishop and Berryman, 2006). The co-construction of the learnt curriculum is a sharing of power by the teacher, as a way of engaging students in learning, and addressing their learning needs and interests. One teacher who was interviewed, experienced teacher Megan, used the term 'co-construction'. Megan was discussing her use of rubrics in her assessments to help students focus on the required learning outcomes. She noted:

> [O]nce I think I've developed a really good knowledge of how to build rubrics myself, I kind of understand the whole thing, I want to move on to co-constructing rubrics with the students. [Megan]

How we teach is also a part of teaching as a political practice. For example, a teacher of science may decide not to use dissection as a pedagogy for teaching science and biology, given the ethical issues (Hug, 2008). In a democracy, we might also teach in a way that models democratic processes. For example:

> I taught a masters'-level course on pedagogy to a class of mainly international students from the People's Republic of China. The content of the course was mainly the classroom pedagogies used in New Zealand schools. I modeled these in their classroom so they could experience these pedagogies, and not just know about them. The teaching activities I used included lecturing for 30 minutes, a teaching activity they were used to, but I also modeled small group discussions, with a group member appointed by the group presenting a summary to the whole class, and cooperative learning activities such as the jigsaw. There were two New Zealand students (and practising teachers) in the class, and the conversation eventually moved around to the link between classroom pedagogy and educating students for living in a democracy, such as New Zealand. An example discussed was how we chose leaders (e.g., choosing who was going to be the spokesperson for each small discussion group, with women as well as men being considered). I was very conscious of the link between pedagogy and politics at that point. [Beverley]

Government policy

Teaching as a political practice is manifested in teachers' critical thinking about and acting on national or state government educational policies. This critique is most visible when government policy goes against the personal and professional values, ethics, morals and aims of teachers, as discussed in Chapter 6 on teaching as a caring practice. Teaching as a caring practice may become devalued, squeezed out and surpassed in daily teachers' work by the imposition of new managerial discourses of governments; in performance monitoring and appraisals; in an overloaded curriculum; in national standards which may lead to 'teaching to the test'; in a climate of performativity rather than professionalism; and in the drive for efficiency, increased accountability and outcomes-based teaching. Caring may also be displaced due to auditing and inspection and mandated pedagogies, as in the United Kingdom, (Hebson et al., 2007; Forrester, 2005; Larson, 2006; Hargreaves and Tucker, 1991). In addition, government policy may be critiqued by educators as promoting the politics of blame. The politics of blame is when government policy blames teachers for student underachievement, with subsequent appraisal policies and assessment of students for accountability purposes being imple-mented. However, rather than the quality of teachers' work, the cause may be in the unequal distribution of wealth and power in society, which is a government responsibility (Thrupp, 2010). Beginning teacher Katie spoke of one contemporary government policy that she disagreed with:

> *[Are there any areas [in which] you would have liked to have more support from the school?]*
> Discipline, again that's [the] school-wide, discipline system. I mean, it's there I admit, but it's just not effective, so it doesn't get used as it should be. The fact that the school accepts money for not expelling students with the government scheme, where they get several thousand dollars each year for not expelling students. [But] it puts it back on us as teachers because these kids are still in our classes and they're taking away the education of other students because they haven't been dealt with effectively. I'm not saying that expulsion is an effective way of dealing with it … [Katie]

Teachers' unions

In New Zealand, the secondary teachers' union (Post-Primary Teachers Association or PPTA) is concerned, among other things, with teachers' conditions of employment and fair employment procedures. Beginning teacher Katie was involved with the PPTA, with her father, also a teacher, having been involved when she was a child. She indicated that she contacted the union for advice, went to meetings, and was the school representative at one stage. She discussed the union with respect to negotiating with her school's principal about her 0.2 time allocation as a beginning teacher:

> … the principal had [the idea] in terms of [my] having a full-time case load, and he had the idea that it [the 0.2 additional non-teaching time allocation] … could be delayed … So I went to the PPTA and they said no, no, it's [a] use it or lose it scheme. So [I] mentioned that to the principal and got [it] changed back down to a 0.8 with that, and they hired another teacher to take on that other class … the expectation that I would be doing full-time stuff, I was quite happy with that, but like I said in my correspondence with the principal, that if I was doing that then I would be wanting some form of remuneration if I was going to miss out on that 0.2 free [non-teaching] time or release time. [Katie]

Politics in the school

Becoming a member of a professional community involves issues of power-sharing with those already in the community. Beginning teachers and teachers on practicum may or may not be included in the membership of a community and therefore have access to teacher knowledge and power and opportunities to develop their teacher identity (Santoro, 1997). Another aspect of politics in a school is that of emotional politics in interactions between teachers and parents (Lasky, 2000). This refers to the positive and negative emotions elicited during teacher–parent interactions. For example, the sense of joy when a teacher is told by a parent that they appreciate their child being in the teacher's class. The positive emotions are related to a gain in power and status, and negative emotions with a loss of power and status (Lasky, 2005).

Three of the beginning teachers explicitly mentioned the internal politics in their schools, which is linked to teaching as a relational practice (see Chapter 2). Beginning teacher Sylvia discussed who in the school took extra-curricular activities:

> *[Can you tell me about any extra curricular activities at the school?]*
> I'm not really doing any at the moment. I have offered to help with some things, but it hasn't really [happened] … it gets a bit political … there's people who have their 'babies' and … there's often people who have been doing it for the last few years, so they're happy to do it, so they can do it. [Sylvia]

Beginning teacher Sandy mentioned the politics of to whom to send misbehaving students:

> *[So the school has a system whereby if a child is misbehaving in your classes there are certain things you do and people you can send them to?]*
> [Yes.] There's things that you can do in your department and things that you can do in the school. So after you've been there a while, you work out that it may be best to do things in your department, leaving the things that the school [does] for later. So I think that sometimes there's all those politics [which] come in as to how you should deal with it and … you learn by experiences. [Sandy]

Beginning teacher Samantha, a mid-career beginning teacher, mentioned politics being a part of any group:

> I mean I've worked in the white collar world … all my working life so I know terrible management from good management, and we've got a really good principal here who is very easy, he's very easy to talk to, very approachable which, you know, so it starts from the top and feeds down. And you've always got … politics in any bunch, where you've got a lot of people, but it's a good school and they've got excellent systems for things like discipline, they've got people who know what they're doing, know what their roles are. [Samantha]

One of the experienced teachers, Megan, discussed how she used politics to get ICT resources for her department:

> In terms of the information technology … how many years ago? It was about two years ago now, I did a huge fundraiser for my department, we raised about fifteen thousand dollars, and that was with the idea that in order to do information technology, communication technology … [doing it] by yourself, it's not going to work because … there's a big financial aspect of it involved.
> So I kind of thought right, if we get this pot of money, and we encourage a lot of people to just do a little bit, [we move] a little bit further forward. Then this is going to make my life easier in the long run. So I led this fundraising and got everybody some data shows in the classroom. So right throughout the Science department now they've all got data shows. … quite interestingly, a lot of staff with these expensive data shows, [the data shows are] sitting in their classrooms, and they've got no idea how to use them initially, but they were quite keen … And I think you just go quietly about your business, and the fact that you're having success in your classroom, other people sort of go, 'oh what have you been doing and how have you been using this?'

so I've really tried to just do some simple things initially just with the Psychology [class]. [Megan]

In summary, teaching as a political practice is a part of teaching, with respect to social justice, the curriculum, government policy, teachers' unions and the politics of a school.

Study and discussion

- Can you give examples from your own teaching of when you engaged in teaching as a political practice with respect to social justice, the curriculum, government policy, teachers' unions and the politics of the school?

11 Rebuilding the bigger picture

In the previous nine chapters, we have discussed teaching as a sociocultural practice with respect to the nine teaching practices: teaching as relational, social, cultural, emotion, caring, ethical, embodied, spatial and political practices. These nine practices have been researched and theorised in the literature as sociocultural practices, meaning that we are viewing them as teaching practices in which mind and action are seen as linked and which are in turn linked with the social, cultural, historical and institutional contexts in which teachers work. The word 'link' is used here to mean that there is an interaction between those that are linked: both determining and being determined. A sociocultural view of teaching assumes that teaching cannot be understood without considering the contexts, because of this interrelatedness and interaction.

In each chapter, one of the nine practices has been foregrounded to attend to the detail of the theorising and research with respect to each practice. However, they are not distinct practices but are interrelated, determining and influencing each other. Whilst foregrounding one practice, the related practices were there in the background, still linked to the highlighted practice. For example, teaching as emotion and caring practices are often discussed together in the literature: a teacher does emotion work to empathise with and care for a student who is crying in the classroom; caring and cultural practices, when a teacher cares that a Māori or Pasifika student for example, achieves academically; cultural and political practices, when a teacher advocates for a student whose cultural practices are mistakenly seen as misbehaviour; emotion and embodied practices, when a teacher has a tight knot in her abdomen after a staff meeting full of conflict between staff and the principal; and social and relational practices when a teacher uses small-group discussion work and cooperative learning activities so as to negotiate the classroom curriculum planning with students.

To give a specific example, the notion of culturally responsive teaching, as summarised in Chapter 4, includes teaching as a:

- Relational practice, with a teacher considering culturally appropriate ways of building relationships with students and parents;
- Social practice, when considering the knowledges needed to construct understandings – for example, of the culturally appropriate practices to use in the classroom and the non-use of notions of ethnic blindness and deficit theorising;
- Cultural practice, when a teacher views a student as a culturally situated person and not as a person who has left their culture at the school gates;
- Emotion practice, when the teacher shows anger in the classroom at the use of a racist put-down by one student to another;

- Caring practice, when the teacher cares about whether the students achieve academically or not, and has high expectations of the students;
- Ethical practice, when the teacher silently reflects on his or her racist views as being unethical and socially unjust in the teaching context;
- Embodied practice, when a teacher becomes aware that their skin colour and other body features are not a barrier to being an effective teacher of a student from another culture;
- Spatial practice, when the teacher understands and enacts the culturally appropriate physical and emotional distance between her or himself and the student;
- Political practice, when the teacher visits local businesses to set up a scholarship fund to help students from families whose culture has not traditionally valued money being spent on tertiary education;

In another example, classroom management may be viewed as a relational practice, with the teacher considering the relationships between her or himself and the students; a social practice, as the kind of language, and how the language is used, is of importance; a cultural practice, as knowing a student's cultural practices can help a teacher make sense of the student's behaviour; an emotion practice, as the teacher may do emotion labour to hide her or his anger at a student's misbehaviour; a caring practice, when a teacher disciplines a student so that his or her attention is refocused on the learning to be done; an ethical practice, as the teacher needs to be aware of unethical practices such as hitting students; an embodied practice, when the teacher somatically feels the frustration and anger of a class that is not responding to requests for on-task work; a spatial practice, when the teacher considers physically separating two misbehaving students who are friends; and a political practice, when the teacher sends an 'out-of-control' student to the principal's office to make the issue of classroom discipline a school-wide issue requiring school-wide policies and strategies, and not solely one associated only with individual teachers.

Lastly, in Chapter 1, the three interview transcripts of beginning teacher Sally indicated that the nine practices were able to be recognised in the talking of one teacher.

The interrelatedness of the nine practices was modelled in Chapter 1 as a jigsaw, to highlight that the pieces together make up the bigger picture that is teaching. The metaphor of the jigsaw is used to emphasise five key points, which are repeated here. First, whilst each jigsaw piece has a picture on it, the picture on each piece is partial. The whole picture on the jigsaw is only visible when all the pieces are in place. In a similar way, if we theorise teaching as a sociocultural practice, we can only understand teaching in its fullness and complexity when we understand the multiple aspects of 'sociocultural', here the nine practices. Hence, the purpose of the jigsaw of the nine sociocultural practices is to make more visible the sociocultural theorising of teaching as a 'coherent structure of interrelated concepts' (Anyon, 2009: 3) to explain and provide an overview of teachers talking teaching.

Second, in a jigsaw, the pieces are related to each other through the shapes of the inter-locking pieces and the partial picture on each piece. Where each piece is placed is related to the other surrounding pieces. Likewise, the nine teaching practices, discussed here as aspects of teaching as a sociocultural practice, are related to and interact with each other. Often, the teachers interviewed discussed two or more practices in a segment of their talking teaching. The teachers tended not to discuss one practice without referring to others of the nine practices.

Third, the sociocultural framework or jigsaw of the nine practices tentatively appears to be a fruitful way to analyse and theorise the talking of both beginning and experienced teachers about their teaching, indicating that the framework is not a narrow, partial perspective of teaching, but is holistic. This aspect is important, for example, when we consider how we will represent qualitative research data (Brown, 1996; Eisenhart, 2006). The theorising using the nine related practices appears to preserve the complexity and richness in the talking and theorising of the beginning and experienced teachers.

Fourth, the use of the framework to analyse the transcript data indicates that the teachers were both describing and theorising when they talked about their teaching.

Lastly, the value of teachers reflecting on, talking about, re-storying and making sense of their lived experiences has been documented in the literature over many years as promoting teacher professional and personal learning and development in the teaching profession, whether it be in initial teacher education or in ongoing in-service learning (Brown, 1996; Loughran *et al.*, 2004, 2008; Palmer, 2007). It is hoped that the framework developed in this book is useful for teachers learning to teach in initial teacher education and for teachers starting more in-depth theorising of teaching at the master's-level programmes.

But having discussed nine practices, one is left wondering if there are not other practices which might also be theorised as sociocultural practices. To leave the model open for further development, it may be best to represent the jigsaw as an uncompleted one:

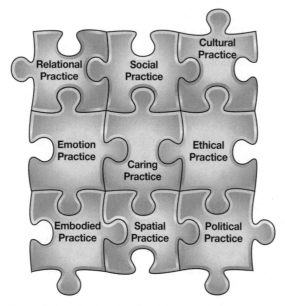

Figure 2 A revised sociocultural jigsaw

In this version of the jigsaw, the replacement of the pieces with straight edges by pieces with interlocking sides suggests that more pieces may be added to expand our theorising of teaching as a sociocultural practice. It opens up the possibility that the nine sociocultural practices discussed in this book are but a partial view of teaching, not a complete one.

Study and discussion

- Explain why there are no straight edges on the revised sociocultural jigsaw.

Appendix

This appendix contains information about the sources of the teachers' quotations in the book. Pseudonyms are given for each teacher, except the author, who is identified by her name, Beverley.

The quotations of the beginning teachers come from the interviews undertaken in the project Making a Difference: the Role of Initial Teacher Education and Induction in the Preparation of Secondary Teachers (Anthony et al., 2008), undertaken in New Zealand in 2005-2007. The author was one of a national project team of twelve.

At the end of 2005, 855 (72%) teacher graduates from the national cohort of graduating initial secondary teacher education students, were asked to complete a survey for the project. On the last survey page, volunteers were sought for three follow up interviews during the first two years of their teaching (2006, 2007). One hundred and sixteen volunteered (although only 100 completed all three interviews). Then ten members of the national project team, were each asked to interview beginning teachers in their region. After obtaining informed consent, the author interviewed ten beginning teachers, who had been allotted to her by the project director, in the Waikato and South Auckland area. The first interview was in June 2006, the second in December 2006, and the third in June 2007. The interviews were done in the author's work office or in an office in the teacher's school. The interviews typically lasted 1 to 1.5 hours. One teacher pulled out of the author's subset of ten beginning teachers for personal reasons. The questions in the interview schedule, relating to teaching experiences, are given below and further details are documented in Anthony et al., 2008. The interviews were audiotaped and transcribed verbatim by a professional transcriber, with the transcripts being confirmed by the teachers. The primary analysis of the survey and interview data was with respect to initial teacher education and induction and the findings reported (Anthony et al., 2008; Kane & Fontaine, 2008).

Later, the author obtained permission from members of the national project team to use the interview transcripts of the nine beginning teachers, whom she had personally interviewed, for the purposes of this book. The author also sought informed consent from the nine teachers, in addition to the original informed consent. Hence, this book is not reporting on the findings of the initial teacher education and induction project, which are documented elsewhere, as cited above. Instead, the use of the interview transcripts for this book represents a secondary analysis by the author. The interview transcripts were seen as a valuable resource as many of the teachers had talked about their teaching during the interviews, as well as their initial teacher education and induction experiences.

The transcripts were analysed for segments that were illustrative of the nine sociocultural practices found in the review of the existing research literature. Hence the quotations are illustrations of existing knowledge of teaching, not evidence to support new knowledge claims. This book is a textbook containing illustrative quotations, not a book documenting research. The author was working down from theory (Anyon, 2009) to categorise the interview transcripts with respect to the nine sociocultural aspects of teaching, rather than thinking upwards from data as in grounded theory.

In chapter 1, the case study quotations are from Sally, a beginning secondary teacher of English in an urban girls' high school. Teaching was her second career. She indicated that she had immigrated to New Zealand 17 years ago. Sally was chosen for the case study as she was the most articulate and had rated her satisfaction with teaching as '4: very satisfied' in all three interviews.

Samantha was a secondary beginning teacher of English, psychology and tourism in a small town high school. Teaching was her second career. She said she had immigrated to New Zealand a few years before undertaking her initial teacher education.

Stephanie was a secondary teacher of science and biology in an urban boys' high school. Teaching was her second career.

Sylvia was a secondary beginning teacher of economics, accounting and social studies in an urban co-educational high school. Teaching was her second career.

Katie taught science and senior biology in two co-educational high schools, having moved at the end of her first year in the project. Teaching was her second career.

Ellie taught English in an urban co-educational high school, with a high proportion of Pasifika secondary students. Teaching was her second career.

Sandy was a secondary beginning teacher of social studies, and teaching was her second career.

James was a beginning secondary teacher of art and photography. He had come specifically to New Zealand to do his initial teacher education, and was intending to teach in several countries, which were culturally distinct from his homeland.

The above 8 teachers could be classified as European/Caucasian New Zealanders. This information is given as readers may wish to use it in reading the chapter on teaching as a cultural practice.

Sarika taught science in an urban co-educational school, with a high proportion of Māori and Pasifika students. Teaching was her second career and could be classified as west-Asian.

The quotations of the experienced teachers were generated by the author and a Canadian colleague on study leave in Hamilton in 2010, interviewing three teachers of science from two local high schools (Bell and Scarff Seatter, 2010). The author interviewed two teachers and Carol Scarff Seatter, one. The teachers were chosen as they were known to the author and her colleague. The questions used came from the interview schedules for the three interviews with the beginning teachers and are those that generated the most talking on teaching. Hence, in the main, only the questions relating to teaching (and not specifically initial teacher education and induction) were used. The interview schedule is reproduced below. Like the interviews with the beginning teachers, no questions were asked about the nine teaching practices of this book. The interviews were from 1-1.5 hours long, and conducted in offices, not classrooms. The audiotapes of the interviews were transcribed by a professional transcriber, and analysed in a similar manner to those of the beginning teachers. That is, the transcripts were analysed for segments that were illustrative of the nine sociocultural practices found in a review of the existing research literature. Hence the quotations are illustrations of existing knowledge of teaching, not evidence to support new knowledge claims. That only three teachers were interviewed is not of concern, as the transcripts of three teachers generated sufficient illustrative quotations for the purposes of the book.

Harry was an experienced teacher of science and physics in an urban co-educational high school. He had taught in New Zealand for 35 years. In recent years, he had held management positions in the high schools in which he was teaching.

Megan was an experienced teacher who had immigrated to New Zealand after teaching in two other countries. She has taught science, physical education and psychology. She was teaching in an urban co-educational high school.

Mary was an experienced teacher of science and biology, with teaching as her second career. She was teaching in an urban co-educational high school.

In addition, where it was thought appropriate, the author, included quotations of her own teaching experiences. Beverley is an experienced teacher of secondary science, tertiary teacher education and supervisor of masters and doctoral research.

All four experienced teachers could be could be classified as European/Caucasian New Zealanders. This information is given as readers may wish to use it in reading the chapter on teaching as a cultural practice.

Interview schedule for the experienced teachers

1   Can you tell me about your background in teaching: how long you have been teaching? Where? What subjects? Which classes you have recently been teaching?
2   Tell me about the good days or experiences of teaching that have recently occurred for you? Why was it good for you?
3   Tell me about the worst days or experiences of teaching that have occurred recently for you? Why was it the worst for you?
4   Tell me about how you address these aspects in your teaching in the classroom:
    Improving learning
    Assessment: formative and summative assessment
    Content knowledge
    Curriculum knowledge
    Diversity of students – Māori, Pasefika, ESOL, gifted and talented, special needs, immigrant students
    Information Communication Technology (ICT)
    Classroom management
5   How has your view of a 'good' teacher changed since you started teaching?
6   What kind of teacher do you aspire to be? In what ways are you developing your teaching at the moment?
7   Can you explain to me how you go about planning and teaching a **topic**, eg. Consumers, light, or volcanoes?

(Adapted from ANTHONY, G., KANE, R., BELL, B., DAVEY, R., FONTAINE, S., HAIGH, M., LOVETT, S., MANSELL, H., ORD, K., PRESTIDGE, B., SANDRETTO, S. & STEPHENS, C. (2008) Making a Difference: The Role of Initial Teacher Education and Induction in the Preparation of Secondary Teachers: Final Report. . Wellington, Teaching and Learning Research Initiative, Ministry of Education/NZ Council for Educational Research.

References

Abell, S. K. (2008) Twenty Years Later: Does pedagogical content knowledge remain a useful idea? *International Journal of Science Education,* 30, 1405–16.

Aitken, V. and Kana, P. (2010) Poipoia kia puawai: a project to explore growth into leadership and cultural appropriacy in preservice teacher education. In Normore, A. (ed.) *Global Perspectives on Educational Leadership Reform: the development and preparation of leaders of learning and learners of leadership.* Bingley, UK: Emerald Group Publishing Ltd.

Allen, P., Leali'ie'e, T. and Robertson, J. (2009) 'In order to teach you, I must know you.' The Pasifika Initiative: a professional development project for teachers. *New Zealand Journal of Educational Studies,* 44, 47–62.

Al-Mahmood, R. (2006) Spatial imaginings: Learning and identity in online environments. *Australasian Society for Computers in Learning in Tertiary Education.* Available online at: http://ascilite.edublogs.org/2006/12/08/spatial-imaginings-learning-and-identity-in-online-environments/ (accessed 8 July 2011).

Al-Mahmood, R. and McLoughlin, C. (2004) Re-learning through e-learning: Changing conceptions of teaching through online experience. In Atkinson, R. *et al.* (eds) *Beyond the Comfort Zone: Proceedings of the 21st ASCILITE Conference.* Perth, 5–8 December.

Anderson, R. C. (2006) Teaching (with) disability: Pedagogies of lived experience. *Review of Education, Pedagogy & Cultural Studies,* 28, 367–79.

Anthony, G., Kane, R., Bell, B., Davey, R., Fontaine, S., Haigh, M., Lovett, S., Mansell, R., Ord, K., Prestidge, B., Sandretto, S. and Stephens, C. (2008) Making a Difference: The role of initial teacher education and induction in the preparation of secondary teachers. Wellington: New Zealand Council for Educational Research.

Anyon, J. (2009) *Theory and educational research: Toward critical social explanation.* New York: Routledge.

Apple, M. (1982) *Education and power.* Boston: Routledge and Kegan Paul.

Ashley, M. and Lee, J. (2003) *Women teaching boys: caring and working in the primary school.* Stoke on Trent: Trentham.

Augoustinos, M. and Walker, I. (1995) *Social Cognition: an integrated introduction.* London: Sage.

Ayers, W. (2004) *Teaching towards freedom: Moral commitment and ethical action in the classroom.* Boston: Beacon Press.

Ayers, W. (2009) Teaching in and for democracy. *Kappa Delta Pi Record,* 46, 30.

Bakhtin, M. (1986) Speech genres and other late essays (trans. V. McGee). In Emerson, C. and Holquist, M. (eds). Austin: University of Texas Press.

Ball, S. (1995) Intellectual or Technicians: The Role of Theory in Educational Studies. *British Journal of Educational Studies,* 43, 255–71.

Bar-Tal, D. and Harel, A. S. (2002) Teachers as agents of political influence in the Israeli high schools. *Teaching and Teacher Education,* 18, 121–34.

Barab, S., Kling, R. and Gray, J. (2004a) Introduction. In Barab, S., Kling, R. and Gray, J. (eds) *Designing for Virtual Communities in the Service of Learning.* Cambridge: Cambridge University Press.

Barab, S., Makinster, J. and Scheckler, R. (2004b) Designing System Dualities: Characterising an Online Professional Development Community. In Barab, S., Kling, R. and Gray, J. (eds) *Designing for Virtual Communities in the Service of Learning.* Cambridge: Cambridge University Press.

Barbour, K. (2004) Embodied ways of knowing. *Waikato Journal of Education,* 10, 227–38.

Barbour, K. N. (2006) Embodied engagement in arts research. *The International Journal of the Arts in Society,* 1, 85–91.

Baskerville, D. (2009) Navigating the unfamiliar in a quest towards culturally responsive pedagogy in the classroom. *Teaching and Teacher Education,* 25, 461–7.

Bauml, M. (2009) Examining the unexpected sophistication of preservice teachers' beliefs about the relational dimensions of teaching. *Teaching and Teacher Education,* 25, 902–8.

Beckett, D. and Hager, P. (2002) *Life, work and learning: practice in modernity.* London: Routledge.

Behrenbruch, M. and Bolger, K. (2006) Building a sustainable future. *Teacher,* 175, 16–19.

Bell, B. (1981) When is an animal, not an animal, *Journal of Biological Education,* 15, 213–18.

Bell, B. (1990) Science curriculum development: a recent New Zealand example. In A. Begg (ed.) SAMEpapers. Hamilton: University of Waikato; 1–31.

Bell, B. (2000) Formative assessment and science education: modelling and theorising. In Millar, R., Leach, J. and Osborne, J. (eds) *Improving science education: the contribution of research.* Buckingham: Open University Press.

Bell, B. (2003) Theorising pedagogy: guest editorial. *Waikato Journal of Education,* 9, 3–9.

Bell, B. (2005a) *Learning in Science: the Waikato research.* London: FalmerRoutledge.

Bell, B. (2005b) Pedagogies developed in the Learning in Science Projects and related theses. *International Journal of Science Education,* 27, 159–82.

Bell, B. (2010) Theorising teaching. *Waikato Journal of Education,* 15, 21–40.

Bell, B. and Baker, R. (1997) Curriculum development in science: Policy-to-practice and practice-to-policy. In Bell, B. and Baker, R. (eds) *Developing the science curriculum in Aotearoa New Zealand.* Auckland: Addison Wesley Longman.

Bell, B. and Cowie, B. (2001) *Formative assessment and science education.* Dordrecht and Boston: Kluwer Academic Publishers.

Bell, B. and Gilbert, J. (1996) *Teacher development: A model from science education.* London: Falmer Press.

Bell, B., Jones, A. and Carr, M. (1995) The development of the recent national New Zealand Science Curriculum. *Studies in Science Education,* 26, 73–105.

Bell, B. and Scarff Seatter, C. (2010) Theorising teaching: three experienced science teachers talk about their teaching. Unpublished research report, University of Waikato.

Bender, T. (2003) *Discussion-based online learning to enhance student learning: theory, practice and assessment.* Sterling, VA: Stylus.

Bernstein, B. (1971) On the classification and framing of educational knowledge. In Young, M. F. D. (ed.) *Knowledge and control: new directions for the sociology of education.* London: Collier-Macmillan.

Beyer, L. E. (1997) The moral contours of teacher education. *Ethics and Teacher Education,* 48(4), 245–54.

Bishop, R. (2005) Freeing ourselves from neocolonial domination in research: A Kaupapa Méori approach to creating knowledge. In Denzin, N. K. and Lincoln, Y. S. (eds) *Handbook of qualitative research,* (3rd edn). Thousand Oaks, CA: Sage.

Bishop, R. and Berryman, M. (2006) *Culture speaks: Cultural relationships and classroom learning.* Wellington: Huia.

Bishop, R. and Berryman, M. (2010) Te Kotahitanga: culturally responsive professional development for teachers. *Teacher Development,* 14, 173–87.

Bishop, R. and Glynn, T. (1999) *Culture counts: Changing power relations in education.* Palmerston North: Dunmore Press.

Bishop, R., Berryman, M., Cavanagh, T. and Teddy, L. (2009) Te Kotahitanga: Addressing educational disparities facing Maori students in New Zealand. *Teaching and Teacher Education,* 25, 734–42.

Bishop, R., Berryman, M., Tiakiwai, S. and Richardson, C. (2003) Te Kotahitanga Phase 1: The Experiences of Year 9 & 10 Maori Students in Mainstream Classrooms. Wellington: Report to the Ministry of Education.

Black, P. and Wiliam, D. (1998) Assessment and Classroom learning. *Assessment in Education,* 5, 7–74.

Bonk, C. J., Kirkley, J., Hara, N. and Paz Dennen, V. (2001) Finding the instructor in post-secondary online learning: pedagogical, social, managerial and technological locations. In Stephenson, J. (ed.) *Teaching and Learning Online: Pedagogies for new technologies.* London: Kogan Page.

Boomer, G., Lester, N., Onore, C. and Cook, J. (eds) (1992) *Negotiating the Curriculum: Educating for the 21st Century.* London: Falmer.

Brouwers, A. and Tomic, W. (2000) A longitudinal study of teacher burnout and perceived self-efficacy in classroom management. *Teaching and Teacher Education,* 16, 239–53.

Brown, T. (1996) Creating data in practitioner research. *Teacher and Teacher Education,* 12, 261–70.

Brown, T., Devine, N., Leslie, E., Paiti, M., Sila'ila'i, E., Umaki, S. and Williams, J. (2007) Reflective engagement in cultural history: a Lacanian perspective on Pasifika teachers in Aoteroa New Zealand. *Pedagogy, Culture and Society,* 15, 107–18.

Bruce, T. (2010) Using Theory to Escape the Descriptive Impasse. *Waikato Journal of Education,* 15, 7–20.

Bullough, R. (2011) Ethical and moral matters in teaching and teacher education. *Teaching and Teacher Education,* 27, 21–8.

Butterworth, L. (2005) Cybersafety: an intrinsic part of the online experience. In Lai, K. (ed.) *e-learning Communities: Teaching and learning with the web.* Dunedin: Otago University Press.

Buzzelli, C. and Johnston, B. (2001) Authority, power, and morality in classroom discourse. *Teaching and Teacher Education,* 17, 873–84.

Campbell, E. (1997) Connecting the ethics of teaching and moral education. *Journal of Teacher Education,* 48, 255.

Campbell, E. (2003) Moral Lessons: The Ethical Role of Teachers. *Educational Research & Evaluation,* 9, 25.

Campbell, E. (2008) The ethics of teaching as a moral profession. *Curriculum Inquiry,* 38, 357–85.

Campbell, N. and Yates, R. (2005) e-Learning and Pre-service Education. In Lai, K. (ed.) *e-learning Communities: Teaching and learning with the web.* Dunedin: Otago University Press.

Causey, V., Thomas, C. and Armento, B. (2000) Cultural diversity is basically a foreign term to me: The challenges of diversity for preservice teacher eduction. *Teaching and Teacher Education,* 16, 33–45.

Cazden, C. (2001) *Classroom Discourse: the Language of Teaching and Learning,* Portsmouth: Heinemann.

Chapman, E. (2003) Alternative Approaches to Assessing Student Engagement Rates. *Practical Assessment, Research & Evaluation,* 8, 13. Available online at http://pareonline.net/getvn.asp?v=8&n=13 (accessed 8 July 2011).

Clandinin, J. (2008) Creating learning spaces for teachers and teacher educators. *Teachers and Teaching,* 14, 385–9.

Clark, E. and Flores, B. (2007) Cultural literacy: Negotiating language, culture, and thought. *Voices From the Middle,* 15, 8.

Clarke, D. (2010a) A less partial vision: methodological, theoretical and cultural inclusivity in classroom research. Paper presented at the symposium Making Difference in Classrooms and Centres: The intersection of Theory and Practice, The University of Waikato, Hamilton, 12 November 2010.

Clarke, D. (2010b) The Cultural Specificity of Accomplished Practice: Contigent Conceptions of Excellence. *Fifth East Asia Regional Conference on Mathematics Education.* Tokyo, 18–22 August 2010.

Clarke, S. (2003) *Enriching feedback in the primary classroom: oral and written feedback from teachers and students,* London: Hodder and Stoughton.

Connolly, F. and Clandinin, J. (1999) *Shaping a professional identity: Stories of educational practice,* New York: Teachers College Press.

Cowie, B. and Bell, B. (1999) A model of formative assessment in science education. *Assessment in Education,* 6, 106–16.

Cranton, P. (2006) Fostering authentic relationships in the transformative classroom. *New Directions for Adult & Continuing Education,* 109, 5–13.

Davis, H. A. (2003) Conceptualizing the role and influence of student–teacher relationships on children's social and cognitive development. *Educational Psychologist,* 38, 207–34.

De Laat, M., Lally, V., Lipponen, L. and Simons, R.-J. (2007) Online teaching in networked learning communities: a multi-method approach to studying the role of the teacher. *Instructional Science,* 35, 257–86.

Delpit, L. D. (1998) The silenced dialogue: Power and pedagogy in educating other people's children. *Harvard Educational Review,* 58, 280–98.

Demetriou, H., Wilson, E. and Winterbottom, M. (2009) The role of emotion in teaching: Are there differences between male and female newly qualified teachers' approaches to teaching? *Educational Studies* 35, 449–73.

Devine, N. (2003) Pedagogy and subjectivity: Creating our own students. *Waikato Journal of Education,* 9, 29–37.

Dorion, K. R. (2009) Science through drama: A multiple case exploration of the characteristics of drama activities used in secondary science lessons. *International Journal of Science Education,* 31, 2247–70.

Dracoulas, S. (2007) Go Live! A library flexible learning space. *Synergy,* 5, 27–31.

Driver, R., Asoko, H., Leach, J., Mortimer, E. and Scott, P. (1994) Constructing scientific knowledge in the classroom. *Educational Researcher,* 23, 5–12.

Dunkin, M. and Biddle, B. (1974) *The Study of Teaching.* New York: Holt, Rinehart and Winston.

Durie, M. (2001) A framework for considering Maori educational advancement. Opening address, Hui Taumata Mètauranga, Turangi. November, 2001.

Dykman, C. and Davis, C. (2008) Online Education Forum: Part two – teaching online versus teaching conventionally. *Journal of Information Systems Education,* 19, 157–64.

Earl, K. and Forbes, D. (2008) Information Communication Technology: Destinations, Highways, Signposts and Speed Bumps. In Mcgee, C. and Fraser, D. (eds) *The Professional Practice of Teaching.* Third edn. Melbourne: Cangage.

Edwards, A. (2001) Researching pedagogy: a sociocultural agenda. *Pedagogy, Culture & Society,* 9, 161–86.

Eisenhart, M. (2006) Representing qualitative data. In Green, J., Camilli, G. and Elmore, P. (eds) *Handbook of complementary research methods in education research.* Washington DC: American Educational Research Association.

Elbaz, F. (1992) Hope, attentiveness, and caring for difference: The moral voice in teaching. *Teaching and Teacher Education,* 8, 421–32.

Endres, B. (2002) Transcending and attending to difference in the multicultural classroom. *Journal of Philosophy of Education,* 36, 171.

England, P. and Farkas, G. (1986) *Households, employment and gender.* New York: Aldine.

Estola, E. and Elbaz-Luwisch, F. (2003) Teaching bodies at work. *Journal of Curriculum Studies,* 35, 697–719.

Filer, A. (ed.) (2000) *Assessment: social practice and social product,* London: RoutledgeFalmer.

Forbes, D. (2005) Formative Interaction in Online Classes. *International Journal of Design Sciences and Technology,* 12, 83–93.

Forbes, D. (in preparation) Online learning in initial teacher education. Waikato, University of Waikato. Unpublished EdD thesis.

Forbes, D. (in press) Listening and learning through ICT with Digital Kids: Dynamics of interaction, power and mutual learning between student teachers and children in online discussions. In Sullivan, K., Czigler, P. and Hellgren, J. S. (eds) *Cases on Professional Distance Education Degree Programs and Practices: Successes, challenges and issues.* Sweden: IGI Global.

Forrester, G. (2005) All in a day's work: Primary teachers 'performing' and 'caring'. *Gender & Education,* 17, 271–87.

Fredricks, J. A., Blumenfield, P. C. and Paris, A. (2004) School engagement: Potential of the concept, state of evidence. *Review of Educational Research,* 74, 59–109.

Galman, S., Pica-Smith, C. and Rosenberger, C. (2010) Aggressive and Tender Navigations: Teacher Educators Confront Whiteness in their Practice. *Journal of Teacher Education,* 61, 225–36.

Gao, S. (in preparation) Teacher Development of English Language Teaching in China: Based on English Language Teachers' Beliefs and Practices in New Zealand. Unpublished PhD thesis. Hamilton, University of Waikato.

Gardener, D. E. (2008) Classrooms and their impact on learning. *School Planning & Management,* 47, IOL18.

Gardner, H. (1983) *Frames of Mind: The theory of multiple intelligences,* New York: Basic Books.

Garner, R. and Gillingham, M. (1996) *Internet Communication in Six Classrooms: Conversations across time, space and culture,* Mahwah, NJ: Lawrence Erlbaum Associates.

Garrison, D. R. and Anderson, T. (2003) *E-learning in the Twenty-first Century: a Framework for Research and Practice.* Abingdon: RoutledgeFalmer.

Garza, R. N. (2009) Latino and White high school students' perceptions of caring behaviors: Are we culturally responsive to our students? *Urban Education,* 44, 297–321.

Gay, G. (2000) *Culturally responsive teaching: theory, research, and practice,* New York: Teachers College Press.

Gay, G. (2002) Preparing for Culturally Responsive Teaching. *Journal of Teacher Education,* 53, 106–16.

Gay, G. (2010) Acting On Beliefs in Teacher Education for Cultural diversity. *Journal of Teacher Education,* 61, 143–52.

Gibbs, C. (2006) *To be a Teacher: Journeys towards authenticity,* Auckland: Pearson Education.

Giles, D. L. (2008a) Experiences of the teacher–student relationship in teacher education: Can the stories uncover essential meanings of this relationship? Australian Association for Research in Education Conference, Brisbane, 30 November–4 December 2008.

Giles, D. L. (2008b) Exploring the teacher–student relationship in teacher education: A hermeneutic phenomenological inquiry. Unpublished PhD thesis, Auckland University of Technology.

Giles, D. L. (2010) Developing pathic sensibilities: A critical priority for teacher education programmes. *Teaching and Teacher Education,* 26, 1511–19.

Gilligan, C. (1982) *In a different voice: Psychological theory and women's development,* Cambridge, MA: Harvard University Press.

Gipps, C. (1994) *Beyond testing: Towards a theory of educational assessment,* London: The Falmer Press.

Gipps, C. (1999) Socio-cultural aspects of assessment. *Review of Research in Education,* 24.

Goldstein, L. (1998) More than gentle smiles and warm hugs: Applying the ethic of care to early childhood education. *Journal of Research in Childhood Education,* 12, 244–61.

Goldstein, L. S. and Freedman, D. (2003) Challenges enacting caring teacher education. *Journal of Teacher Education,* 54(5), 441.

Goldstein, L. S. and Lake, V. E. (2000) 'Love, love, and more love for children': exploring preservice teachers' understandings of caring. *Teaching and Teacher Education,* 16, 861–72.

Goleman, D. (1996) *Emotional Intelligence,* London: Bloomsbury Publishing.

Gomez, M. L., Allen, A.-R. and Clinton, K. (2004) Cultural models of care in teaching: a case study of one pre-service secondary teacher. *Teaching and Teacher Education,* 20, 473–88.

Gonzalez, C. (2009) Conceptions of, and approaches to, teaching online: a sudy of lecturers teaching postgraduate courses. *Higher Education,* 57, 299–314.

Gore, J. (1993) *The struggle for pedagogies: critical and feminist discourses as regimes of truth.* New York: Routledge.

Greenleaf, C., Hull, G. and Reilly, B. (1994) Learning from our diverse students: Helping teachers rethink problematic teaching and learning situations. *Teaching and Teacher Education,* 10, 521–41.

Gruenewald, D. (2003) The best of both worlds: a critical pedagogy of place. *Educational Researcher,* 32, 3–12.

Gulati, S. (2008) Compulsory participation in online discussions: is this constructivism or normalisation of learning? *Innovation in Education and Teaching International,* 45, 183–92.

Hale, A., Snow-Gerono, J. and Morales, F. (2008) Transformative Education for culturally diverse learners through narrative and ethnography. *Teaching and Teacher Education,* 24, 1413–25.

Hall, A. (2001) Professionalism and Teacher Ethics. In Mcgee, C. and Fraser, D. (eds) *The Professional Practice of Teaching.* Second edn. Palmerston North: Dunmore Press.

Hall, A. (2008) Professional Responsibility and Teacher Ethics. In Mcgee, C. and Fraser, D. (eds) *The Professonal Practice of Teaching.* Third edn. South Melbourne: Cengage Learning.

Hall, A. and Bishop, R. (2001) Teacher ethics, professionalism and cultural diversity. *New Zealand Journal of Educational Studies,* 36, 178–202.

Hammond, M. (2005) A review of recent papers on online discussion in teaching and learning in higher education. *Journal of Asynchronous Learning Networks,* 9(3), 9–23.

Hara, N., Bonk, C. J. and Angeli, C. (2000) Content analysis of online discussion in an applied educational psychology course. *Instructional Science,* 28, 115–52.

Hargreaves, A. (1998) The emotional practice of teaching. *Teaching and Teacher Education,* 14, 835–54.

Hargreaves, A. (2000) Mixed emotions: Teachers' perceptions of their interactions with students. *Teaching and Teacher Education,* 16, 811–26.

Hargreaves, A. (2001a) Emotional geographies of teaching. *Teachers College Record,* 103, 1056.

Hargreaves, A. (2001b) The emotional geographies of teachers' relations with colleagues. *International Journal of Educational Research,* 35, 503–27.

Hargreaves, A. (2005) Educational change takes ages: Life, career and generational factors in teachers' emotional responses to educational change. *Teaching and Teacher Education,* 21, 967–83.

Hargreaves, A. and Tucker, E. (1991) Teaching and Guilt: Exploring the feelings of teaching. *Teaching and Teacher Education,* 7, 491–505.

Harré, R. (ed.) (1986) *the Social Construction of Emotions,* Oxford: Basil Blackwell.

Harré, R. and Parrott, W. G. (eds) (1996) *The Emotions: Social, cultural and biological dimensions,* London: Sage.

Hattie, J. and Timperley, H. (2007) The power of feedback. *Review of Educational Research,* 77, 81–112.

Hebson, G., Earnshaw, J. and Marchington, L. (2007) Too emotional to be capable: The changing nature of emotion work in definitions of 'capable teaching'. *Journal of Education Policy,* 22, 675–94.

Hemara, W. (2000) Maori pedagogies: a view from the literature. Wellington: New Zealand Council for Educational Research.

Hennessy, S. (1993) Situated cognition and cognitive apprenticeship: implications for classroom learning. *Studies in Science Education,* 22, 1–41.

Hew, K. F., Cheung, W. S. and Ng, C. S. L. (2009) Student contribution in asynchronous online discussion: a review of the research and empirical exploration. *Instructional Science,* 38(6), 571–606.

Hill, J. and Hawk, K. (2000) Making a difference in the classroom: Effective teaching practice in low decile, multicultural schools. Albany Auckland: Massey University, for the Ministry of Education.

Hirst, E. and Cooper, M. (2008) Keeping them in line: choreographing classroom spaces. *Teachers and Teaching,* 14, 431–45.

Ho, A. (2009) Educational leadership for international partnerships between New Zealand and East Asian Chinese higher education institutions. Unpublished EdD thesis. Hamilton, New Zealand.

Hochschild, A. R. (1983) *The Managed Heart: Commercialization of Human Feeling.,* Berkeley: University of California Press.

Hohepa, M., McNaughton, S. and Jenkins, K. (1996) Maori pedagogies and the roles of the individual. *New Zealand Journal of Educational Studies,* 31(1), 29–40.

Holmes, B. and Gardner, J. (2006) *e-Learning: concepts and practice.* London, Sage.

hooks, bell (2003) *Teaching Community: a pedagogy of hope,* New York: Routledge.

Hug, B. (2008) Re-examining the practice of dissection: What does it teach? *Journal of Curriculum Studies,* 40, 91–105.

Hume, A. and Berry, A. (2010) Constructing CoRes – a strategy for building PCK in pre-service science teacher education. *Research in Science Education,* 41(3), 341–55.

Humpage, L. (2009) A 'culturally unsafe' space: The Somali experience of Christchurch secondary schools. *New Zealand Geographer,* 65, 73–82.

Husu, J. and Tirri, K. (2003) A case study approach to study one teacher's moral reflection. *Teaching and Teacher Education,* 19, 345–57.

Hwang, S. and Roth, W.-M. (2010) The (embodied) performance of physics concepts in lectures. *Research in Science Education,* 24 April, 1–17.

Ibrahim, H., Small, D. and Grimley, M. (2009) Parent/school interface: Current communications practices and their implications for Somali parents. *New Zealand Journal of Education Studies,* 44, 19–30.

Isenbarger, L. and Zembylas, M. (2006) The emotional labour of caring in teaching. *Teaching and Teacher Education,* 22, 120–34.

Jarman, E. and Worton, C. (2008) Creating spaces that are 'communication friendly'. *Mathematics Teaching,* 209, 31–4.

Jarvenpaa, S. and Leidner, D. (1998) Communication and trust in global virtual teams. *Journal of Computer-mediated Communication,* 3, Nov/Dec, 791–815.

Jenlink, P. M. and Jenlink, K. E. (2008) Creating democratic learning communities: Transformative work as spatial practice. *Theory Into Practice,* 47, 311–17.

Jewson, N. (2007) Communities of practice in their place: some implications of changes in the spatial location of work. In Hughes, J., Jewson, N. and Unwin, L. (eds) *Communities of Practice: critical perspectives.* London: Routledge.

Jordon, S. (2001) Embodied pedagogy: The body and teaching theology. *Teaching Theology & Religion,* 4, 98.

Ka'ili, T. (2005) Tauhi va: nurturing Tongan sociospatial ties in Maui and beyond. *The Contemporary Pacific,* 17, 83–115.

Kalavite, T. (2010) Fononga 'A Fakahalafononga: Tongan students' journey to academic achievement in New Zealand Tertiary Education. Unpublished PhD thesis. Hamilton, New Zealand, University of Waikato.

Kana, P. (2003) Nga Hua O Te Noho Marae: Preservice teacher education students' experience of learning in a marae context. Unpublished MEdLeadership thesis. Hamilton, University of Waikato.

Kana, P. and Aitken, V. (2007) 'She didn't ask me about my grandmother': Using process drama to explore issues of cultural exclusion and educational leadership. *Journal of Educational Administration,* 45, 697–710.

Kane, R. and Fontaine, S. (2008) How prepared are New Zealand Secondary Teachers? Results from a National Graduate Survey. *New Zealand Journal of Education Studies,* 40(1),43.

Katz, L. G. (1980) Mothering and teaching: some significant dimensions. In Katz, L. G. (ed.) *Current topics in early childhood education.* Norwood, NJ: Ablex.

Katz, M., Noddings, N. and Strike, K. (eds) (1999) *Justice and caring: The search for common ground in education,* New York: Teachers College Press.

Kelchtermans, G. (1996) Teacher Vulnerability: understanding its moral and political roots. *Cambridge Journal of Education,* 26, 307–24.

Kelchtermans, G. (2005) Teachers' emotions in educational reforms: Self-understanding, vulnerable commitment and micropolitical literacy. *Teaching and Teacher Education,* 21, 995–1006.

Khoo, E. (2010) Developing an online learning community: A strategy for improving lecturer and student learning experiences. Unpublished DPhil thesis. Hamilton, University of Waikato.

Kidd, J. K., Sanchez, S. Y. and Thorp, E. K. (2008) Defining moments: Developing culturally responsive dispositions and teaching practices in early childhood preservice teachers. *Teaching and Teacher Education,* 24, 316–29.

Kind, V. (2009) Pedagogical content knowledge in science education: perspectives and potential for progress. *Studies in Science Education,* 45, 169.

Kling, R. and Courtright, C. (2004) Group Behaviour and Learning in Electronic Forums: a socio-technical approach. In Barab, S., Kling, R. and Gray, J. (eds) *Designing for Virtual Communities in the Service of Learning.* Cambridge: Cambridge University Press.

Kramer Schlosser, L. (1992) Teacher distance and student disengagement: school lives on the margin. *Journal of Teacher Education,* 43, 128–40.

Ladson-Billings, G. (1995) Toward a theory of culturally relevant relevant pedagogy. *American Educational Research Journal,* 32, 465–91.

Larson, A. (2006) Student perception of caring teaching in physical education. *Sport, Education & Society,* 11, 337–52.

Lasky, S. (2000) The cultural and emotional politics of teacher–parent interactions. *Teaching and Teacher Education,* 16, 843–60.

Lasky, S. (2005) A sociocultural approach to understanding teacher identity, agency and professional vulnerability in a context of secondary school reform. *Teaching and Teacher Education,* 21, 899–916.

Lave, J. and Wenger, E. (1991) *Situated learning: legitimate peripheral participation,* Cambridge: Cambridge University Press.

Leach, J. and Moon, B. (eds) (1999a) *Learners and Pedagogy,* London: Paul Chapman Publishing.

Leach, J. and Moon, B. (1999b) Recreating Pedagogy. In Leach, J. and Moon, B. (eds) *Learners and Pedagogy.* London: Paul Chapman Publishing.

Leathwood, C. (2004) Doing difference in different times: Theory, politics, and women-only spaces in education. *Women's Studies International Forum,* 27, 447–58.

Lee Hang, D. (2011) Fa'afatāmanu talafeagai mo lesona fa'asaienisi: O le tu'ualalo mo a'oga a faia'oga saienisi fa'aōliōli. A culturally appropriate formative assessment in science lessons: Implications for initial science teacher education. Unpublished EdD thesis, Hamilton, University of Waikato.

Lemke, J. (1990) *Talking science: Language, learning and values,* Norwood, NJ: Ablex.

Lim, L. and Renshaw, P. (2001) The relevance of sociocultural theory to culturally diverse partnerships and communities. *Journal of Child & Family Studies,* 10, 9–21.

Locke, T. (2007) E-learning and the reshaping of rhetorical space. In Andrews, R. and Haythornthwaite, C. (eds) *The SAGE Handbook of E-learning Research.* London, Sage.

Locke, T. and Daly, N. (2007) Towards Congeniality: The place of politeness in asynchronous online discussion. *International Journal of Learning,* 13, 121–34.

Loughran, J., Berry, A. and Mulhall, P. (2006) *Understanding and developing science teachers' pedagogical content knowledge,* Rotterdam: Sense Publishers.

Loughran, J., Hamilton, V., La Boskey, V. and Russell, T. (eds) (2004) *International handbook of self-study of teaching and teacher education practices,* Dordrecht: Kluwer.

Loughran, J., Mulhall, P. and Berry, A. (2008) Exploring Pedagogical Content Knowledge in Science Teacher Education. *International Journal of Science Education,* 30, 1301–20.

Lowe, P. (2004) The effect of co-operative work and assessment on the attitudes of students towards science in New Zealand. Unpublished PhD, SMEC, Curtin University of Technology, Australia.

Lumpkin, A. (2007) Teaching as an ethical profession. *Phi Kappa Phi Forum.* 87 edn.

Lynch, K., Carbone, A., Arnott, D., Jamieson, P. and World Conference on Computers in Education (2002) A studio-based approach to teaching information technology. *Computers in education 2001: Australian topics: selected papers from the seventh World Conference on Computers in Education.*

Macfarlane, A. (2000) Listening to Culture: Maori principles and practices applied to support classroom management. *SET 2,* 23–8.

Macfarlane, A. (2004) *Kia hiwa ra! Listen to culture: Maori students' plea to educators.* Wellington: New Zealand Council for Educational Research.

Macfarlane, A., Glynn, T., Cavanagh, T. and Bateman, S. (2007) Creating Culturally-safe Schools for Maori Stduents. *The Australian Journal of Indigenous Education,* 36, 65–76.

MacIntyre Latta, M. and Buck, G. (2008) Enfleshing embodiment: 'Falling into trust' with the body's role in teaching and learning. *Educational Philosophy and Theory,* 40, 315.

Mansell, H. (2009) Collaborative Partnerships: An investigation of co-construction in secondary classrooms. Unpublished PhD thesis. Hamilton, University of Waikato.

Mao, C.-J. (2008) Fashioning curriculum reform as identity politics: Taiwan's dilemma of curriculum reform in new millennium. *International Journal of Educational Development,* 28, 585–95.

Massey, D. (2005) *For Space,* London: Sage.

May, S. and Sleeter, C. (eds) (2010a) *Critical Multiculturalism: Theory and praxis,* New York: Routledge.

May, S. and Sleeter, C. (2010b) Introduction: Critical Multiculturalism. In May, S. and Sleeter, C. (eds) *Critical Multiculturalism: Theory and praxis.* New York: Routledge.

Mayes, T. (2001) Learning technology and learning relationships. In Stephenson, J. (ed.) *Teaching and learning online: Pedagogies for New Technologies.* London: Kogan Page.

Mayes, T. (2006) Theoretical perspectives on interactivity in e-learning. In Juwah, C. (ed.) *Interactions in online education: implications for theory and practice.* London: Routledge.

Metge, J. (2008) Maori Education 1958–1990: A personal memoir. *New Zealand Journal of Educational Studies,* 43, 13–28.

Middleton, S. (1993) *Educating Feminists: Life histories and pedagogy,* New York: Teachers College Press.

Middleton, S. (1998) *Disciplining sexuality: Foucault, life histories, and education.* New York: Teachers College Press.

Middleton, S. and McKinley, E. (2010) The gown and the korowai: Maori doctoral students and spatial organisation of academic knowledge. *Higher Education Research and Development,* 29, 229–43.

Mila-Schaaf, K. (2006) Va-centred social work: Possibilities for a Pacific approach to social work practice. *Social Work Review,* 18(1), 8-13.

Milner, H. R. (2005) Stability and change in US prospective teachers' beliefs and decisions about diversity and learning to teach. *Teaching and Teacher Education,* 21, 767–86.

Moll, L. (2001) Through the mediation of others: Vygotskian research on teaching. In Richardson, V. (ed.) *Handbook of Research on Teaching: Fourth Edition.* Washington DC: American Educational Research Association.

Moore, G. T. and Lackney, J. A. (1995) Design Patterns for American Schools: responding to the reform movement. In Meek, A. (ed.) *Designing places for learning.* Alexandria, VA: Association for Supervision and Curriculum Development.

Mullis, I. V. S., Martin, M. O., Foy, P. (with Olson, J. F., Preuschoff, C., Erberber, E., Arora, A. and Galia, J.) (2008) TIMSS 2007 International Mathematics Report: Findings from IEA – Trends in International Mathematics and Science Study at the Fourth and Eighth Grades. Chestnut Hill, MA: TIMSS & PIRLS International Study Center, Boston College.

Murray, C. and Pianta, R. C. (2007) The importance of teacher–student relationships for adolescents with high incidence disabilities. *Theory Into Practice,* 46, 105–12.

Myers, J. P. (2009) Learning in politics: Teachers' political experiences as a pedagogical resource. *International Journal of Educational Research,* 48, 30–9.

Naring, G., Briet, M. and Brouwers, A. (2006) Beyond demand-control: Emotional labour and symptoms of burnout in teachers. *Work & Stress,* 20, 303–15.

Nash, R. (2003) Progress at school: Pedagogy and the care for knowledge. *Teaching and Teacher Education,* 19, 755–67.

New Zealand Ministry of Education (2007) *The New Zealand Curriculum.* Wellington: Learning Media.

New Zealand Ministry of Education (2009) *Ministry of Education Statement Priority Outcomes 2009-2014.* Wellington: Ministry of Education. Available online at: http://www.minedu.govt.nz/NZEducation/EducationPolicies/PasifikaEducation/PasifikaEducationPlan/MinistryStatement.aspx. Accessed 8 July 2011.

New Zealand Ministry of Education (2010) Down the back of the chair: Ministry of Education's catalogue of teaching and learning resources for schools. Wellington: Ministry of Education.

New Zealand Teachers Council (2007) *Graduating Teacher Standards: Aotearoa New Zealand.* Wellington: Teachers Council.

New Zealand Teachers Council (2010) *Code of Ethics.* Wellington: Teachers Council. Available online at http://www.teacherscouncil.govt.nz/required/ethics/index.stm/ (accessed 5 July 2011).

Newberry, M. (2010) Identified phases in the building and maintaining of positive teacher–student relationships. *Teaching and Teacher Education,* 26, 1695–1703.

Nguyen, P.-M., Terlouw, C., Pilot, A. and Elliot, J. (2009) Co-operative learning that features a culturally appropriate pedagogy. *British Educational Research Journal,* 35, 857–75.

Nias, J. (1996) Thinking about feeling: the emotions in teaching. *Cambridge Journal of Education,* 26, 293–306.

Nieto, S. (2000) *Affirming diversity: The sociopolitical context of multicultural education (3rd edn),* White Plains, NY: Longman.

Nieto, S. (2010) *The light in their eyes: Creating multicultural learning communities. 10th anniversary edition,* New York: Teachers College Press.

Noddings, N. (1992) *The challenge to care in schools,* New York: Teachers College Press.

Noddings, N. (1999) Care, justice and equity. In Katz, M., Noddings, N. and Strike, K. (eds) *Justice and Caring: the Search for Common Ground in Education.* New York: Teachers College Press.

Noddings, N. (2001) The Caring Teacher. In Richardson, V. (ed.) *Handbook of Research on Teaching, 4th edn.* Washington DC: AERA.

Noddings, N. (2003) Is teaching a practice? *Journal of Philosophy of Education,* 37, 241–51.

Nuthall, G. (1997) Understanding student thinking and learning in the classroom. In Biddle, B., Good, I. and Goodson, I. (eds) *The International Handbook of Teachers and Teaching.* Dordrecht: Kluwer.

O'Connor, K. E. (2008) 'You choose to care': Teachers, emotions and professional identity. *Teaching and Teacher Education,* 24, 117–26.

Openshaw, R. (2007) A sense of deja vu across the Tasman. What Australians might learn from the New Zealand experience with the Te Kotahitanga professional development programme. *Education Research and Perspectives,* 34, 24.

Ovens, A. P. (2008) Physical education facilities: Planning for the future. *New Zealand Physical Educator,* 41, 7.

Palloff, R. and Pratt, K. (2003) *The Virtual Student: a profile and guide to working with online learners,* San Francisco: Jossey-Bass.

Palloff, R. and Pratt, K. (2005) *Collaborating Online: Learning Together in Community,* San Francisco: Jossey-Bass.

Palmer, P. (2003) Teaching with Heart and Soul: Reflections on Spirituality in Teacher Education. *Journal of Teacher Education,* 54, 376–85.

Palmer, P. (2007) *The Courage to Teach: Exploring the Inner landscape of a teacher's life. Tenth anniversary edition.* San Francisco: John Wiley & Sons.

Pere, R. (1982) Ako: Concepts and learning in the Maori tradition. Hamilton: University of Waikato.

Perez, S. A. (2000) An ethic of caring in teaching culturally diverse students. *Education,* 121, 102.

Phuong-Mai, N., Terlouw, C., Pilot, A. and Elliott, J. (2009) Cooperative learning that features a culturally appropriate pedagogy. *British Educational Research Journal,* 35, 857–75.

Pinar, W., Reynolds, W., Slattery, P. and Taubaum, P. (1995) *Understanding Curriculum: an introduction to the study of historical and contemporary curriculum discourses,* New York: Peter Lang.

Pointon, P. and Kershner, R. (2000) Making decisions about organising the primary classroom environment as a context for learning: The views of three experienced teachers and their pupils. *Teaching and Teacher Education,* 16, 117–27.

Rawlins, P. (2010) Student participation in formative assessment for NCEA. *New Zealand Journal of Educational Studies,* 45, 3–16.

Richards, H., Brown, A. and Forde, T. (2006) *Addressing Diversity in Schools: Culturally Responsive Pedagogy,* Arizona State University, Tempe, Arizona. National Center for Culturally Responsive Educational Systems (NCCREST).

Roberts, E. and Lund, J. (2007) Exploring E-learning Community in a Global Postgraduate programme. In Andrews, R. and Haythornthwaite, C. (eds) *The SAGE Handbook of E-learning Research*. London: Sage.

Roberts, G. (2003) Teaching using the web: Conceptions and approaches from a phenomenographic perspective. *Instructional Science*, 31, 127–50.

Rodriguez, A. J. (2006) The politics of domestication and curriculum as pasture in the United States. *Teaching and Teacher Education*, 22, 804–11.

Rogoff, B. (1993) Children's guided participation and participatory appropriation of sociocultural activity. In Woznial, R. A. F. K. (ed.) *Development in Context: Acting and Thinking in Specific Environments*. Hillsdale, NJ: Lawrence Erlbaum Associates.

Rogoff, B. (1995) Observing sociocultural activity on three planes. In Wertsch, J., Del Rio, P. and Alvarez, A. (eds) *Observing Sociocultural Studies of the Mind*. Cambridge: Cambridge University Press.

Roth, W.-M. (2005) *Talking Science: Language and learning in science classrooms*, Lanham, MD: Rowman & Littlefield.

Royal, Te Ahukaramū Charles (2009) *Papatūānuku – the land – The importance of Papatūānuku*, Te Ara – the Encyclopedia of New Zealand. Available online at http://www.TeAra.govt.nz/en/papatuanuku-the-land/1 (accessed 3 July 2011).

Salomon, G. (ed.) (1993) *Distributed Cognitions: psychological and educational considerations*, New York: Cambridge University Press.

Salomon, G. and Perkins, D. (1998) Individual and social aspects of learning. *Review of Research in Education*, 23, 1–24.

Samu, T. W. (2006) The 'Pasifika Umbrella' and quality teaching: Understanding and responding to the diverse realities within. *Waikato Journal of Education*, 12, 36–49.

Samu, W. T. (2010) Pacific Education: an Oceanic perspective. *Mai Review*, 1. Available online at http://www.review.mai.ac.nz/index.php/MR/article/view/311/379/ (accessed 8 July 2010).

Sanger, M. and Osguthorpe, R. (2011) Teacher education, preservice teacher beliefs, and the moral work of teaching. *Teaching and Teacher Education*, 27, 569–78.

Santoro, N. (1997) The Construction of Teacher Identity: an analysis of school practicum discourse. *Asia-Pacific Journal of Teacher Education*, 25, 91–9.

Santoro, N. and Allard, A. (2005) (Re)Examining identities: Working with diversity in the pre-service teaching experience. *Teaching and Teacher Education*, 21, 863–73.

Schon, P. (2005) *WholeHearted: Stories by teachers who are committed to bringing wholeness and heart to their teaching and learning*, Palmerston North: Kanuka Grove Press.

Segall, A. (2004) Revisiting pedagogical content knowledge: the pedagogy of content/the content of pedagogy. *Teaching and Teacher Education*, 20, 489–504.

Shahjahan, R. A. (2009) The role of spirituality in the anti-oppressive higher-education classroom. *Teaching in Higher Education*, 14, 121–31.

Shapira-Lishchinsky, O. (2011) Teachers' critical incidents: Ethical dilemmas in teaching practice. *Teaching and Teacher Education*, 27, 648–56.

Shapiro, S. (2010) Revisiting the teachers' lounge: Reflections on emotional experience and teacher identity. *Teaching and Teacher Education*, 26(3), 616–21.

Shapiro, S. B. (1997) *Pedagogy and the politics of the body: critical praxis*, London: Garland Publishing.

Sharma, R. and Juwah, C. (2006) Developing competencies for online and distance education teaching. In Juwah, C. (ed.) *Interactions in Online Education: Implications for theory and practice*. London: Routledge.

Shaunessy, E. and Alvarez McHatton, P. (2009) Urban students' perceptions of teachers: Views of students in general, special and honors education. *Urban Review*, 41, 486–503.

Shields, C., Bishop, R. and Mazawi, A. E. (2005) *Pathologising practices: The impact of deficit thinking on education*, New York: Peter Lang.

Shulman, L. (1987) Knowledge and new reforms: foundations of the new reforms. *Harvard Educational Review*, 57, 1–22.

Shulman, L. and Shulman, J. (2004) How and what teachers learn: a shifting perspective. *Journal of Curriculum Studies,* 36, 257–71.

Siteine, A. (2010) The allocation of Pasifika identity in New Zealand classrooms. *Mai Review,* 1. Available online at http://www.review.mai.ac.nz/index.php/MR/article/view/301/383/ (accessed 8 July 2011).

Sleeter, C. (2010) Confronting the Marginalisation of Culturally Responsive Pedagogy. *Cultural Responsive Pedagogies Symposium,* University of Waikato, Hamilton, New Zealand, 21–22 November.

Smith, G. (1997) The development of Kaupapa Maori: theory and praxis. Unpublished PhD thesis, University of Auckland, New Zealand.

Snook, I. (2003) *The ethical teacher,* Palmerston North: Dunmore Press.

Stacey, E. and Wiesenberg, F. (2007) A study of face-to-face and online teaching philosophies in Canada and Australia. *Journal of Distance Education,* 22, 19–40.

Stephenson, J. (2001a) Learner-managed learning – an emergent pedagogy for learning online. In Stephenson, J. (ed.) *Teaching and learning online: Pedagogies for new technologies.* London: Kogan Page.

Stephenson, J. (ed.) (2001b) *Teaching and learning online: Pedagogies for new technologies.* London: Kogan Page.

Strachan, J. (2005) Working out of my comfort zone: Experiences of developing national women's policy in Vanuatu. *Delta,* 57, 47–66.

Strike, K. A. (1990) Teaching ethics to teachers: What the curriculum should be about. *Teaching and Teacher Education,* 6, 47–53.

Stuckey, B. and Barab, S. (2007) New Conceptions for Community Design. In Andrews, R. and Haythornthwaite, C. (eds) *The SAGE Handbook of E-learning Research.* London: Sage.

Sutton, R. and Wheatley, C. (2003) Teachers' emotions and teaching: A review of the literature and directions for future research. *Educational Psychology Review,* 15, 327–58.

Swartz, E. (2009) Diversity: Gatekeeping knowledge and maintaining inequalities. *Review of Educational Research,* 79, 1044.

Tallent-Runnels, M., Thomas, J., Lan, W., Cooper, S., Ahern, T., Shaw, S. and Liu, X. (2006) Teaching courses online: a review of the research. *Review of Educational Research,* 76, 93–125.

Tanner, C. (2008) Explaining relationships among student outcomes and the school's physical environment. *Journal of Advanced Academics,* 19, 444.

Tate, P. M. (2007) Academic and relational responsibilities of teaching. *Journal of Education,* 187, 1.

Taylor, S. S. (2009) Effects of studio space on teaching and learning: Preliminary findings from two case studies. *Innovative Higher Education,* 33, 217–28.

Teven, J. (2001) The relationship among teacher characteristics and perceived caring. *Communication Education,* 50, 159–69.

Thaman, K. H. (2006) Draft Paper Nurturing Relationships: A Pacific perspective of teacher education for peace and sustainable development. *UNESCO Experts meeting on ESD.* Samutsongkram, Thailand.

Thompson, D. A. (2000) Teaching what I'm not: Embodiment, race, and theological conversation in the classroom. *Teaching Theology & Religion,* 3, 164.

Thompson, M. (2007) From Distance Education to E-learning. In Andrews, R. and Haythornthwaite, C. (eds) *The SAGE Handbook of E-learning research.* London: Sage.

Thrupp, M. (2010) The politics of being an educational researcher: minimising the harm done by research. *Waikato Journal of Education,* 15, 119–33.

Tippins, D., Tobin, K. and Hook, K. (1993) Ethical decisions at the heart of teaching: making sense from a constructivist perspective. *Journal of Moral Education,* 22, 221–40.

Tronto, J. (1998) An ethic of care. *Generations,* 22, 15–20.

Van Eijck, M. and Roth, W.-M. (2010) Towards a chronotopic theory of 'place' in place-based education. *Cultural Studies of Science Education,* 5, 869–98.

Van Houtte, M. (2007) Exploring trust in technical/vocational secondary schools: Male teachers' preference for girls. *Teaching and Teacher Education,* 23, 826–39.

Villegas, A. M. and Lucas, T. (2007) The culturally responsive teacher. *Educational Leadership*, March, 28–33.

Vogt, F. (2002) A caring teacher: Explorations into primary school teachers' professional identity and ethic of care. *Gender & Education*, 14, 251–64.

Vygotsky, L. (1978) *Mind in Society: the development of higher psychological processes*. Cambridge, MA: Harvard University Press.

Walshaw, M. and Anthony, G. (2008) The teachers' role in classroom discourse: A review of recent research into mathematics classrooms. *Review of Educational Research*, 78, 516–51.

Watkins, M. (2007) Disparate bodies: The role of the teacher in contemporary pedagogic practice. *British Journal of Sociology of Education*, 28, 767–81.

Webb, K. and Blond, J. (1995) Teacher knowledge: The relationship between caring and knowing. *Teaching and Teacher Education*, 11, 611–25.

Weinstein, C., Tomlinson-Clarke, S. and Curran, M. (2004) Toward a Conception of Culturally Responsive Classroom Management. *Journal of Teacher Education*, 55, 25–38.

Weinstein, C. S. (1998) 'I want to be nice, but I have to be mean': Exploring prospective teachers' conceptions of caring and order. *Teaching and Teacher Education*, 14, 153–63.

Wertsch, J. (1991) *Voices of the Mind*, Cambridge, MA: Harvard University Press.

Wertsch, J., Del Rio, P. and Alvarez, A. (1995) *Sociocultural Studies of Mind*, Cambridge: Cambridge University Press.

White, B. (2003) Caring and the Teaching of English. *Research in the Teaching of English*, 37, 295–28.

White, J. (2010) Dialogic–Dilectic: Epistemological alignment or ontological provocation in schooling. PESA Conference, December 2010. Perth.

Wilcox, H. N. (2009) Embodied ways of knowing, pedagogies, and social justice: Inclusive science and beyond. *NWSA Journal*, 21, 104–20.

Wilensky, U. and Reisman, K. (2006) Thinking like a wolf, a sheep, or a firefly: Learning biology through constructing and testing computational theories – An embodied modeling approach. *Cognition & Instruction*, 24, 171–209.

Winch, C. and Gingell, J. (1999) *Key Concepts in the Philosophy of Education*. London: Routledge.

Wright, N. (2010) e-learning and implications for New Zealand schools: a literature review. Wellington: Ministry of Education. Available online at: http://www.educationcounts.govt.nz/publications/ict/77614/ (accessed 8 July 2011).

Young, E. (2010) Challenges to conceptualising and actualising culturally relevant pedagogy: How viable is the theory in classroom practice? *Journal of Teacher Education*, 61, 248–60.

Zembylas, M. (2002a) Constructing genealogies of teachers' emotions in science teaching. *Journal of Research in Science Teaching*, 39, 79–103.

Zembylas, M. (2002b) 'Structures of feeling' in curriculum and teaching: Theorizing the emotional rules. *Educational Theory*, 52, 187.

Zembylas, M. (2003) Emotions and Teacher Identity: a poststructural perspective. *Teachers and Teaching: Theory and Practice*, 9, 213–38.

Zembylas, M. (2004a) Emotion metaphors and emotional labor in science teaching. *Science Education*, 88, 301–24.

Zembylas, M. (2004b) The emotional characteristics of teaching: an ethnographic study of one teacher. *Teaching and Teacher Education*, 20, 185–201.

Zembylas, M. (2005) Discursive practices, genealogies, and emotional rules: A poststructuralist view on emotion and identity in teaching. *Teaching and Teacher Education*, 21, 935–48.

Zembylas, M. (in press) Investigating the emotional geographies of exclusion at a multicultural school. *Emotion, Space and Society*.

Zhang, Q. and Zhu, W. (2008) Exploring emotion in teaching: Emotional labor, burnout, and satisfaction in Chinese higher education. *Communication Education*, 57, 105–22.

Index